BUT HE'LL REI
AN AUTOBIO

Old men forget: yet all shall be forgot,
But he'll remember, with advantages,
What feats he did that day.
(Shakespeare, *King Henry V*, act 4 sc.iii; with
acknowledgements to Duff Cooper)

To Ann
with love

But He'll Remember: an autobiography

David Rubinstein

William Sessions Limited
York, England

ISBN 1 85072 220 X

'Begin at the beginning, and go on till you come to the end: then stop.'

(Lewis Carroll, *Alice's Adventures in Wonderland*, 1865, ch. 12)

Printed in 11 on 12 point Plantin Typeface
from Author's Disk
by Sessions of York
The Ebor Press
York, England

Contents

Illustrations

Preface

' A DECENT RESPECT to the opinions of mankind' or at least
such of it as might come across this book demands some
justification for the arrogance of writing an account of one's life.
An explanation is all the more necessary when the writer is an
historian who knows well that most published autobiographies
would be more accurately classified as fiction than fact.

I have been thinking for some time of writing the story of my
life, as it seems to me that someone who has witnessed and closely
followed many of the dramatic events of our time might have a story
to tell of interest to others, even though he has himself played the
humblest of roles. The world into which I grew up and lived until
early middle age, if it has not wholly disappeared, is sharply different from the present one; what were once thought of as titanic
political and social controversies seem to have vanished. It was not
ever thus. Moreover, there should be some interest in the story of
one who has been lucky enough to enjoy three careers and live in
three different countries.

There is another, more mundane reason for these memoirs. In
the summer of 1997 when I began to write them I was coming to
the close of my final year of employment, spent in the hospitable
environs of the Université du Littoral in Boulogne-sur-Mer. I was
temporarily cut off from the London libraries whose facilities have
enabled me to engage in scholarly research since the 1950s. An
autobiography is one of the few types of work in which a would-be
serious writer who lacks the imagination to write novels, plays or
poetry can engage without immediate recourse to a research library.
Chapters 1 to 5 were drafted in Boulogne, chapters 6 to 10 in
London in autumn 1997. Chapter 11 and 12 were written during
my long-delayed visit to the United States and as I travelled home
in spring and summer 1998, and in autumn 1998 I reread and
revised the entire manuscript.

It is customary for historians to thank those people and institutions who have made it possible for them to complete their research. Such considerations are less significant in the case of an autobiography, though I have had to check many details in local and national libraries and I am grateful for the cheerful assistance I have had from librarians. But anyone bold enough to write such a work is likely to have built up considerable personal debts, and this is certainly true in my case. I have drifted apart from many of my friends over the years as geographical considerations and changing interests have led to relinquishing some old friendships and beginning new ones. Nonetheless, certain relationships have been (or were) constant in my life for many years and to the people concerned I owe a particular debt of gratitude. These include above all Ann Holt to whom I have been married since 1974, my sons Peter, John and Paul, and the following friends: Bob Gaebler, Tom Greene, Chris Hall, Peter Jackson, Nicholas Tucker. My life would have been very much poorer without their affection and support and I am grateful to them. Ann read the entire manuscript in draft and Tom read chapter 2; their criticism and advice have been invaluable. I am once again deeply indebted to David Martin, on this occasion for reading the proofs. I am also grateful to the following people for assistance with particular points: Roger Adley, Claire Britcher, Clive Davies, Fiona Duffy, Wendy Marlow, Charlotte Prager, Paul Rubinstein, Richard Snaith, Colin Speakman, Joanne Todd, Sarah Topping, Nick Tucker, Ellen Weld, Louise Williams and Peter Williamson.

One final word. I have provided as much documentation as possible to substantiate my story. But much of it depends on my own memory, which is certain to be faulty in some particulars. Everyone mentioned by name is intended to resemble a person living or dead, and if I have misrepresented or traduced anyone I apologise sincerely. I can only say that any mistakes have not been deliberate and that I have tried to give as fair, truthful and unadorned a picture of my life and experiences as I could without causing needless offence or pain to myself or others.

DAVID RUBINSTEIN
Boulogne-sur-Mer, London, Salem (Oregon), York
November 1998

CHAPTER 1

Childhood and Youth: 1932-50

LIKE MANY AMERICANS I am not of Anglo-Saxon origin. Three of my four grandparents were dead when I was born; their failure to reach old age was a common experience of those born in the third quarter of the nineteenth century. My paternal grandfather, who lived until I was in my teens but whom I never knew, was born in Lithuania and emigrated to England, where he lived for a period and practised as a rabbi or a minor religious functionary. My grandmother came from a family which had lived in South Africa but had moved to England where she married my grandfather (in London) and where her eldest child was born (in Sheffield). My father had English cousins of whom he knew nothing, except that they taught ballet dancing. My maternal grandfather was born in Hungary, my grandmother probably in Sweden. Being deeply suspicious of 'thinking with the blood' I have never made an effort to dig into family history, preferring to devote my researches to the less tainted and more rewarding history of other people's families.

My mother liked to tell her children that we were descended from a long line of beggars (i.e., rabbis) on our father's side and thieves (i.e., pedlars) on hers. When I became interested in politics and society I amended that dictum to conclude that I had middle-class antecedents over many generations, for what better typified the bourgeoisie than beggars and thieves?

My paternal grandparents moved to Athens, Georgia, which must have been an odd choice in the 1890s; southern, small and providing little opportunity for a congregation for a young rabbi. So far as I know, not only my father but his two older brothers, his

1

younger brother and his sister were all born there. My grandmother drew on her English experience to name her sons Percy, Douglas and Laurence, and her daughter Evelyn (or Eveline, depending on my aunt's whim at various stages of her life).

Why she should have picked Beryl as a name for my father is not clear, and it led to a good deal of curiosity and occasionally mirth, especially after I moved to England. This is because Beryl, which is a name (like Beverley or Marion) less sex-divided in the United States than in Britain, is my own first name, though never one by which I have been known. (My naturalisation papers read 'Beryl David, known as David', my passport 'David' tout court.) I believe that Beryl also has some significance in the Jewish religious calendar, being connected with the month of October; my father was born on 26 October 1898. (On the same day Florence, Lady Harberton, was refused admission to the Hautboys Inn in Ockham, Surrey, wearing her knickerbockered cycling outfit known as rational dress; I was later to write an account of this once-famous incident.) Although he was to leave Georgia and his later home in Florida while still youthful, my father never lost his southern accent.

My mother was born in Cleveland, Ohio, on 15 December 1903, into a family who were part-owners of the Landesman-Hirschheimer department store, which no longer existed when I was a child. She too was one of five (Landesman) children, of whom she was the youngest; the others were Zella, Geoffrey, Helen and Dorothy. Unlike my father's family, both the children and the parents were close, and the siblings remained close all their lives. Zella and Dorothy moved after marriage to New York and Helen to Los Angeles, but the sisters remained in touch with each other and Uncle Geoff stayed in Cleveland, in virtually daily contact with my mother.

This was not easy for my father, whose character differed sharply from my uncle's. My guess is that they had to learn to like each other and that Uncle Geoff's relationship with my mother was conducted more during the day when my father was away at work than in the evening or at weekends. Uncle Geoff was a freelance photographer, which gave his working day a good deal of flexibility; my father worked several miles away in 'downtown' Cleveland. The fact that I never saw him and Uncle Geoff openly at odds says a good deal for both of them and for their common love of my mother. Uncle Geoff was breezy and boyish, saying anything to anyone, with little sense of person or occasion. (He also had a fairly haphazard attitude to money, so that his sisters felt forced to replenish his bank account from time to time.) My father had a very strong sense of appropriate behaviour, while Uncle Geoff had strong opinions on most things; as I grew into adolescence I did not always find it easy to be with either of them. It must be said, however, that Uncle Geoff who had his own son two years younger than myself had a better idea of how to treat young boys than my father, who had hardly had a childhood at all. One example of the difference between them was that Uncle Geoff, like his sisters and her childhood friends, always called my mother 'Chick', a nickname my father detested. My parents always called each other 'hon' (for 'honey') in American fashion.

I do not know of any musical history in my paternal family before my father. Aunt Evelyn writing to me on 10 August 1964 insisted that 'our family was like any average family', apart from her brother Beryl. What struck her was not the unusual character of her family but how many teachers it produced. I have learned little about them apart from a few details of my grandfather's professional career. Certainly my father was committed to the piano from earliest childhood. I have some biographical notes sent by Aunt Evelyn to my mother (undated but postmarked 1 June 1955) about the hours which he had had to devote to the piano as a child: 'It was *so* hard for such a little fellow to practise the required six hours a day on a piano, but evidently our father, who was his teacher, seemed to think it highly necessary.' When he was seven years old he began to play professionally and from the first had high praise from critics. My grandfather gave up his religious position and toured with my father, arranging also for him to study with the noted contemporary piano pedagogue Alexander Lambert (1862-1929).

Aunt Evelyn may have been right in saying that the family was 'average'. She herself worked all her life for the Bell Telephone Company in Atlanta. In the same 1964 letter she told me that she had 'never cared to be a supervisor. It only pays $100.00 a month more and is not worth all the extra studying at night and also the hatred of the girls who work under you as is the case many times.' Evelyn was the only one of his siblings whom my father had any wish to see in later life. Two of his three brothers did not have careers worthy of note, but Douglas, who ran away from home to join the army, rose to the rank of colonel.

I recall several stories which my father told from these early years. One was of buying enormous watermelons for a nickel, five cents, which was then worth about 2½d.; by the time I worked at weekends and holidays in a grocery shop in the 1940s they were selling for three dollars each. He told us that he flushed the first dollar he had ever earned down the lavatory, which suggests that Athens had, unfortunately for my father, better sanitation than one might have expected at that period.

He also told us that my grandfather was sitting on a train smoking when a stranger passed by and saw the packet of cigarettes. 'I'll have one of those', he said, grabbing a cigarette. 'No, you won't', said my grandfather, grabbing it back. Uncle Percy, the eldest child in the family, who later became a doctor, was regarded by my own branch of the family as a black sheep, for reasons which remained undisclosed. (He too remained undisclosed for some decades.) His life of crime, however, apparently began when he hid in a lavatory for an entire night to gain free admittance to the circus. 'You're not clever enough to be dishonest', my grandfather told my father, advice which is worth remembering across the generations. These last two stories suggest that the there was more to be said for the old man than his children were wont to believe.

In about 1911, when my father was touring with my grandfather, he came to the notice of Irma, the lovely and vivacious wife of Isidore Zacharias, a wealthy Florida lawyer and property developer. Mrs Zacharias was a talented violinist and patron of music whom I remember having met only once, in the first week of 1958 shortly before her death. She felt, she told me, that my father was being exploited and mistreated by his own father. Indeed, according to the recollection of her son Jerrold (1905-86), who later became a leading American physicist, 'the boy was so miserable that he considered planning to run away and never again play the piano' (Jack Goldstein, *A Different Sort of Time: the life of Jerrold R. Zacharias, scientist, engineer, educator*, 1992, p. 4). The account may have been exaggerated, but undoubtedly he was depressed and unhappy before Mrs Zacharias came to his rescue.

She came to an arrangement with the rabbi whereby she effectively purchased my father and brought him up in her home with her own two children. He was there given the love and care of which he had been deprived. He wrote to Mrs Zacharias on 6 September 1918, shortly before his twentieth birthday: 'Without you to look on & give encouragement my life would be nothing, as it was before the night at the Duval Theatre', presumably the occasion of their first meeting. 'I am your grandmother', Mrs Zacharias later told me, much to the indignation of my mother, who had never liked her and was probably jealous of her. But in fact her comment was scarcely more than the truth, since my father signed his letter 'Votre fils adoptif'. The arrangement was less happy for her own children. Jerrold recalled being neglected by his mother in favour of the newcomer (Goldstein, pp. 4, 11) and her daughter Dorothea, who was groomed to marry my father, was I believe greatly distressed when the match failed to take place.

As he continued with his career after moving in with the Zachariases, my father did not live the life of a normal adolescent, even as then understood. Mrs Zacharias took him with her own children to study in Berlin on more than one occasion before the outbreak of the Great War with the composer-pianists Ferrucio Busoni (1866-1924) and José Vianna da Motta (1868-1948). She brought her family back to the United States not because of the war, she said, but because Busoni had developed an interest in my father which was more than paternal.

Some time after the United States entered the war in 1917 he narrowly escaped being conscripted, as he wrote to Mrs Zacharias in the letter previously quoted: 'Everyone who looks to be of the draft age is being held up on the street & asked for registration cards. Those who cannot give satisfactory answers are taken to jail and held there until they can prove their identity...And my practising, & my work, twelve years of it!' (It is hard not to conclude that I was the son of a draft dodger, the first though not the second time round.) In the same year (1918), however, he accompanied the famous Belgian violinist Eugène Ysaÿe (1858-1931), to whom he was 'mon cher compagnon de route', on one or more American tours, so he must have been highly visible to the conscription authorities had they wished to find him. Subsequently he continued his professional career, touring in the United States.

In 1921 he was engaged by Ernest Bloch (1880-1959), composer and the founder-director of the Cleveland Institute of Music, to teach in the piano faculty of the institute. Thus began a connection with Cleveland which was to end only with his death. The year 1925 was of crucial importance to him. He became head of the piano department of the Cleveland Institute. He made his London debut in June at the Queen's Hall, playing Saint-Saëns with the London Symphony Orchestra and giving a recital of Bach, Mozart, Chopin and Ravel a few days later. *Musical Opinion* wrote of the latter occasion that he was 'truly a great player and received a frenzied ovation' (July 1925, p. 1007). And he married my mother, a union which may have reinforced his (or her) determination that he should spend more of his time in one place and less in touring.

Elsa Landesman had been educated in Cleveland schools and subsequently attended Wellesley College, an upper-crust women's college in Massachusetts to which my sister Ellen followed her in due course. I recall my mother as an intelligent and educated woman, and her library before her marriage substantiates the recollection; her leather-bound edition of Shakespeare is one of my prized possessions. (My father had had a much more sporadic education, having had no regular schooling since he was seven years

My mother, probably some time in the 1930s.

6

old, but he loved Dickens and his love passed to me; so did his leather-bound complete set of the author's books, published in 1901-02.) I remember thinking with the unforgivable arrogance of youth how intelligent and well educated she was for someone who had spent all her life in Cleveland. I also thought when I was a child how different and superior my parents were to my friends' parents, who generally had had much less education and were much less interesting – to me, at least.

My mother was keen, even obsessive, about correct English, and her precise pronunciation of the language resulted in occasional queries in her place of birth as to whether she was English. Grammar and correct use of words were important to her; I can still recall her 'this is she', when she answered the phone, followed by an all too obvious total bewilderment on the part of her interlocutor. (But it was surely more graceful than the nasal '*spea*-king' of her American contemporaries.) Ann suggests that her love of correct English may owe something to the fact that she was a first-generation Anglophone; that may well be the case, and it is also true that that generation of Americans at least was much more careful of its grammar and syntax that its British contemporaries. It was to be a shock to me when I eventually realised how much more informal in behaviour, mores and speech the English were than Americans. (An English family told me when I was hitch-hiking in the 1950s that Americans never used a small word when a large one would do, never spoke simply when there was a complicated alternative; it was a seminal moment for me.)

I know little of my mother's childhood other than that it seems to have been happy and that she made friends including Gladys Goldfinger and Charlotte Young (later Bates) who remained life-long intimates. She was, one might say, the lighter side of the marriage; a woman of charm and beauty. I have a photograph of her taken before the second war looking like Marlene Dietrich and an even earlier one looking like Theda Bara. My father was a much more intense, more rigid, more judgmental sort of person. My mother's life revolved around him and at least one of her sisters thought that she had sacrificed the gaiety and enjoyment of her life to him. She may have been right but I never forgave my aunt for telling me so within three months of my father's death.

My mother must have been unhappy at Wellesley. Otherwise it is impossible to account for the fact that she left the college to be married nearly half-way through her final (in the American system, the fourth) year. I doubt that she ever regretted it and perhaps she thought that if she did not marry when she did my father would have lost interest, even though she did not accept his offer of marriage at once. It was a family joke that he proposed to every young woman he met; that one of them had asked for time to make up her mind but that he had left the town where he was performing the next morning and never saw her again.

My parents were married at the Temple, Cleveland, by Abba Hillel Silver (1893-1963), later a leading American Zionist, on 29 December 1925. The date is one of some resonance in English/British history; Thomas à Becket was murdered on 29 December 1170, W.E. Gladstone was born on the same day in 1809, the Jameson Raid took place on 29 December 1895 and the Luftwaffe firebombed the City of London in one of the worst raids of the Blitz on 29 December 1940. It was certainly a date of resonance in my family history; my father was to die on 29 December 1952, aged 54, and Rabbi Silver officiated at his funeral. (In the Roman Catholic calendar it is also my saint's day and forty years after my father's death my first grandchild, Dora, was born the following day.)

Whether or not my father ruined my mother's life, as Aunt Helen believed, she was certainly the best thing that ever happened to him; providing him with a stable, loving home, being an excellent hostess and generally sharing his own views (but by no means slavishly) on music (which she loved), religion (which they rejected) and politics (both were virtually unqualified supporters of Franklin D. Roosevelt and the New Deal). Though in conformity with the orthodoxy of her day she never engaged in paid employment, she had serious intellectual interests which she duly passed to her children, who spent much more time with her than with our sometimes remote father. My father, on the other hand, provided my mother with an entry to professional and cultural circles which her own commercial background did not offer. I find it hard to believe, however, that he could have found so good a wife elsewhere, or that she would not have married another successful professional man if she had wished to do so.

The favoured suburbs of Cleveland lie east of the city, on which they look down from the first foothills, so it is said, of the Appalachian Mountains. Cleveland proper crouches on the flat

8

land below, south of Lake Erie; the 'west side' had a high proportion of people of central and eastern European origin who were employed in the steel works which were the city's principal industry. In my childhood the population of the city was about 900,000 and Cleveland was the sixth largest city in the country, but as the years passed and white families moved out of Cleveland proper, its numbers steadily declined. The suburbs added another fifty per cent or so to the population of the conurbation in the 1940s. (The same process of urban decline and suburban growth has of course affected Britain.)

My parents lived for almost the whole of their married life in Cleveland Heights, a suburb of about 60,000 people some six miles east of the centre of Cleveland and perhaps half that distance from my mother's birthplace. So far as I know her childhood home is still standing, now in an area populated almost exclusively by inner-city ethnic minorities. It is not a district, I was told when last there (now many years ago), where white people would choose to suffer a disabling defect in their cars. They lived for a year in New York in the mid-30s when my father had a sabbatical, most of which he spent writing an opera; upon their return they moved a few streets away from their previous home in Cleveland Heights, to a house in which they lived until my father's death. My mother lived in the same house until her own death in 1963 and after that time Ellen, who had returned to Cleveland with her own family after our mother fell seriously ill in the early sixties, lived for a long period in what I liked to think of as the ancestral home.

It was an unusual neighbourhood with a very high proportion of professional people prominent in the life of Cleveland. Our neighbours were of English, Scottish, German and other 'acceptable' European origins, including Irish. There were many Catholics in the neighbourhood, as there was a Catholic church and school nearby, and a few Jewish families. There were, however, no black families, and this was true, so far as I know, of the whole of Cleveland Heights. Most of the Catholics were of Irish origin (my closest friend in early childhood was named Phil (then known as Pidgy) Clancy, and I first watched television in his house; Clancy meant 'seer of the clans', he told me.) It caused a considerable frisson on the street when the first family of Italian origin moved in.

Ellen was born on 17 January 1930; I followed on 7 August 1932, the same year that my father was made director of the

Cleveland Institute of Music, a position which he held until his death in 1952. I was born on a Sunday, but I do not think that I could ever have been described as bonny or blithe, good or gay. I still have three letters which my mother received from her sister Zella and two of her closest friends congratulating her on my birth. Her friend Ruth Edwards described me as 'the heir to the throne', an inappropriate title for a subsequent republican, while Charlotte Bates, writing to 'Dear Chick, old bean', referred to my mother's previous belief that she would never be the mother of a boy.

Many aspects of my childhood conduced to happiness. We children had intelligent parents, devoted to and dependent on each other, who cared deeply for us. (I can recall only once when they quarrelled in front of us, and that was at the end of a long day's car journey when we were all exhausted.) Uncle Geoff was a constant visitor, and during the war when my father was in the army my mother's sister Dorothy lived with us; her husband was in the navy. We adored Aunt Dot, and for a period almost had two mothers. We took for granted all the material comforts which most Europeans at the time would hardly have believed possible; a detached home with gardens front and back, central heating, consumer durables such as a car, washing machine and (at the end of the war) a dishwasher. My parents were passionately concerned about political developments and most of their friends were also strong New Dealers, though I was discomfited by one who told me that he had been a strikebreaker in the British General Strike of 1926. Ellen and I were exposed from earliest infancy to a heady mixture of intellectual, political and cultural influences which were to be determining influences on my life.

We also had resident domestic servants until American entry into the Second World War; it was in fact that war which largely ended this type of status in the United States as elsewhere, propaganda to the contrary. We had long and happy holidays at the less fashionable end of Cape Cod until interrupted by the war; my father composed and wrote in the morning and we all swam in warm inland lakes and the (relatively) warm sea, ate clam chowder and other delicious shellfish. In Cleveland we went to concerts and plays in the numerous professional and semi-professional theatres of the city. My father had a wide acquaintance in the musical world and we met or were told of our parents' meeting celebrated names who

(Left to right) Beryl Rubinstein, pianist (1898-1952), Jascha Heifetz, violinist (1901-1987), hostess?, Artur Rodzinski, conductor (1892-1958), Arthur Loesser, pianist (1894-1969); Cleveland, probably about 1940.

included Jascha Heifetz (1901-87), the most famous violinist of the day. Georg Szell (1897-1970), who refashioned the Cleveland Orchestra, was a family friend. I remember the eminent Swiss violinist André de Ribaupierre (1893-1955), a former colleague of my father's in Cleveland and best man at my parents' wedding. He had climbed the Matterhorn five times, on three of them with his violin strapped to his back to play when he reached the summit. It is impossible to describe how heroic he seemed to a small boy who had never 'been anywhere'. I can only say that his influence was one of the factors which roused in me a longing to travel which wartime conditions made even more burning.

My parents did not belong to the social aristocracy of Cleveland. They would not have wished to do so and they bore the wrong surname. But their friends were among the city's musical and cultural elite and they also knew many wealthy music lovers among the city's business leaders. The subsidies of such people were important if not essential for the survival of the Insitute of

Music, which was a private institution. One such friend was Mrs Hickox, who was already elderly in my childhood and who as a child had witnessed the German Uhlans marching through Paris in 1871 after the Franco-Prussian war. It was one of the counts against me in childhood that I had said 'guts' in front of Mrs Hickox. Britain was always less rule-bound than the United States, but we are now thankfully in a world less restricted by convention than we were then. (However, I believe that I never committed a public faux pas as devastating as one of my Swarthmore contemporaries who, at home during the Christmas holiday, said: 'no shit!' in reaction to a story which he found surprising. In the frozen silence which ensued he was forced to leave the dinner table.)

I remember once in about 1942 attending with my mother an extravaganza of patriotic music and sketches in aid of the war effort. (There were several such in wartime.) A little old man came on stage and to thunderous applause sang: 'This is the army, Mr Jones.' Who was it who had received such an ovation, I asked my mother. She replied that the little old man was Irving Berlin, then in his fifties. He was to live for nearly another fifty years; I was ten.

The United States being a collection of cultures, we had food from everywhere. Cleveland Heights was literally above the area called Little Italy; I recall one delicious Italian meal paid for by my wealthy Uncle Lee from California; there were six or eight of us at table and the bill, we were given to understand, came to a staggering $30 or so, about £18 at present exchange rates.

My great passion as a child was sport. My father was interested in it too and sometimes played with me; he taught me to play tennis and I enjoyed the game for many years. Not far from my home was a piece of empty ground which Americans called a 'vacant lot' (it later became a car park), and which was a centre for baseball (spring and summer) and American football (autumn and winter). There were lots of boys in the neighbourhood, most of whom attended the nearby Catholic 'parochial' school called St Anne's, and I was never short of a game. Baseball was my great love. Cleveland had a good professional team, the Indians, and my father and I went often to see them play. The old names come to my mind: Lou Boudreau, Rollie Helmsley, Roy Weatherley, Oris Hockett ('Sockit, Hockett', we screamed) and above all Bob Feller, the pitcher (bowler) who was a national star and with whom (thanks to a contact of Uncle Geoff's) I was photographed when I was about nine. I remember my father once commenting as we watched the Indians that Boudreau could not possibly hit a ball effectively with his peculiar posture, his bottom high in the air. Boudreau responded by nearly hitting the ball out of the park. 'What do you think now?', I asked my father. 'Nearly a home run' (a six), was his not unreasonable response.

My recollection is that professional baseball and football continued during the war, some at least of the players being unfit for military service but fit for the equally or more demanding requirements of professional sport. (This may be unfair.) I was a good sportsman and was usually picked for teams for which I applied; by the time I was in my mid-teens, however, my interests had shifted elsewhere. All that remained of my childhood obsession with sport, which, until mid-adolescence far exceeded my interest in anything else, was a reasonably fit body and a love of the out-of-doors.

Boxing was a sport which normally found little favour in my family home, though little was said about it; this was my parents' way. (I was generally given to understand that things of which they

David with Bob Feller, baseball star, Cleveland, about 1941.

13

disapproved were matters of taste, not of conviction, though how can the two be differentiated?) But Joe Louis, the 'Brown Bomber', was a hero amongst all white liberals, especially after defeating in the first round the Nazi Max Schmeling. My father would be practising the piano in the evening, as was his wont, and shortly before the fight he would wander into the adjacent room and turn on the radio. Joe Louis always won and there was quiet jubilation in the Rubinstein household.

Another pleasure of childhood was our trips to visit my mother's childhood friend Charlotte Bates, who lived with her husband and three children in a flat-roofed house on the shores of Lake Erie. Kenneth Bates was an artist who worked in enamel, and their home was light and bright as befitted their interests. They owned their own stretch of the lake shore, and though their home was only a few miles from the famously polluted centre of Cleveland (the Cuyahoga River, which ran through the centre of the steel district, was reputed to be the only river in the world which constituted a fire hazard) the lake was clear and inviting by the time it reached them. We went to see the Bates family regularly, always on the 4th July when we ritually let off fireworks, and I as regularly incurred universal disapproval by kicking sand into the barbecued meals.

In short, I had everything in childhood which should have made me happy, but I was often not. I was never a conformist, by which I mean that I have seldom felt a fully integrated member of any group. I was so undisciplined in school, constantly chattering, constantly disturbing others, that teachers despaired of me. Only my skill in baseball and other games prevented me from being bullied. My relations with Ellen were and have always remained frustrating; sometimes intimate, sometimes fraught. (We have consequently spent long periods out of touch with each other, though these periods have always ended in reconciliation.) I felt with some justice that she was happier, better liked and more successful than I was, and perhaps the consequent feelings of jealousy have never wholly worn off. Certainly she has always found it much easier to make and keep friends than I have done. In short, my need for friendship was almost equalled by my ability to alienate people.

I was frequently in trouble with my mother ('David, don't make me nag like a fishwife', she would say; I wish she could have lived to see the beautiful and charming fishwives of Boulogne), and as time passed my relations with my father deteriorated. I do not think that he was much bothered about my total lack of interest in music, though I developed a passion for it (alas, only as a listener) when I was about 17. He was much more bothered about my lack of interest in anything with intellectual content, my long periods of boredom, my total absorption in sport. For one who had had no proper childhood and had worked since he was seven years old such behaviour was obviously difficult to understand or endure.

I was unsure of myself and emotional, easily hurt and lacking protection against the outer world. One April Fool's day in my early childhood Ellen hid the family newspaper and when my father asked for it replied that she did not know where it was. He searched for it, not realising that he was the victim of a prank. I watched with mounting agony and finally burst into uncontrollable sobs. My father had been only slightly perplexed by the absence of the newspaper, but the whole family was alarmed by my gross over-reaction. On this occasion it had been directed against the supposed suffering of my father, but I was also very good at exaggerating my own supposed slights.

My mother was deeply concerned about my lack of self-control. She mooted more than once the possibility of sending me to one of the private schools which served the Cleveland middle class (most of the pupils attending by the day rather than boarding), but I was adamant that I would not go to a 'snob' school and she did not really believe in private education, so the point was not pressed.

My adventures at summer camp, that curse of the American middle classes, were by no means wholly negative, but there was much which I could not learn to do, as manual dexterity was beyond me, unlike my father, who was an enthusiastic amateur carpenter. (I have lamentably passed on the inability to make anything more complicated than bookshelves to my sons.) I was squeamish about first aid (though this did not stop me regularly donating blood in later life until I developed high blood pressure), and in consequence I was unable to join the long canoe-cum-camping journeys from Camp Mishawaka (boys only) located in an idyllic part of northern Minnesota near the source of the Missippi River. The trips went over the border and were consequently known as 'Big Canadian' and 'Little Canadian'. I did learn to canoe, however, and to swim, and played tennis and baseball ardently. I had the same problems

15

and enjoyments in my period as a Boy Scout. And my love of the outdoors was strengthened; the more I reflect about summer camp the more I realise I learned from it.

I learned a lot also from some of the 'counsellors', especially John Dickerson, a sensitive and liberal soul not much older than myself who had a family connection with the Cleveland Institute of Music. The death in childhood of his cousin Harriet (known as Mickey), a near neighbour in Cleveland Heights and loved by everyone, was an extremely distressing experience; Aunt Dot's sudden death in her mid-forties soon after she left our home upon the return of her husband from the war was of course even more traumatic.

One of the directors of the camp was Kent Curtis, whose family connection with the Dickersons had resulted in my attending Mishawaka in the first place. He was hugely popular among the boys, who loved his piano playing as he led community singing, often of his own songs. The story of the commuter who missed the 5.15 train home from his office ('Talk about your subway, talk about your "el", talk about your streetcar lines as well; but if you're living out where the grass is green, you've gotta go home on the 5.15.') and his subsequent escapades was a special favourite.

Earlier I had attended Red Raider camp outside Cleveland and learned to ride horseback, though I never quite overcame my initial terror of horses. Red Raider was owned and run by Fox Smith, a man of enormous charm and the good looks of a film star. I idolised him as did everyone else, and enjoyed the rides home in the camp bus, often driven by Fox, as it struggled up the hills east of Cleveland. He led us in singing and I remember several songs from the period: 'John Jacob Jingleheimer Smith: that's my name too' was one of them. Another was a rather grisly number about the neighbours' cats and dogs being ground to sausages in 'Johnny Rebeck's machine' ('Oh, Mr Johnny Rebeck, how could you be so mean'). The one I remember most vividly contained several verses about particular objects such as lollipop ('That's the only decent kind of candy, candy, man who made it must have been a dandy, dandy'; the American slang of the 1940s comes back like a dream). One verse was about Red Raider itself. 'That's the only decent kind of ca-mp, ca-mp; man who made it must have been a...' Wickedly encouraged by Fox, half or more of the bus shouted 'tramp', while I joined the others who screamed 'champ'. We did enjoy ourselves.

16

The most painful single recollection of my early childhood was also connected with Red Raider. Located as it was east of the eastern suburbs of Cleveland, it catered mostly for day campers, but there was a boarding section in which I was enrolled in 1942 when I was ten. It was my first sojourn away from home. During the first week or so I enjoyed myself enormously, but after a visit from my parents I developed uncontrollable homesickness of a type which I have fortunately never experienced subsequently. It was a real illness from which I found it impossible to recover. Finally, my parents took me away on the face-saving grounds that my father was going into the army and that I should be with my mother in his absence. They must have hesitated before sending me to camp in Minnesota, from which I could not return home, but fortunately the earlier problems did not recur.

In short, my recollections of unhappiness in childhood, though real, are somewhat hard to identify. Everything, I repeat, which should have made me happy was in place; my frequent unhappiness and failure to relate to other people were largely of my own making. There was, however, one objective cause of unhappiness, the war, for which my father volunteered in his mid-forties, in marked contrast with his efforts to avoid conscription in 1917-18. Having studied in Berlin he may have felt little reason in 1917 to hate Germany, and though neither of my parents had German relatives they probably regarded Germany as the home of music and, generally, civilisation. The seizure of power by Hitler and subsequent events must have been a source of great anguish to them. When they did not want us children to understand them they spoke German at the dinner table, though alas my mother's anguished 'bitte schön' when my father was particularly hard on me in adolescence was before long as easy to understand in German as in English.

My father, who was a captain, was used mainly in a morale-boosting role, singing as he marched with the troops and playing for them. (He was later to feel that his talents were being used simply as an antidote to the boredom of high-ranking officers.) He came home from time to time on leave and we saw him off from the railway station. On one occasion my mother wept, and I asked her why she was distressed, since she had previously kept up appearances before Ellen and me. 'This time he's going abroad', she

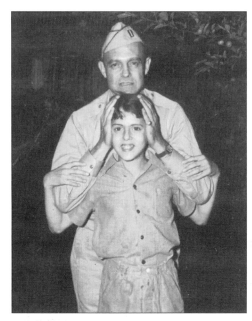

My father and I, Cleveland Heights, June 1944 (my father in US Army captain's uniform).

replied. In fact he was going to North Africa and before he returned home he had travelled some 20,000 miles in his support work for the troops. An obituary notice in a Cleveland paper published a recollection of him which has always moved me to tears. It was an account of his playing in the North African desert all the popular music that the soldiers wanted. 'A young GI jammed up against the piano platorm bawled: "Hey can you play 'When I Jump Off in Cairo, Illinois a Delegation at the Station will Meet Me?'" Sure, said the captain... "Hey", said another lad, "play 'Margie'. We want to sing." The captain played "Margie".' ('The captain played everything', *Cleveland News*, 6 January 1953)

He served in Italy, and another of my early memories was a letter of his to my mother saying that he had seen a 'most interesting natural phenomenon'. American officers censored their own mail, Vesuvius was then in eruption and this was the first time that my mother had known where he was. (One imagines that if the Gestapo had been anxious to locate Beryl Rubinstein or his regiment they would have been as little deceived by this description as my mother was.) The *Cleveland News* obituary also recalled him playing during the siege of Monte Cassino, 'that bloody and forlorn battle...The booming and whizbanging of the big guns went on incessantly. The rain also leaked on the piano keyboard and now and then the captain had to wipe and warm his hands so he could go on playing for the bearded, frozen, punchy GI's who stood in a kind of numb silence around him, speaking only to voice requests.'

I should add that my father must have worked hard to identify the tunes the troops asked of him, for he was never interested in popular music. (Asked by one of my friends who was his favourite composer, he replied that he thought Beethoven was 'pretty good'.) When on holiday one summer after the war we visited the Shannon family; Kay had been one of my mother's Wellesley contemporaries. Her husband Percy played a recording of Cole Porter's *Kiss me, Kate* for my previously sceptical father; he thought it utterly marvellous. Apart from that experience I think that his only experiment with popular music was the work of George Gershwin.

I am bound to say that for me the war meant mainly that my father was replaced in the house by Aunt Dot. There was rationing but I do not remember it affecting me. Readers need not be told that Americans did not suffer invasion or bombing. I grew up slowly and was not really interested in the outside world much before the American election of 1948, when I was 16. I knew that there was a war on and who the enemy was, but I was far more interested in my personal concerns than in any outside matters. As I turned thirteen years old the day after the first atomic bomb was dropped on Hiroshima, this lack of concern was perhaps not wholly reprehensible.

Nevertheless, I could not escape introduction to politics nor, indeed, to religion. As I have said, my parents were uncompromising New Dealers as were most of their friends. Cleveland Heights was a prosperous suburb and most people there were conservatives who supported the Republican Party. In 1940, when I was eight, I came home and told my parents that I (like almost all my schoolmates) supported Wendell Wilkie, the Republican candidate in that autumn's presidential election. I was told firmly that I did not, that like the rest of the family I supported Roosevelt. Memory says that I went back to school to announce my new allegiance but that there was only one other Democrat in my class.

Ellen and I with our parents at home in Cleveland Heights, probably about 1945.

I recall my father's politics mostly in the context of his attempts to restrain my increasingly extreme left-wing views in later adolescence. I don't think that he was consciously influenced by the fact that his musical institute was partly dependent on contributions from wealthy people some of whom were probably very conservative, but he felt rightly that my political beliefs were callow in the extreme. My mother was a proud American, patriotism in those years being still associated with the melting pot of American legend, the 'last best hope' of humanity, and the country which stood aloof from European fascism. (The New Deal had also roused a new wave of patriotism, but it should also be remembered that there was a good deal of American-style fascism and racism in the period.)

The United States being a country of strong politicians and weak parties, she regarded herself as an independent, but she was an independent who always voted for the Democrats. She was always a passionate believer in the individual deciding for him or herself, on the basis of personal conviction, not simply according to the dictates of environment or heredity. 'Why don't they *go* to Moscow?', she would demand of Chekhov's *Three Sisters*. It was inevitable that growing up in a home like mine at such a critical period of European and American history I would be infected by the political disease.

I must have been no more than 16 when I realised that I was a socialist, defined as the abolition of such private property as permits one person to dominate another's life, and the abolition of social classes. Socialism, which I regard as tautological to qualify as 'democratic', seemed to me in adolescence to be nothing other than common sense. It seems so still, fifty years later, not despite but because of all the changes which have occurred during the period.

I came to political consciousness in the early years of the Cold War, when anti-Communist hysteria was very strong. I was greatly influenced by the Alger Hiss perjury case, which Alistair Cooke rightly called 'a generation on trial' (in his book of that title published in 1950) and which has fascinated me ever since. Oddly, the trial of Julius and Ethel Rosenberg largely passed me by, but I remember the beginnings of Richard Nixon's political career, in which he built a career on abusing his opponents as fellow-travellers or crypto-Communists. In my late adolescence and early twenties Senator Joseph McCarthy was at the height of his fame and power. Democrats were stigmatised by their political opponents as guilty of '*creeping* socialism'. All of this was a major influence in disillusioning me with my own country.

I was never a Communist, and indeed when I became a student in Britain many of my colleagues looked on me as a moderate if not a CIA spy, but I was more conscious of the failings of my own country and its political system than those of a country at the other end of Europe, suffering the effects of a war in which it had done most of the fighting and dying, and which claimed to be the workers' state. From my mid-adolescence Britain, which had not succumbed to the kind of open anti-Communist hysteria prevalent in the United States, seemed to me a haven of good sense in the English-speaking world, particularly as it had been governed for six years after the war by a political party which called itself socialist.

21

As to religion, it posed little problem for my parents because they did not believe in it. They were conscious of being Jews ('that's me', I remember my father saying once, beating his chest: 'Jew, Jew, Jew', rather than the softer 'Jewish') and having a Jewish inheritance, particularly in the age of Hitler. My father, the rabbi's son, never ate bacon or ham, though the rest of the family did, and I recall my bewilderment on Cape Cod when my parents found to their dismay that a packed lunch prepared for us by our holiday hotel consisted of ham sandwiches.

But in terms of religious practice they were convinced agnostics. They moved in a cosmopolitan world of music and culture and most of their friends were Christians by background. At that time country (golf, etc.) clubs (and sometimes indeed summer camps) were usually divided on grounds of religious affiliation. In some communities Jews were unwelcome as neighbours, but I recall virtually nothing of this kind in Cleveland. My parents belonged to no Jewish social organisations and sent Ellen and me to summer camps which did not discriminate on grounds of religion. I do not recall my mother making any moral statement on the matter; it was all a matter, she said typically, of personal preference.

Evidently they felt, in a country which divided public education from religion, that Ellen and I should have some sort of religious education. We were Reform Jews (i.e., as liberal and undogmatic as we could be while still retaining some ties with the faith of the past) and hence belonged to an institution called the Temple, not a synagogue. To my mother fell the duty of accompanying us there once a year on the Jewish Day of Atonement. I hated it. (So, I imagine, did she.) Why, I cannot say, but I felt at once that this was not the place for me, that I did not want to be cut off from the rest of humanity on grounds not of my own choosing. I also felt that if one did believe in God it was disappointing to have only one; the classical or Norse multiplicity of deities seemed much more fun.

When we reached the age of 12 or 13 both Ellen and I refused to continue attending the Temple, and we attended school on all the Jewish holy days; my parents certainly had no objection and I am sure that my mother felt a sense of relief that she no longer had to take us to atone for our sins of the previous year. With a single exception, when a friend and I in our undergraduate days visited all the different churches we could find near our university, I have never subsequently attended any act of Jewish worship and almost never been inside a synagogue. I have always been glad not to have suffered compulsory religion as a child but I have also regretted my consequent impressionistic knowledge of the Bible.

The early years after the war, when I grew from childhood into adolescence, were also the aftermath of the horror of the Nazi concentration camps and the foundation of the state of Israel. I was too young to know what was happening, but my parents, though obviously concerned, were not Zionists and felt that the foundation of a Jewish state was at best a regrettable necessity. By the time I became politically conscious I shared their views and was early convinced of the gross injustice to the Arab population caused by the foundation and early history of Israel.

Like my socialism, my opposition to Zionism and a state based on a particular religion has never wavered. Only my religious affiliation has varied over time. Without altering the view that Christian theology is a matter not of divine truth but of anthropological or historical interest, I have come to appreciate the importance of religion in human lives and the need of it in my own.

I should add that though Zionism had its most powerful support in the United States, in my youth American Jewry was far more divided than, I suspect, it was in Britain. Large numbers of Jews were fully assimilated into American life and I think that American Jews, despite periodic manifestations of discrimination, felt themselves to be unqualified citizens of their country before their British counterparts did. The longer period of assimilation was inevitable in Britain which was until after 1945 much more ethnically homogeneous than the United States. One's surname in the latter country did not automatically imply fixed beliefs or ways of behaviour. One could go into a cafe and ask for a ham sandwich, to be greeted with the query: 'on rye bread or white?' The melting pot was not in theory or in practice a device whereby young Central or Eastern Europeans, Asians or Afro-Caribbeans could become young Anglo-Saxons and I have never stopped believing in it.

My family observed Christmas in ways similar to their Christian neighbours, with trees and presents. It was customary in our social circle for people to buy presents for their friends' children, so that Ellen and I received thirty or so presents from almost as many people. The surfeit of family and greed eventually aroused an antagonism on my part to Christmas which I have never lost. But I remember suggesting to my mother one December that we put a wreath outside our door and my surprise and embarrassment when she replied: 'But we are a *Jewish* family!'

We learned Christmas carols at school, which I imagine is no longer the case in the United States. Christmas was already such a secular holiday that I don't think this had any impact on our religious convictions, and there were no nativity plays. I was always grateful to have learned Christmas carols, though surprised when I came to live in England to discover that the tunes of several of them differed from the American versions. Ann and I usually attend a midnight mass on Christmas Eve and have been lucky enough to attend the service of Lessons and Carols at King's College Cambridge more than once; I find Christmas as a religious experience both moving and happy.

At the age of fifteen I entered high school, as was the norm in the American system, and remained there for three years. Cleveland Heights was still a lily-white suburb and there were only a few families who did not belong to favoured ethnic groups among the 2000+ pupils. I had one school friend from my Saturday grocery job who came from an Italian family and there were others like him, but not many of them.

I found out about girls at this time but I was too timid and prudish to be much of a success with them; I was 17 before I discovered that any girl actually liked me 'that way', though they were mostly younger girls who did not know me. I remember that when I was new to high school I met Jeanie Berko, a charming young woman slightly older than I who was generally known as Beanie, from the transposition of the initial letters of her names. 'I'm tired', she said to me one day. I replied that I was too, I suppose because I had nothing else to say. 'I will *not* say: "Let's go to bed"', she replied, as if wearied through repeating the phrase too often. I thought to myself: 'I'm in a different league now.' I was still an enthusiast for sport, at least in my first year, and used to watch the high school (American) football team, which attracted more support than the baseball side: 'Two bits, four bits, six bits, a dollar, all for Heights High, STAND UP AND HOLLER!'

It was in high school, however, that I found that I was not a sportsman but an intellectual. High time too, my parents must have thought, as they had despaired over my lack of interest in anything other than sport. My father, who worked so constantly, had tried to interest me in history and gradually he had some effect. William Morris, later to become one of my heroes, wrote that he was taught 'next to nothing' at school. I cannot say the same, but the teaching I underwent had less impression on me that my total immersion in the Heights Players, the dramatic society.

The school's intelligentsia, as we liked to think, were Players. We put on 'major productions' for the wider public every year, but what was far more educational for the participants was the short plays which we put on weekly for ourselves. I was introduced to many authors I had not come across before and enjoyed acting. We also had a Players' magazine in which we criticised productions and wrote about related subjects. This was my first experience of independent writing and our talks and parties were my introduction to serious or semi-serious discussions with my contemporaries. (I went to bed later on a regular basis when I was 17 than I have ever done since.)

It was through the Players that I began the experience of growing up. I owe as much to them as to any other group of people with whom I have ever been in contact. When I entered high school I was little more than a child. When I left I was a sentient human being, and the major reason was my exposure to Heights Players. I think with much affection of these friends of long ago: Harry Ritchie, Eddie Bordo and Marv Metschis, whose *Twelfth Night* was a seminal and unforgettable experience for us all; Sue and Peggy Brown, Jack Dennis, Rosemary Catalano, Maggie Wadsworth, Dorothy Tobkin, Cammie Wettlaufer, Larry Kaufman, Bob Lazar, Bill Herzog, Eileen Gelfand, Rhoda Robboy and others.

I also remember 'Doc' (Dinah) Evans, the teacher who had responsibility for the Players with her assistant Leonard Freyman. And above all I remember Mary Dyas, one of my greatest school chums. Mary was no actor, but she was one of the few of us who was totally committed to the theatre and intended to make it her career. I remember her saying to me that I would not be a professional actor or manager but that the theatre needed an intelligent audience and that I should be sure to be among their number. I hope that I have been, and certainly I have gained much pleasure from the theatre over the years. Mary, who was a Catholic, and I were inseparable for a period and we were both deeply distressed when she was told by her mother that she should not 'go out so much with Jewish boys', i.e., me. I never had any kind of sexual relationship with her and I seldom or never saw her after I left Cleveland Heights for university, but my debt to her is enormous. I hope she flourished behind the scenes of Broadway or wherever else she ended up.

It was in high school that I made my first girlfriend, Anne Bowden. We were very close and the relationship brought me both intimacy and intense happiness. I owe Anne a great deal for what she gave and taught me, but the relationship did not survive the end of my first year away from home. (We did not meet again until by an extraordinary chance she and I were both in Salem, Oregon, in the summer of 1998 and she responded to an article which I had written in *The Oregonian*.) It was because of Anne that I made my first foreign journey, for she was of Canadian origin and the family retained a Canadian home. I visited her twice on the shores of Lake Ontario; apart from Cape Cod, summer camp in Minnesota, occasional visits to New York and one to Washington, going to see Anne was virtually my only trip away from Cleveland before I went to university.

I recall cycling with a school friend when I was about 15 to the Ohio-Pennsylvania border, a return journey of 150 miles or so. I lost some money in a slot machine (illegal in Cleveland and probably the state of Ohio but legal in Pennsylvania) and then cycled back again. Although I grew up within 200 miles of Niagara Falls I did not visit them then or subsequently. Was this due to the fact that people travelled less in those days? Wartime petrol rationing? The fact that my father was in the army for a period? Or my parents' feeling that anything which attracted so many visitors must be meretricious? I don't know.

It was also in high school that I formed my first close male friendship, a relationship which was indirectly to form a link in the chain which was to lead me to emigrate. My friend was Bob Gaebler, who came from a less wealthy family than mine and lived in a less prosperous part of Cleveland Heights. (His mother was the only person I can recall who was in considerable awe of mine.)

Much of what I learned about life as a boy of 15 to 17 I learned with Bob and for a period we were inseparable, though in fact we shared few interests or convictions. It is I suppose not surprising that I, who came from a wealthy family, should have been a socialist from adolescence, while Bob, who had to work his way through a much less fashionable university, has long been wedded to free enterprise and The American Way. But our different backgrounds and interests and our reduced intimacy in later life do nothing to reduce my debt to him.

When we were not with girls, which was much of the time, and sometimes when we were, we spent much of the weekend with each other. We went often to the cinema and one of my most vivid memories of these years was of Ealing comedies with Alec Guinness; *Passport to Pimlico, Kind Hearts and Coronets, The Card, The Lavender Hill Mob* and others. After the film we would go to the back door of a bakery and buy a loaf of hot bread, which we would devour while talking about the film and about Life. We hatched a plan at one stage to become intellectual farmers outside Paris which, needless to say, failed to bear fruit. We were town boys, knew nothing of Paris or farms and little about intellectuals either. On another

Carol and Bob Gaebler, newly-weds, Chicago, March 1961.

occasion we went to see *Gone with the Wind*, a third-rate film which the British (and indeed French) fashion for American kitsch has helped to make a cult. Our excuse was that we were very young, but we were so excited by the film that we walked afterwards the six miles from downtown Cleveland to our homes.

I also saw with Bob, my parents or occasionally with girls other British films such as *I Know Where I'm Going* with Wendy Hiller, *A Matter of Life and Death* with Roger Livesey, Laurence Olivier's *Hamlet* which I saw four times and almost memorised and *The Red Shoes* with Moira Shearer and Marius Goring. (I remember my parents discussing in the car on the way home from *The Red Shoes* whether the impresario, played by Anton Walbrook, had been in love with Moira Shearer. 'A man does not smash a mirror with his fist unless he is in love with a woman', my father pronounced gravely, which was presumably just the suspension of disbelief at which the film-makers aimed.)

In my youth and long afterwards Britain was not generally seen in the United States as the mother country, but the feeling of admiration for British endurance and survival against Hitler is impossible to exaggerate. Also, the educated classes were anglophiles to a man or woman for reasons not easy to analyse but which had much to do with admiration for British history, literature and culture, from Shakespeare to Shaw and Graham Greene. Any educated person had read in youth Lewis Carroll, Edward Lear, Robert Louis Stevenson, Edith Nesbit, Kenneth Grahame, A.A. Milne, P.L. Travers. Any educated person read English books and idolised Winston Churchill. This admiration of all things British was a feature of the United States which amused and pleased British visitors as perhaps it still does.

I should add that admiration for Britain was combined with staunch anti-imperialism, though the United States had already begun its own history as the great post-1945 imperial power. In particular Americans of my generation and whatever their ethnic origin believed in the unification of Ireland as an article of faith – and I still do, a conviction which undoubtedly owes something to my contacts with young people of Irish extraction in my youth. The harm done to Ireland by the famine of 1846, the British response and mass Irish emigration to the United States had a permanent effect on Anglo-American relations. It is a point too conveniently forgotten when British opinion-formers consider naive American reactions to the Irish question.

Cleveland Heights was not the wealthiest suburb of Cleveland; Shaker Heights was. But in 1950 when I left school (we said 'graduated from high school', even though we had no national or even local school examinations) virtually every pupil in my graduating class went to university or, as we said, to college. I recall my astonishment at meeting a girl in my graduating class working in a bank when I was in my first year at university. She was the only member of my wider circle who had left school at 17 or 18 for permanent employment. It is true that Bob Gaebler had to work for a year on steamers on the Great Lakes to earn enough money to start his university career and there were others like him, but he always intended to become a student, and did.

However, while most people from my school went to university, there was a distinct pecking order in the choice which they made or was presented to them. Broadly, the further one went from home and the further east, the more prestigious was the institution. Private institutions were more highly regarded than public ones. The least favoured were the many Ohio state universities, with which my parents threatened me if I 'didn't work'. My engagement with school work came just in time to save me from such a fate.

I applied to three universities. One was Oberlin, which was highly thought of but ruled out as being in Ohio and not far from Cleveland. The second was Harvard. In those days at least one did not tour the United States being interviewed at the institution of one's choice. Instead, my father took me, metaphorically cap in hand which must have been an odd experience for him, to the home of a wealthy (much wealthier than we were) Harvard graduate named Johannes Fleek for an interview. Mr Fleek recommended me, and my father was somewhat disgruntled when I decided that I did not want to be a 'Harvard man'.

Instead, I went to Swarthmore College, in the environs of Philadelphia, which was the suggestion of my mother. Swarthmore was a co-educational institution, like Oberlin but unlike Harvard, and had under a thousand students. It had been founded in 1864 by Quakers, a sect my mother much admired though I am not sure how much she knew about them. Certainly I never met a Quaker before going to Swarthmore. But though it had high academic standards it was not an Ivy League institution and one would not gain undesired prestige in later life for having attended it. Indeed, during the remaining years of my life in the United States a common reaction to my telling people that I was a student at Swarthmore was the reply: 'But I thought it was a *girls*' college!' (I still hear echoes of the same comment in England.)

They may have been confusing it with Bryn Mawr, which, with the men's college at Haverford, formed the remaining Quaker-inspired institutions in the Philadelphia area. Many of the students came from the same sort of homes that I did: left-liberal, intellectual, cultured; a sizeable proportion from New York City. It was probably more true in my case than in most others' that my choice of university, ill-informed as it was, was to have an enormous influence on the rest of my life.

CHAPTER 2

Swarthmore: 1950-4

I FIRST WENT TO Swarthmore College in September 1950, soon after my eighteenth birthday. In the American fashion I spent four years there and left with a BA. I had never been to Swarthmore before, never even to Philadelphia. I knew no one there. I had left Anne Bowden in Cleveland. Not for the first or last time I took refuge in self-pity.

In reality there was nothing to be distressed about, except for leaving Anne. Swarthmore has a most beautiful campus, in effect a landscaped park, gardens and woods which are a delight for walking and the study of nature alike. The campus also houses the home of Benjamin West (1738-1820), the painter who, like me, moved to England in youth and never returned. I always thought it a pity that he was such a ghastly painter.

Philadelphia, though far from being the city of brotherly love of its name, is a fascinating place and the 'cradle of American independence'. (I was told at an early stage that its town hall, topped by a statue of William Penn, was a monument to Penn's phallus; once again I told myself that I had begun to grow up and had moved into a new world.) Philadelphia is a much larger, older and more interesting city than Cleveland. Its historic attractions included Independence Hall where the American Declaration of Independence was signed in 1776, the Liberty Bell of the same period and a number of other eighteenth-century buildings, including the home of Betsy Ross (1752-1836), who is credited with being the designer of the first American flag with stars and stripes. Benjamin Franklin was buried in the churchyard of Christ Church, one of the city's oldest surviving (Anglican) churches (1754), and pennies were traditionally thrown on his grave. I was pleased when visiting Philadelphia in May 1998 to observe that the tradition continued. There were several Quaker meeting houses; the independent 'Free Quaker Meeting House' dated from 1783.

Philadelphia had several theatres and a magnificent symphony orchestra conducted by Eugene Ormandy. This last meant a great deal to me since I had suddenly and belatedly realised the joys of serious music in my final year in school. I became an avid and frequent though, alas, ignorant member of the audience. A ticket for the Philadelphia Orchestra cost 80 cents in the amphitheatre, and the orchestra's home at the Academy of Music with its fine acoustics was my introduction to the nineteenth-century European-style hall of music. It was at the Academy of Music that I heard several thrilling performances of Beethoven's Ninth Symphony.

The city has a fine art gallery and a museum with unique ancient remains, a fact unknown to me until after I had become a school teacher in London and collected postcards and pamphlets to help me teach ancient history. In short, Philadelphia unlike Cleveland was a metropolis, its importance apparently unimpeded by the fact that it was less than a hundred miles from New York.

The 500-mile rail journey from Cleveland could have been taken nearly a century before; it is difficult to believe that in the age of the motorway and the aeroplane there are still students who travel from Cleveland to Philadelphia by train. (There was in 1998 only one train a day in each direction and an arduous and impracticable change was required.) It passed through the beautiful hills of Pennsylvania and the steel works of Pittsburgh. Near Altoona the train negotiated the celebrated Horseshoe Bend in which one could see simultaneously both front and rear of the train. If I took the night train I arrived at North Philadelphia station before 7.0 in the morning and transferred to a suburban train to the main terminus, Thirtieth Street, from which I took another suburban train to Swarthmore. The trains were punctual. I never missed an 8.0 a.m. class and indeed, could just rush through breakfast in the college refectory before it began.

It was on these night journeys that I 'slept with Ruthie Wolfe'. Ruth Wolfe was the only other Clevelander in my year at Swarthmore; she came from the much more working-class West Side. She was a good travelling companion and our journeys

32

together were always pleasant; seats on the train reclined and we could get a certain amount of sleep. Our circles at Swarthmore, however, were wholly different, and I virtually never saw her except on the move between Philadelphia and Cleveland.

It did not take me long to make friends or at least a friend. This was John Purnell, son of a car dealer from a Chicago suburb. As he was shy of women and I had a girlfriend in Cleveland we spent a great deal of time together in our first year and also in our second, when my relationship with Anne Bowden had ended. John and I learned a great deal together and from each other, visiting cultural centres in Philadelphia and every religious establishment in the 'village' (more properly, suburb) of Swarthmore. I don't remember much about these visits except that the Episcopalian Church (the American equivalent of the Church of England) had much the best choir. Swarthmore itself is an upper-middle class area, but we also visited the working-class town of Chester a few miles away to attend the synagogue. It was not Reformed, and the service went on and on. Eventually we could stand no more and left. As previously mentioned I have never attended another Jewish religious service.

Swarthmore then had only about 900 students, a number which has increased to about 1300 since my day. About half the students were men, half women. There were four black students in my year, one American and three Nigerians. The American did not survive the full four years to graduation. Many students in each year became engaged to each other or to students in other years while undergraduates, giving the college the somewhat self-conscious nickname of 'the little Quaker matchbox'. But the rules which British universities called 'in loco parentis' were severe. Indeed, the reader at the end of the twentieth century will hardly believe the social and sexual conditions under which we lived.

There was strictly no visiting between the men's and women's halls of residence except on Sunday afternoons, when it was apparently assumed that the libido was not in evidence. At some point early in my student life the exception was ended, apparently because it had been 'taken advantage of' in a manner unacceptable to the authorities. (This was a considerable feat in view of the fact that most students shared bedrooms in the halls of residence, and bathrooms and toilets were used by all the students on a given floor.) Although love affairs were common they infrequently went 'all the way'. My guess is that the majority of students of my generation graduated in a virginal state. Almost everyone lived in a hall of residence limited to a single gender. We ate in a common refectory so that, unfortunately, we had no opportunity to learn to cook.

Women students had to be in their halls of residence, even on Saturday nights, by 1.30 a.m., earlier on most other nights. There was no time limit for the men but it was (correctly) assumed that without female companionship they too would return to their halls. I should add that the village of Swarthmore, like many others in the United States, was 'dry'; there was nowhere to buy alcohol and it was strictly forbidden on the college campus. (I used to bring in cheap wine and keep it in my cupboard, but I usually had nobody to drink it with so there was little incentive and I eventually gave it up as a bad job.)

Students were forbidden to marry, though an exception was made for a pair of brilliant students in my year named Ralph Brown and Peggy Rash. One student was reputed to have been fitted for a Dutch cap (I hardly knew what it was), but our innocence was generally great. It is necessary to remember not only American puritanism which was real enough, but also the fact that I was at university well before the advent of the birth control pill; pregnancy would have been a catastrophe for the students involved. This aura of innocence, protection and restriction was one facet of life in a country in which divorce was more common than elsewhere, and in which pornography and prostitution were widely available even for sheltered Swarthmore students down the road in Philadelphia.

My description resembles those of the Cambridge women students of the 1890s about whom I was to write years later. Like those Cambridge women, however, we had no objection to our chains. Like them we felt that we had a great deal of freedom and relished it. It was less than twenty years after my graduation in 1954 that I was told, in Hull, of a women finalist who had, unusually or uniquely, remained a virgin by choice. But even in the 1950s sexual taboos were not so strong in Britain.

I have written that my introduction to intellectual and cultural life outside my own home came from the Heights Players. Attending Swarthmore was immensely more exciting intellectually, and I owe a great deal to my tutors and fellow students for opening my eyes to a new world. A number of the tutors were on the political left, even socialists, and a few of the students shared their convictions. The first tutor who made an impact on me was Murray Stedman, who taught party politics and convinced me without trying that the British system of voting for parties was vastly superior to the American one where parties were weak and one often voted for a candidate one liked rather than for a party. (Mr Stedman was a 'character'; he liked to think that one of his claims to fame was that one of his ancestors had been a horse-thief.)

In addition, I thought that the American system which confused the head of state with the head of government, set one house of Congress against the other and gave supreme powers to an unelected judiciary to interpret a constitution designed for the eighteenth century, was a recipe for frustrating the will of the people and benefiting only the forces of reaction. The fact or at least the claim that in Britain one voted for a party which had laid out its manifesto and hence stood for clear principles made a deep impression on me. So too did the principle of parliamentary sovereignty. In Britain nine appointed judges could not declare acts of the legislature unconstitutional if they felt that a particular act was politically undesirable. The fact that the Supreme Court could also be more progressive than the legislature on occasion, as in the civil rights decisions of the 1950s, did not shake my belief in party government. (Hence the later passion in certain circles in Britain for judge-made law masquerading as civil rights has never appealed to me.)

I was to learn after Mrs Thatcher came to power in 1979 that the reality of party government was an elected dictatorship, that the legislature had lost its power to the Cabinet and that the Prime Minister was far more than *primus inter pares*. But I remain convinced that the American system of separation of powers is open to manipulation and abuse and that voters should have a clear idea of what each party stands for. The fact that this is not the case in the United States must have contributed a good deal to the lack of political interest evident in that country. On the other hand, if both parties are obsessed with claiming the centre ground, as today in Britain, party government loses much or even all of its purpose.

British socialism, British heroism after 1939, British history and culture, British party politics, the anglophilia prevalent at Swarthmore added up to a powerful combination. When one adds to it the alarming growth of the power of Senator Joseph McCarthy and his supporters, and the anti-intellectual atmosphere of the United States in those years, my eventual move to Britain seems inevitable, almost as though I had no active choice in the matter. I remember Murray Stedman saying to a few of us: 'The place for socialists in times like this is on university campuses.' The students who shared my views and I were deeply disillusioned, but what he said was probably no more than the most elementary common sense.

There are few things more exciting in life than the opening of new worlds to intelligent but ignorant students. I had excellent teachers; Paul Beik (and his charming, shy wife, who was one of the college librarians), Laurence Lafore, James Field and Mary Albertson in history, which was my own subject, Murray Stedman, Paul Ylvisaker, David Smith at the end of my student life (David and I were later friendly in London) and above all Roland Pennock in political science, which was my subsidiary subject. I had the greatest respect and liking for Roland Pennock and his wife Helen and was in touch with Roland until his death in 1995. (Retention of friendship with one's tutors is less common in the United States than in Britain, or at least it was then.) At the time they had two marriageable (or perhaps recently married) daughters and I remember my regret that I never met either of them so that I could not become a candidate to be a Pennock son-in-law. The Pennocks senior were Quakers and used plain speech ('thee' and 'thou') to each other. They were delightful people, neither pompous nor arrogant, unlike many academics I knew later. When my mother visited me at Swarthmore after my father's death they showed the greatest (and of course wholly unexpected) kindness and compassion by inviting her to stay with them.

Mr Pennock (the tutors at Swarthmore were rarely called by their first names, though seldom by their full academic titles) had written a book called *Liberal Democracy: its Merits and Prospects* (1950), which was one of the many books which opened new worlds to me. It was densely written, had (we told each other) only one joke and that was in the first sentence ('My dear', said Adam to Eve, 'we live in an age of transition', p. 3). Nonetheless, it was readable and impressive. I remember that in my second year I rashly locked horns with Mr Pennock over the virtues of socialism and capitalism before a sizeable group of students who all, memory says, remained silent. I was annihilated. I lacked the knowledge and the means of expressing myself which would have enabled me to argue my corner. That experience when I was 19 taught me that one cannot hope to win arguments simply through deploying emotion; or it would have taught me that lesson if I had been prepared to learn it. At least it taught me not to take on Mr Pennock in his own subject.

Came the American presidential election of 1952, when the parties gave the electorate the relatively left-wing (and, reputedly, intellectual) figure of Adlai Stevenson for the Democrats against the war hero Dwight D. Eisenhower for the Republicans. Eisenhower was conservative though not reactionary. We thought in our intolerant way that he was weak and mindless, preferring golf to reading like so many other political leaders, it should be added, before and since. (In retrospective there may have been more to be said for Eisenhower than we were willing to allow, notably the American reaction to the Suez crisis of 1956. That lay in the future.) My Swarthmore friends supported Stevenson almost without question or exception. But Roland Pennock voted for Eisenhower. I cannot now remember why, but I remember the anguish in my circle when the news was disclosed. That too taught me a lesson, one which, I admit, I have learned even more imperfectly than the need to argue coolly and factually. Mr Pennock was all things that were good, an admirable man in every respect. But he supported Eisenhower. It must be possible to be a Republican (or even, later, a Tory) but simultaneously an intelligent, decent and kindly person.

The American education system as I knew it had many vices. In schools and in many universities the quality of the teachers was not high and demands on the students were low. Universities of necessity made up for the limited knowledge of their students by broad survey courses. These obviously had their limitations, and the American penchant for 'great books' and 'great men' (sic) is in part the result. But a general education, in the company of intelligent and eager fellow-students and tutors also has much to be said for it, especially in widening the horizons and enthusiasm of students.

37

Having spent over half of my working life as a British academic I am convinced that what is most important in higher education is not knowledge but intellectual enthusiasm. This is produced by the American system at its best, whereas the British system of specialisation from the age of 16 teaches many facts but can kill intellectual curiosity. This has been recognised by the so-called 'new universities' of the 1960s and the former polytechnics in their wider curricula which have now infiltrated the older universities. On the other hand it is hard to think that the educated British public as a whole is less liberally minded or intellectually curious than its American counterpart, and I think in particular of the anti-Communist hysteria of the 1950s, the period about which I am writing.

Be that as it may, I certainly had a broad education at Swarthmore. My degree was in modern history, but, partly under Roland Pennock's influence, I took nearly as many courses in political science as well as some in economics. In the first two of my four years I also took English, French (for most of the period), and isolated courses in mathematics, astronomy, psychology and philosophy. I remember little of the mathematics or astronomy and not much of the psychology other than the student expression 'Get the Gestalt!', but the philosophy made rather more impact, quite apart from the two-toned shoes of the lecturer, Mr Firth. I was particularly impressed by the opposition between the idealism of the eighteenth century Bishop Berkeley and the realism of the twentieth century philosopher Bertrand Russell. (If a tree fell in the forest and nobody heard it, did it make a sound?) I had not yet met the celebrated limerick which neatly summarised the idealist argument:

> Dear Sir, Your astonishment's odd:
> *I* am always about in the Quad.
> And that's why this tree
> Will continue to be,
> Since observed by Yours faithfully, God.

The greatest gift of Swarthmore College to those of us who flattered ourselves that we were the intellectual elite of an intellectually elite establishment was independence of mind. I had a head start coming from a family with a similar perspective. It must be said that I have learned over the decades that human beings are very largely the products of their social class, education, occupation, religion (whether explicitly accepted or not) and nationality.

Yet there is, as my mother was fond of saying, an individual spark in each of us which enables one to choose one's convictions and behaviour. (The limits of this typically liberal approach were shown in her belief that her domestic servants should be as honest and committed in their work as, say, my father was in his.) Be that as it may, I have always striven, often uncomfortably but consistently, to avoid the fate of the man portrayed by Maurice Hare (1886-1967) in another limerick:

> There once was a man who said, 'Damn!
> It is borne in upon me I am
> An engine that moves
> In predestinate grooves,
> I'm not even a bus I'm a tram.'

That fierce belief in individualism has reinforced my equally fierce – and entirely consistent – belief in socialism throughout my life.

I learned an enormous amount at Swarthmore. The whole of the intellectual world opened before me and I drank it in. I remember working on an essay the whole of one night out of sheer passion for the subject; the essay was not due for some days. I had not then met the English cult of effortless superiority, in origin an upper-class phenomenon but expressed at the level of the university teacher by colleagues who gained Firsts while 'doing no work for three years'. I worked and worked hard and so did everyone else in my circle. Swarthmore was an odd place inasmuch as each year cohort had little more than 200 students, but many remained largely unknown to each other. A relatively small group, however, knew each other intimately.

This had advantages. I made more close friends at Swarthmore than I have ever made since, though I have not seen most of them since my graduation in 1954. They were Milt Cummings, Gordon Togasaki, John Jacobson ('bring me back a Nye Bevan badge', he said before my first visit to England in 1952), Walt Clark, Dave Lang, Jon Fine, Johnny Strauss, George Struble, Jerry Beker and others. We learned an enormous amount from each other, and I should add that though some of my fellow male students were visibly uninterested in women as sexual partners, there was no hint of homosexuality in my student days; if you were gay you were silent about it. This is of course another feature of life which has greatly improved since that time.

Jerry Beker, who was from Philadelphia, carried out social work in his spare time as he had done before coming to Swarthmore. His severe speech impediment, while sometimes embarrassing to strangers, was wholly absent when he talked to children. He was an engaging lad, whose favourite phrase was: 'I'd rather die.' I once complained to him that he and another friend (a New Yorker) talked too much about their schools, to which his reply was: 'Horace Mann and Central High; Cleveland Heights, I'd rather die.' Perhaps he was right.

Mike Dukakis, a year behind me, was later governor of Massachusetts and still later Democratic candidate for the American presidency. ('It must have been those long hours in the Swarthmore library that did it!', he wrote to me in 1974, when he was elected governor. Many of us could have written in the same terms.) By the time he stood for president in 1988 he had become 'Mike the Greek', but I knew nobody who thought of him as such in my day. Our attitude in the fifties seems to me much healthier than the modern passion for 'roots with everything'. The slogan on American coins and banknotes is 'e pluribus unum', and if a nation is to survive harmoniously it is surely important for its peoples that their similarities should be more significant than their differences.

My closest friend in my last two years at Swarthmore was Tom Greene. My greatest single enduring regret about leaving the United States, apart from my unceasing feelings of guilt about leaving my widowed mother 3000 miles away, is that I have seen so little of Tom in the years since we graduated in 1954. He was the son of a professor at Dartmouth University, a tall, handsome lad who, as our graduating class handbook (a cloying, embarrassing feature of the American system) said, was 'a ladies' man, but doesn't know it'. His family traces its American ancestry to the mid-seventeenth century or earlier, though I did not learn that until many years later; as I have said in the case of Mike Dukakis, we were not much interested in our fellow students' origins. Tom and I breakfasted together virtually daily in our final year, and I gained a great deal in both intellectual and personal terms from these sessions.

Tom became a diplomat, stationed mainly in the Indian subcontinent, so that our paths would have crossed relatively infrequently (but much more often than they did) even if I had remained in the United States. But I sometimes wonder at the insouciance

Tom Greene, my mother and I, near Chipping Norton, September 1955.

with which I tossed aside my American residence and nationality and moved as an adult to a country where I knew nobody. I have often been asked, of course, why I settled in England and it has sometimes been embarrassing to say that my reasons were mainly political, for the people who enquire are often not socialists. But the flippant reply which I have frequently been tempted to make, that I moved when I was too young to realise what I was doing, is not without a scintilla of truth.

Being part of a closely knit group of students had its drawbacks and I would not have wanted a child of mine to attend so small and ingrown an institution as Swarthmore. It was said that if you walked into the dining room once with a girl no one paid any attention. If twice with the same girl, in the eyes of fellow students you were engaged. The women finalists lived in Worth Hall; which lights in the hall were shining on Saturday nights? (That is, which women had no current boyfriends?) In any event there was an unwritten but generally observed rule; do not phone Worth on Saturday nights. Force-fed as we were it is not surprising that so many students married each other, but the lack of privacy from which the inmates suffered could not have been a good way to grow up. Little Quaker matchbox perhaps, but little Quaker goldfish bowl, certainly.

41

About half of my time at Swarthmore was spent studying British history. Through it I developed a stronger and more conscious love for everything British than I already possessed. Laurence Lafore traced from memory a map of the Thames as it passed through London on his living room carpet for his history seminar, reinforcing my passion to visit Europe, Britain, London. I remember Mary Albertson telling us one day in 1952 that George VI was dead, which caused a considerable frisson in the class. Many of us had a most unhealthy and politically inconsistent reverence for the British monarchy, which in my case lasted until well after I had begun to live in Britain. (As Tom Greene reminds me, this reverence for British royalty has become an enduring feature of American life.) I also remember despising one of my fellow students for calling Sir Herbert Samuel 'Sir Samuel' in a seminar on the General Strike, familiarity with the British honours system also being a curious area of knowledge for a soi-disant socialist.

Gladstone was my hero and I accepted the Whig interpretation which saw the historical process as one of constant, gradual improvement. (Now that I am older and more cynical I think that there is much to be said for the witty but relatively candid Disraeli.) My mother gave me the three-volume life of Gladstone by John Morley (1903) for my nineteenth birthday, and the book has never lost its value to me. The study of modern British social history was then in its infancy, but I was much taken by George Dangerfield's *Strange Death of Liberal England*, then largely unknown in his native Britain (it was first published in the United States in 1935) but later popular in this country too.

Another of my Swarthmore friends was Dave Peel, who later became a librarian. We took a seminar in English history from the eighteenth century, from which we picked up and used with relish the radical catchphrases of whatever period we were studying. When we met in corridors or on campus our initial watchword was 'Wilkes and Liberty!'. Later in the course we met to the warcry of 'Votes for Women!'. It was stimulating and fun, if rather juvenile.

I learned much from my teachers, academically and otherwise. James Field, teaching American history, pointed out that American foreign policy had always been inspired by what Americans took to be morality, rather than the considerations of national interest employed by cynical European powers. The United States thus often did more harm than other countries in the name of good. While I was an undergraduate American intervention (egged on by Britain) to topple the elected regime of Mohammad Mosaddeq in Iran and destroy a reforming government in Guatemala were cases in point. Another which impinged far more on my daily life was the crude anti-Communism which was the dominant feature of American political life during my years at Swarthmore and long after.

I thus learned at an early age that Americans were not hypocrites but innocents, unaware that morality for some is crude power politics for others; morality kills. Presumably making immense economic gains from the two world wars encouraged this feature of the American psyche. Woodrow Wilson said in 1919: 'America is the only idealistic nation in the world' (*Oxford Dictionary of Political Quotations*, 1996, p. 392). The same dangerous twaddle was still being spouted in 1992 by Henry Kissinger of all people: '[M]oral purpose has motivated every American war this century' (quoted in John Pilger, *Hidden Agendas*, 1998, p. 43). And President Clinton is a master at the same art of self-interested self-deception. Mr Field was even more accurate than he could have known.

Mr Lafore commented to us one day that people who said that their student days had been their happiest were unhappy people. I have always agreed with him. I was on balance happy at Swarthmore, sometimes very happy, and I was alarmed recently when a contemporary told me that he had not enjoyed his student life. Did I contribute to his unhappiness? Was I really unhappy too? I think not, but I have never thought of my undergraduate life as anything other than preparation for the real world, and I grew very sick at times of the apparently unending years as a student.

Swarthmore had some Quaker staff, including Roland Pennock, and a meeting house on the campus. Every Thursday we had a compulsory gathering or 'collection' of the whole college in a building called Clothier Hall. It had a large tower, dated from earlier in the twentieth century and was derided by those who claimed to know about these things as 'collegiate Gothic'. At the start of the hour we had a two-minute silence in the Quaker tradition; this was the only overt Quaker influence on us, and I do not remember more than one or two Quaker fellow-students if any. I attended Quaker meeting on the campus on several occasions. As I did not believe in God and was more interested in doing than in reflecting I found the meeting boring and did not attend often. It may have had a more profound influence on me than I thought; I attended Stratford-on-Avon meeting early in my residence in England and never forgot the Friends, some of their beliefs (in simplified form) and especially their activity in the peace movement. I like to say that any religious education I ever had was Quaker, but the statement is at best misleading; I learned more about the Bible from a course on Milton's *Paradise Lost* than from any direct exposure to religious teaching.

Though not of a reflective disposition I was attracted by many aspects of Christianity as I learned about them. It has long been one of my regrets that I have had to learn what I know about Christian history and theology as an adult, that I know so few hymns and did not attend church (as opposed to Friends' meetings) regularly till I was aged 64 and then only for a year. (In spite of this regret, I cannot believe that compulsory religious education is beneficial either to society or to the individual.) I joined the Student Christian Movement at Swarthmore, in the United States as in England a liberal movement, distinct from the more fundamentalist Student Christian Association. In an age when Americans were more commonly agnostic than in subsequent years I lined up on the side of those who thought religion was, in the alleged belief of the Anglo-American minister Moncure Daniel Conway (1832-1907), '...not devoid of interest, Although it be not true' (*St James's Gazette*, 17 December 1881). There was something in me ready to take a more active role in religious observation in the right circumstances, but the circumstances did not arise for over thirty years. However, my interest in the influence of organised Christianity, its buildings, art and music, grew stronger with the years.

I do not remember any Jewish, Israeli or Hebrew society in my day at Swarthmore, though there were many Jewish students. The strong emotions aroused by the creation of the state of Israel had subsided and the Suez crisis still lay in the future. I was a member of the Cercle Français, at least for a period, and played baseball and tennis from time to time, though not for the college sides. By this time I had largely lost interest in professional sport, and

Swarthmore was not a college which placed huge store by its baseball and football sides. (I was even part of somebody's sociology survey because I was among the few who worked in the college library on a Saturday afternoon when the football team was at home to Haverford, our supposed arch-rival.)

What is more interesting is that I remember few if any students who had a grand passion for professional sport. (This may also say something about the circles in which I moved.) Nobody so far as I can remember went home to Philadelphia or New York at weekends to watch sporting events, much less further afield. It was a new experience for me when I came to England to find grown men and sometimes women caring deeply for sport, travelling the country to follow their side, and in the case of one friend, a classics graduate from Liverpool University, choosing his daily newspaper on grounds of its sports coverage. Among these sports enthusiasts are my three sons, but my own feeling about sport is expressed in St Paul's words: 'When I became a man, I put away childish things.' (I *Corinthians* xiii. 11) My sons have educated me to a certain level about football and everyone in England has to have some rudimentary knowledge of cricket, but my lack of interest in sport has been a stumbling block, if not a severe one, to assimilation to my adopted country.

The 'collection' held in Clothier Hall on Thursdays after the two-minute silence was filled by lectures and performances of various kinds. I had developed an interest in public speaking at school and took part in the finals of a speaking competition before the whole college on one occasion. My subject was the vast one of democracy and I was congratulated after it was over by Paul Beik, my history tutor. He pointed out, however, what I had realised even as I said it, that I had used the phrase 'manhood suffrage' to mean 'universal suffrage'. Then and later I found that speaking extempore has its defects as well as its virtues. The college must not have been listening on this occasion, fortunately, for my gaffe aroused no titters or guffaws. In any case it was common in those days to assume that 'he' included 'she'.

Swarthmore was a liberal establishment, as I have suggested, something of a haven in an hysterical world. It did, however, have an engineering school which attracted conservative students, and more generally the expense of attending a private institution with high academic standards meant that virtually all the students in the college were from well-off homes. American universities were and still are cursed by so-called Greek letter societies; fraternities and sororities, to which were attracted – what shall I say? – the wealthiest, most conservative and most sport-conscious students in the various universities.

Swarthmore had no sororities but it had five fraternities exclusive to particular religious or social backgrounds. About 40 per cent of the men in each year group belonged to them. They were less pernicious than elsewhere for at Swarthmore nobody lived in the fraternity houses, though these buildings were useful centres, specially when the weather was cold, for courting couples. The absence of alcohol, in addition, reduced their charms as social centres and their attractions to members and their girlfriends. Some members treated their fraternities with less than total seriousness. Phi Delta Theta men sang: 'Phi Delta Theta, piss-poor fraternity'. (It was the most exclusive of the fraternities.) When I asked Chuck Valsing, a universally popular student and a fraternity member, if I was eligible to be admitted to Delta Upsilon, (known as DU; 'D stands for dirty, U for underwear'), he replied: 'Why not? They let the fucking barriers down for me, why wouldn't they let the fucking barriers down for you?' (This was difficult to answer. It was also Chuck who allegedly met a girl in the corridor when, stark naked one Sunday afternoon, he returned to his room after a shower. What did he say? What could he say? 'Hi', and proceeded on his way.)

Nonetheless, it seemed morally wrong to me for organisations to be based on policies of exclusiveness, not to be open to anyone who wanted to join them. (This was a sentiment to which I have adhered and which has incurred some ridicule and/or hostility in my later life.) And so, in my second year I took on the Swarthmore establishment almost singlehanded and of course lost, though I had fun and stirred up a good deal of publicity. I wrote to the college paper, *The Phoenix*, on which my friend John Purnell was prominent and which he later edited, urging the abolition of fraternities. It was certainly the biggest controversy engendered in my years at Swarthmore and there was lively debate on both sides.

A deputation of us went to see John Nason, the college president (or Vice Chancellor), who made it abundantly clear that financial grants to the college made by its old students who belonged to fraternities were far too precious to lose. Such former students usually went into business and had both the money and the inclination to give to their old college which shallow intellectuals often lacked. Fraternities were perhaps inconsistent with Swarthmore's history and traditions, but the funds they generated were more important. But the fact that a sizeable number of male students was siphoned off into fraternities was an aspect of the division of the student body by political conviction, subject specialism, personal interests and chance. These divergences, it is true, would probably have meant in any case that many students were little more than names to other classmates. (I also recall that none of my friends were smokers, which may be more than coincidental.)

The mobilised left had lost the campaign but as a later age was to say our consciousness had been raised and this, my first political struggle, was a useful preparation for the more serious politics in which I was to engage in Britain. I was always, however, grateful for British universities' greater contact with the world outside the university system as well as their absence of fraternities and sororities (one might perhaps say except for Oxbridge), which smacked more of the world of F. Scott Fitzgerald than of a modern society.

I should add that students were not allowed to keep cars on the beautiful Swarthmore campus, and this prohibition then aroused little or no opposition. There was no room, and the beauty of the campus would have been wrecked by hundreds of cars. This meant that much of the surrounding area was inaccessible to us, including George Washington's celebrated winter headquarters at Valley Forge, but as I have said, there were no murmurs. Since my day there has been a campaign for student cars on campus which has been partially successful. I suppose that that the transfer of attention from a political to a personal issue illustrates the evolution of society from the idealism of the 1950s to the 'me-first' attitude of later generations.

It must be said that my political contacts while at the little Quaker ivory tower ten miles from Philadelphia were minimal. I belonged to Students for Democratic Action, a left-liberal body close to the Democratic Party. I went once on a mission to the poor of Philadelphia, papering the walls of somebody's sitting room and finding that kind of charitable work degrading both to the recipient and to me. I went to one meeting of socialists in Philadelphia.

47

I cannot now remember who sponsored it, but I believe that it was not a Communist-front organisation. I bought at the meeting *Socialist Britain* (1949; British edition, *The Triple Challenge*, 1948) by Francis Williams, a leading apologist for the Attlee government, and another by Léon Blum, the former French prime minister, expressing his socialist beliefs from his prison cell in 1941. It was called, in English, *For All Mankind*. I think that I attended no more such meetings, however; perhaps I learned about the group late in my undergraduate life, or perhaps Philadelphia was too far away for active involvement.

Another political event which I attended was a conference of students from all over Pennsylvania. I moved a resolution advocating the public ownership of the means of production, distribution and exchange. 'But that's socialism', somebody said. 'That's right, that's why I'm advocating it' I replied. I lost again, but again it was fun and good experience. Mike Dukakis the future presidential candidate was also a participant; he may even have been on my side in the debate.

The year 1952 was to be momentous for me. That summer I visited Europe for the first time. Ken Snyder, a neighbour in Cleveland Heights who was slightly older than I was, had visited Europe the previous summer, cycling his way round various countries. 'I can do that', I thought. Then: 'I *want* to do that.' It should be remembered that at this stage I had been as far north-west as Minnesota to summer camp, as far north as Anne Bowden's summer home in Ontario, east to New York, Philadelphia and Cape Cod, south to Washington on a visit with only Ellen as chaperone when we were hardly more than children. (It had been an exciting and formative trip, my introduction to the great monuments of the nation's capital. I was just old enough to understand, perhaps after explanation, a tour guide's sneering reference to the pile of timber in the back garden of John L. Lewis, the pugnacious leader of the coal miners.) I had also visited Virginia when my father was stationed there in the army and seen places which had connections with the Confederate leader Robert E. Lee.

Later, while still at Swarthmore, I was to visit California after my father's death, attend congressional hearings in Washington (my friend George Struble and I hitch-hiked there and back and I was deeply impressed to hear a manufacturer praise trade unions as a stabilising influence) and visit Thomas Jefferson's home in Monticello, also in Virginia. The weather was cold and the fish pond on the estate frozen over, or so I thought. I jumped on it and went through the ice above my knees, doing no harm to myself but dripping water all over the house when my fellow-students and I went round it. (Act first, think afterwards, is a modus operandi from which I found it more difficult to extricate myself than from the fish pond.)

But in the summer of 1952 I had visited only the top right-hand quarter of the United States and crossed the border into Canada. I would not say that I was steeped in European history and culture; at the age of 19 I was steeped in nothing. But I was desperate to *go somewhere*, especially to Britain. I talked my parents into paying for me despite an initially inept démarche, and John Purnell into accompanying me. Our relations were no longer very good. We were too close, we had seen too much of each other, by now we rubbed each other up the wrong way. We made separate contacts while crossing the Atlantic, or perhaps I made a lot and left John isolated.

After an initial fortnight in England we split and went our several ways, John to Germany and I as far north as Inverness and then to France and Switzerland. After our return to Swarthmore we did not speak to each other during our final two years, my first important and most dramatic rupture with a friend. Our fathers both died in our third years at university, but not even these tragedies brought us together. In later years I wrote to John, by then a parish priest in Massachusetts, but his replies were perfunctory and soon stopped. It is easier to break a friendship than to repair it.

Despite the ending of this friendship, a rupture which had been brewing for months, the eleven weeks of my first trip abroad were the most exciting of my short life. The trip began excitingly. Bob Gaebler joined me in New York and we visited the United Nations and other highspots. He and my Aunt Zella saw me off and I have a photograph of the two of them at the front of a huge crowd watching the boat sail out of New York harbour. I have another of myself wearing an overcoat and gloves in the heat of a New York June. The ship itself was the French Liner *Liberté*, formerly the German *Europa*, and I thought it was marvellous, even in third class. The

The crowd watching the departure of the Liberté, New York Harbour, *June 1952. Bob Gaebler (leg through railing) is third from the left in the front row; my Aunt Zella is behind him.*

food was delicious; my mother was a good cook but I had never eaten food of this quality before, and to have wine every day (without extra payment) was a new experience. I won a table tennis tournament on board ship and was given as a prize a medal which I still possess. Over thirty years later I visited a museum in Amboise, a charming town in the Loire Valley near Tours, which had a display of items relating to transatlantic liners; there was a specimen of my medal. It was my first experience of being an historic monument.

The crossing was romantic and exciting and I was almost beside myself when we passed the Scilly Isles on the final afternoon. I had no sleep that night. The next morning, 17 June 1952, I first set foot on British soil, in Plymouth. Unlike Nikolaus Pevsner, whose *Buildings of England* book on South Devon was published the same year, my cursory diary of the trip does not mention the fact that the city had been flattened by bomb damage. I had arrived in a

50

Britain slowly emerging from shortages and rationing, in which anyone with dollars felt like a monarch.

I explored England as thoroughly as I could in a few weeks on a bicycle, from Land's End to the Scottish border. I was overcome by everything I saw, both ancient churches and secular buildings, and the quiet and beauty of the hedgerowed, motorway-less England of those days. I loved London, then still slowly recovering from wartime damage, and took tram rides in the week that trams (alas) disappeared from the London streets. I found Scotland even more appealing than England. I crossed Loch Leven on the old Ballachulish ferry and was stunned by its beauty. I said as much to some Roman Catholic priests on the ferry only to suffer the rebuke: 'Young man, have you ever seen California?' (They were Americans, of course; I had *not* seen California.) Later I cycled through Glen Coe and earlier I had visited Edinburgh, which I thought the most attractive city I had ever visited. (I still think so (with one or two 'equal firsts'); my heart lifts whenever I see Arthur's Seat and arrive at Waverley Station.)

I often stayed in youth hostels but sometimes I slept in a sleeping bag underneath the stars and occasionally in bed and breakfasts, which in those far-off days cost on average 8s. 6d. per night. I stayed in the YMCA in Edinburgh when two Scots came in, clumping about and swearing with every other word. I pointed out that I was trying to sleep and asked them to be quiet, and the sequel was that we engaged in a long and interesting conversation, in which swear words were notable by their absence. I still think Scotland the most beautiful country I have ever visited and, forty-odd years later feel that if I can visit Scotland frequently I do not need to go anywhere else – apart from France, of which much more later.

To see so much antiquity was, to put it mildly, an exciting experience for a 19-year old who had 'never been anywhere'. Cleveland had celebrated its one hundred and fiftieth anniversary only in 1946, but few of its buildings predated 1880. Even Philadelphia with all its stimulus and excitement only went back in its surviving artefacts to the eighteenth century. But what I remember more than countryside or buildings was the friendship shown to me wherever I went, in England, Scotland and Wales alike.

The proprietor of a cycling shop told me of a young woman named Eileen Goll who wanted an American pen-friend; it was to be me until I returned to live in England. (She wrote to me about the national tragedy of the deaths of King George VI and the aged Queen Mary in quick succession; even in my unregenerate monarchist days this seemed to me an exaggerated view.) Jimmy Wood, a young Scot I met cycling, invited me to stay in his home then and on subsequent visits to Scotland. A family whom I asked if I could sleep in their barn (I think in the vicinity of the Lake District) in my sleeping bag said that they were worried about disease to their livestock but invited me to sleep in the house.

I had written to the Gladstone family; Charles Andrew Gladstone (1888-1968) was the Grand Old Man's grandson and lived in the family home at Hawarden Castle near Chester; I had found his address in *Who's Who*. Mr Gladstone invited me to stay at Hawarden Castle, an impressive great house of which ancient fragments remained, hot and sweaty as I was straight from my bicycle. He also inscribed and gave me a little book of photographs of *Mr Gladstone and Hawarden* taken by Robert Banks of Manchester between 1889 and Gladstone's death in 1898; it is still in my library. I was rather disappointed, however, to find out that in his view from the great house Gladstonian Liberalism had been absorbed by the Churchillian Conservative Party rather than, as I thought, into socialism. I had not yet realised how fully, in the Marxist phrase, social being determines consciousness.

My enduring recollection of this first visit to Britain was that everywhere I went I was treated like a guest or a friend. When I returned to New York I was met by Bob Gaebler and we went to one of the stations to ask for railway tickets. 'Can you tell me which platform is for Cleveland?', I asked. 'Nope', was the clerk's full reply (and in truth it was a stupid question because I should have gone to Enquiries). 'I am back home', I told Bob.

I also had one or two political adventures while in Britain. The main one was hearing Winston Churchill speak in the House of Commons as Prime Minister. He used the acronym 'snafu' in relaying the American explanation for intensifying the Korean conflict by bombing the Chinese-North Korean border the previous week. The British government had been neither consulted nor informed. Presumably deliberately and to my delight he mispronounced the acronym which he said was new to his vocabulary. He also pointed out the common sense inherent in the diplomatic recognition of

Communist China, a step which the American government was wholly unwilling to take. '[I]f you recognise anyone', he said, 'it does not mean that you like him. We all, for instance, recognise the right hon. Gentleman the Member for Ebbw Vale' (Aneurin Bevan) (503 *HC Deb.*, 5s., 1 July 1952, cols 277, 286) I found no Nye Bevan badge but his book *In Place of Fear* was published that year, and I bought and read it. I also had a conversation with a Communist or fellow-travelling newsagent, which was an event in my young life, the first such discussion I had ever had.

I wrote daily ecstatic postcards, interspersed with air letters, to my parents; I still have them all as well as the short diary already mentioned, mostly filled with superlatives. My mother told my father that when I reached the Continent I would be even more dazzled, but my father replied that since I had liked Britain so much I would like the Continent less. He was right.

I enjoyed much of what I saw in France, though the long straight lines of poplar trees in northern France made me feel lonely. But I found to my surprise and relief that I could make myself understood in French and enjoyed my visits not only to Paris and its environs, which I thought even more exciting than London, but other places as well. These included Tours, where I celebrated my twentieth birthday, Chartres, Reims, Fontainebleau, Bourges and the chateaux of the Loire Valley which I was to see again in quite different circumstances thirty years later. I finally cycled into Geneva, met some friends of Ellen's (she had studied there for a year not long before), cycled round the lake, returned to Geneva, sold my bike and after a further short stay in Paris took the *Liberté* again, this time from Le Havre, across the Atlantic. I had cycled 2619 miles in seven weeks and spent another two weeks in London and Paris. I had greatly enjoyed the Continent, but after my six weeks in Britain I could think of nothing but returning there.

My father died on 29 December 1952, about four months after my return from this first trip to Europe. He was a chain smoker and died, relatively and mercifully quickly, from lung cancer. He had never been ill previously and his illness and death were an unbearable shock, all the greater because wholly unexpected. (Tom Greene reminds me that when I left Swarthmore for home a week or so before Christmas I was concerned about my father's illness but had no idea that it would prove fatal.) Smoking and lung cancer were only beginning to be associated at the time. His death was an event in the musical life of Cleveland and the nation, and also in Cleveland social life. He was only 54. Though my Aunt Dot had died about the time of my thirteenth birthday, my father's death was of course a much greater tragedy in my life. I don't know how I would have got through the ordeal had it not been for the constant friendship and loyalty of Bob Gaebler, to whom I remained extremely close although he was at university in our native state of Ohio and I was not. Certainly it was a period of high emotion and I was near hysteria some of the time.

During the following summer vacation Bob and I worked in a grocery warehouse loading lorries from 6.30 p.m. till 2.0 a.m.; the pay was good but it is hard to imagine anything more wounding to my mother than for me to absent myself most evenings in the first summer of her widowhood. I was young and selfish, and I had much to learn. Ellen had married in April 1952, during my father's lifetime, but by the time of his death she was living in New England with her husband and unable to give my mother practical support.

Ellen, Cleveland, February 1952.

54

This was natural and inevitable in a newly-wed, but I failed to fill the breach. My mother and I did see a good deal of each other that summer, but it was the evenings when she naturally needed me most and the evenings when I was absent.

During the Swarthmore academic year 1952-3 I met Joan Friendly. She, a New Yorker, was in her first year, I in my third. She was the great love of my young life. I do not know really what to say about this relationship. My friend Dave Lang once said, in the sexist language of the 1950s, that I saw every woman I met with an apron in the kitchen (i.e., as my future wife) and certainly I was anxious, even desperate, to marry and establish a home. I was also desperate to be engaged to Joan, but it was not to be. I wanted to live in England and she was not happy at Swarthmore, I think mainly because of its goldfish bowl aspects. She left Swarthmore fairly early in her college life for Radcliffe College, the woman's affiliate of Harvard University, but in the end she remembered her period at Swarthmore as fondly or more so than her years at Radcliffe.

Perhaps I should say that though Joan and I were in love we had definite and clashing plans for our lives. I had decided after my return from my cycling safari in 1952 that I wanted to study in Britain if not necessarily to emigrate there. Joan had her own life to lead, though it seemed much less important to me at the time than my own. I should also say that we were both young, hotheaded and passionate, which is to say that we quarrelled quite a lot of the time. If we had married we would probably have learned to control our tempers, but it is hard to see the marriage lasting into the mass divorce era of the 1970s and after. As it is, she and I have remained friends through correspondence over the decades.

I should mention in connection with Joan that she gave me for my 21st birthday in August 1953 the then newly-published correspondence of Oliver Wendell Holmes (1841-1935), the American Supreme Court Justice, and Harold Laski (1893-1950), the British political scientist and public figure. This book made more of an impact on my intellectual development than anything I had ever read. Holmes with his enormous erudition, his memory going back to the American Civil War in which he had been wounded, his friendship with British and American political, legal and literary leaders over the generations, his sometimes world-weary observations about philosophy, history and politics; Laski with his comments on his wide reading, on British and American political developments, his tall stories. I had certainly never read anything like these letters before, and I was just knowledgeable enough about the events they discussed to be utterly entranced by the book. I have never forgotten and often quoted or elaborated on Holmes's dictum that the cause of human antagonism was 'fundamental differences of taste, especially national ones'; policies could be compromised, 'taste' could not (*Holmes-Laski Letters*, ed. Mark DeWolfe Howe, 1953, p. 990, also pp. 862, 1238).

I graduated in the summer of 1954 with a good degree and was one of relatively few students in my year elected – not to a fraternity but to another so-called 'Greek letter' organisation, Phi Beta Kappa. This was an organisation of people who had secured academic honours; its membership and 'key', whatever that may be, was supposed to secure the recipients preferential treatment in scholarly circles in later life. I was a solemn young American who had not forgotten the anti-fraternity campaign of two years earlier. I still believed that one should belong to no organisation which was not open to all on the basis of conviction or preference, and I declined membership, to my mother's consternation. She asked me what my father would have said. I said 'we would have had a row' but added that I was unwilling to yield to my father dead what I would have been unwilling to have yielded to him living. For all the self-conscious rectitude attached to my decision I still feel that it was a fault in the right direction. There were, however, no consequences. I moved to England two months after graduation and have hardly heard of Phi Beta Kappa since. It was fortunate for me that British universities do not go in for this manner of rewarding their graduates.

Somewhat earlier than this event I had had to make up my mind what I was going to do after Swarthmore. I had no idea as to my future career. One of the few things I knew was that I did not want to be an academic, towards which career I seemed to be heading, and which American postgraduate education would, I thought, have made inevitable. I also knew that I wanted to live in Britain, at least for a period. I did not care for the student's life in its more parasitic aspects, but being a foreign student was at least a way of putting off decisions, as so many of us have found. I was also influenced by Aunt Zella whom I visited occasionally in New York at weekends and who shared my left-wing politics. She suggested to my receptive ear that life would be more politically congenial to me in Britain than in the United States.

I could not decide between Edinburgh and London. I applied to both. I imagine that at that stage of the dollar shortage those institutions would have welcomed any young American with a degree into their postgraduate schools, largely made up in any case (in London at least) of foreigners, mostly Americans. Be that as it may, I decided to study at the London School of Economics for a doctorate. I knew that the Scottish MA (Hons) was a four-year undergraduate degree but I cannot remember why I thought of taking it, since I was about to complete a four-year undergraduate degree of my own. Perhaps at that stage Edinburgh was not offering a doctorate to history students. And I may have sensed that it was easier to be a foreigner in a great, cosmopolitan capital than in a city like Edinburgh with a strong sense of national identity. In any event I decided on London though not without preliminary indecision.

For a young socialist with a somewhat inflated idea of the left-wing past of LSE this was a logical move. I was clear in my own mind that I was not going to London solely as a student but also to decide whether or not I wished to make my home in Britain. I did not know how and where I wished to pass my life but I was already half-convinced that whatever I did it would not be in the United States. I hope I have made clear that a combination of political, cultural and romantic reasons brought me to England and that my whole life and its associations before the summer of 1954 came together to make the move inevitable. What seems odd to me in retrospect is not that I was to move permanently to England but that in the United States of my youth, with its anti-Communist hysteria on one side and anglophilia on another, I was the only person in my circle who did so.

When I came to England in August 1954 I was just 22. I was not to know that, apart from basic training (square bashing) and specialist training (as a typist) in the American army in the last four months of 1957 I would not spend more than three weeks together in my native land until 1998, or as much as a year there during the remainder of my life (so far).

It did not occur to me that my mother might not want to finance what turned out to be my definitive departure from both my home

57

in Cleveland and my native country. ('But I was [two]-and-twenty, No use to talk to me.') She had been widowed for less than two years when I left the United States. The fees at LSE were virtually non-existent but I had to live, and though my father had left me some money my mother was in charge of its administration until my twenty-fifth birthday. My view of mothers must have been that they were there to be exploited. In any event I crossed the ocean without reflecting that I might have done something to ameliorate her loneliness rather than adding to it.

Paul Beik was teaching at Columbia University that summer of 1954. I visited him before I left New York for London, this time on the Cunard liner *Queen Mary*. I complained to him that I had graduated with a good degree and knew practically nothing. (When Tom Greene, Milt Cummings and I went into Philadelphia we used to say that when we got our degrees we would be of less use to society than the man who cut out doughnuts before an admiring crowd in a Philadelphia shop, piled them on to his thumb and then plunged them into the frying pan.) 'Of course', said Mr Beik, 'an undergraduate degree is only a smattering.' Being a kindly man he did not ask: 'What did you expect?'

Thus chastened I boarded the ship, where I was seen off by my mother and a group of college friends. I liked the *Queen Mary* too, though not the food, and made a number of friends with whom I kept in touch for some years. I told the cabin steward that I was going to England because I was a socialist. (Perhaps I expected, wrongly, that he would be one.) 'You will have plenty of mates there', he said, correctly.

CHAPTER 3

The LSE Years: 1954-6

I LEFT NEW YORK on 11 August 1954. The next day there was a surprise move in the American Senate to ban the Communist Party and make membership in it or co-operation with it illegal. The move was led by two of the Senate's leading 'liberal' Democrats of whom more was to be heard in later years, Hubert Humphrey and John F. Kennedy. (Though this attempt by Democrats to flaunt their anti-Communist credentials was supported unanimously in the Senate, the final version was somewhat watered down, principally because the American government thought that it could learn more about the Communist Party if it was not driven underground.) I had not been tempted to join the party (and indeed would not have known how to), though I was later to sympathise from the sidelines with its British counterpart, particularly during my years of self-imposed exile from the Wilson Labour Party. Nevertheless, I was outraged by this assault on civil liberties by those who should have been its most ardent protectors when I learned about it on board ship. I thought to myself: 'I am leaving just in time.' I was then unaware that British Communists too could suffer for their beliefs, though in most cases less than their American comrades.

What I did know was that there were gross social and racial injustices in the United States (we did not think much about gender injustice in those days) and that anti-Communism was a convenient cloak for the preservation of inequality of all kinds. I knew also in a general way that, as E.J. Hobsbawm was to comment much later: 'Among democratic countries it was *only* in the USA that presidents were elected...against communism, which in terms of domestic politics was as insignificant in that country as Buddhism in Ireland.' (*Age of Extremes*, 1994, p. 237)

It was Mr Field's explanation of foreign policy based on morality brought up to date. Any analysis of American policy since 1945 is inevitably highly coloured by one's political views and, in my case, by a natural desire to justify to myself leaving permanently my native country. But my conviction, however influenced by my own personal experience, is that American policy has been disastrous throughout the world since 1945. I believe that the United States has done all it could to choke off incipient democratic and socialist movements in the developing world; that the Vietnamese war was an aberration only in deploying massive numbers of ground forces; that the American view of developing-world regimes has been determined solely by the degree of their allegiance to the ideology and policies of the United States; that the United States has stood in the way of peace in the Middle East by its blind support of Israel; and that without the actions of the United States, the liberal movement in the Soviet Union would have begun earlier and taken more benevolent forms than it did at various periods from the 1960s.

American foreign policy has been based on the morality of anti-Communism; the British, under governments of both parties, have supported whatever the Americans did as an attempt to preserve some of their old importance. Douglas Hurd was later as Foreign Secretary to refer in a fatuous phrase in 1993 to this subordination to the Americans as 'allow[ing] Britain to punch above its weight in the world' (*Oxford Dictionary of Political Quotations*, 1996, p. 185). The Suez experience of 1956, when the United States and the Soviet Union both strongly opposed Anglo-French aggression in Egypt, should have established once for all that without American backing Britain's weight in the modern world was no more than marginal. (And no doubt it did.) Naive, two-dimensional blundering by the Americans was backed by their profligate expenditure on weapons in a hungry world; its counterpart was the cynical British calculation that national self-interest lay in acting as the willing satellite or goad of the United States.

I began my residence in Britain on 17 August 1954, when the *Queen Mary* landed at Southampton. Again, the voyage across the Atlantic was romantically exciting and again I had no sleep the final night. (Prosaic travel by air is a sad substitute for crossing the Atlantic by ship for the young and unattached.) I went to the YMCA, located close to the British Museum, where I stayed for a short period and used its accommodation agency to find a flat in Highgate. I did not know what a favoured part of London that was and how stimulating my brief residence there was to be.

For a variety of reasons I changed my digs quite a lot in my student days; from Highgate to Belsize Park, to Kilburn, to Stockwell in South London. Although I often cycled to LSE, I tried to live no more than a sixpenny bus or tube ride away, an attempt foiled by the constantly rising prices of London Transport. All my accommodation was in stark contrast to my comfortable home in Cleveland; a single room, shared kitchen and bath, no central heating, no telephone. In fact I was to live in London for nearly ten years without central heating, including the cold winter of 1962-3, without really being aware that I was doing so. Great is youth; though I think that I have always sought comfort or luxury less than many of my contemporaries. Perhaps it was a training for life after 1971, in what many of my friends regarded as slum houses and without a car.

From the start I fell in love with London. I thought of Cleveland as boring, Philadelphia as much more interesting, New York (which I did not know well) as an intimidating mixture of wealth, poverty and enormous buildings. London was huge but there were then few high buildings except churches. It seemed both more relaxed and more intimate than New York, because the tourist attractions were not concentrated in a geographically restricted area. The river was enchanting. There were concert halls and theatres galore, though the Queen's Hall had been burnt down in the blitz. (The Festival Hall and its later sister halls must never have been an adequate substitute.)

In the City there were still many bombed sites; I was told that feral cats prowled in them. There were parks and open spaces, above all Hampstead Heath, which no American city of my limited experience could rival, and many old buildings had survived the war. I have either lived in London or visited it regularly for 44 years as I write, and I have difficulty in separating my memories by decade. But I felt at once that this was a place where I could feel at home, more than anywhere I had ever lived. This feeling was to endure for many years.

In 1954 the cost of living was cheap for someone with a dollar income, for these were still the years of the almighty dollar. What I do not remember was great poverty or sordid living conditions. These were the hopeful years of rebuilding after the war. Harold Macmillan and his Conservative colleagues had promised to build 300,000 houses a year and were doing so. The National Health Service had taken root. New schools were being built and I was to teach in three of them in the next decade. It is true that the long British tradition of blaming each other, and above all the trade unions, for the country's relative economic decline had already begun. But for whatever reason I was never conscious of a lower standard of living in Britain than the one I had enjoyed in the United States.

It was very heaven to be young, politically committed in an intensely political age, conscious of how much formal learning lay ahead of me and with a new country to explore. I immediately joined the Labour Party; my first party card, which I still possess, was initialled by Ian Aitken, who then wrote for the left-wing *Tribune* and was ultimately to become the avuncular political editor of the *Guardian*. I visited Transport House, then the home of the Labour Party where I was given a lengthy private tour of the building by Peter Shore, at the time a youthful party employee and later a Cabinet Minister in the Wilson and Callaghan governments. (Years later, now an established British academic, I was to study party history in the Transport House library.) There was much else besides politics in my life. I returned to Edinburgh for the festival, the first of many visits to Edinburgh for the festival (and otherwise) over more than forty years. I was, to my embarrassment, thrilled by the Military Tattoo and continued to be thrilled by it long afterwards.

I found very quickly that it was far easier to be a political non-conformist in England than in the United States, even in a liberal establishment like Swarthmore. The anti-Communist United States as I had experienced it was a place in which everyone was supposed to do the same things and think in the same way, as Pete Seeger pointed out brilliantly in the song 'Little Boxes' (written by Malvina Reynolds, 1962).

In Britain one was respected for being different. Part of the reason was that social class ties were overtly much stronger in

Britain; while the working class found strength in solidarity, among the middle class political differences were strong and accepted without question. A society composed of different strands expected and tolerated difference. The years since the 1950s have seen that situation change radically. Universal television, galloping Americanisation, greatly increased prosperity and growing depoliticisation have led to much greater conformity in Britain. It must be admitted that a society overtly divided on class lines has strengths as well as weaknesses, and that universal aspiration to a position in the middle class can stifle some spirits even as it liberates others.

And so I went to the London School of Economics in October 1954. It was certainly the most astonishing experience of my young life. The buildings of LSE, now more numerous than in my day, are unimpressive to look at, but they were intellectually and politically intoxicating. LSE had been founded in 1895 by the Webbs; Shaw, only four years dead in 1954, was also to be an inspiration but the hard cash of Charlotte Payne-Townshend who married him in 1898 was of more importance in the early years. The school had been the home of socialist thinkers and writers from its inception and its library was, as it remains, one of the best if not the best social sciences library in the English-speaking world.

Its left-wing reputation owed much to the influence of Harold Laski, who, born 37 years after Shaw, had also died in 1950. It was also due to students from India and the colonies who had studied there and subsequently become independence leaders in their own countries. In fact the reputation was partly bogus by the 1950s, because the real intellectual leaders among academic staff were the political scientist Michael Oakeshott and the economist Lionel Robbins, who were national leaders of conservative thought. The left-wing tradition was, however, real inasmuch as there were strong Communist, Socialist and Labour Societies. Soc-Soc, as the Socialist Society was known, was reputed to be a Communist front; perhaps it was, but it had many talented and committed socialist student members.

I joined Lab-Soc, partly because to do so was at that time already a statement for a young American, partly because (like many people born and educated in Britain) I misunderstood the essentially reformist nature of the Labour Party. I was then a

Bevanite, a left-wing non-Communist socialist, and I have retained this political stance all my life despite increasing despair about the Labour Party and occasional temptations over the years to join the CP. I have often wondered about the subsequent political affiliations of some of my more left-wing fellow students of the time. Certainly while I was a political moderate among student socialists at LSE, I am now a political radical amongst the friends of my youth.

In my early days I met Rodi Okorodudu, a Nigerian who had worked on building sites in Manchester before coming to LSE to take the trade union studies course run by Ben Roberts (another well-known LSE figure) for students who came directly from the shop floor. I also met Les King who was a student on the same course and his wife Mary. They were from Ashton-under-Lyne, in that peculiar corner of England where Cheshire, Lancashire, and Derbyshire meet and Yorkshire is not far away. Les had been a signalman on the railways before coming to London to work on London Transport. All three remain my friends, my oldest English

Les and Mary King, David, at the King home near Chesham, October 1998.

friends. Rodi was to marry Brenda Middleton, a Yorkshire student in the Lab-Soc - Soc-Soc circles in which I moved. Brenda's early death in 1993 was a tragedy above all to Rodi and their children, but also to everyone who knew her.

It was easy to make friends at LSE. Constance Saville told me years later at Hull as a self-evident truth that as someone on the political left my social relationships were laid out for me in advance. She was certainly not far wrong. If you were a socialist your likes and dislikes were predictable and you knew exactly where to find other people who thought like you. You had a circle and a social life ready-made. This is certainly one of the advantages or perhaps compensations of a life on the left. I made no male friends at LSE as close as those at Swarthmore, but I remained friendly for some years with and think warmly of Peter Fletcher, Jim Sharpe, Gabriel Newfield and others. I also made a few American friends including Bill Gwyn and David Smith, both of whom later became prominent American academics.

David, as I have already mentioned, became a junior tutor towards the end of my Swarthmore years and came to London to complete his doctorate, if my memory is correct. We had a good many stimulating political discussions from which I learned a good deal. Why does his repeated use of the phrase 'the same old horse-hair sofa' come to my mind? Perhaps it was his way of emphasising the importance of material possessions and not turning one's back on a bourgeois life style. If so, he was of course correct, irrelevant as it may have seemed to a student leading a happy life in digs and largely unconscious of any personal need of wealth.

The friend to whom I owed most was probably David Harris, a British postgraduate who was somewhat older than I was and much less naive. He convinced me quickly and completely that altruism was not a quality which should motivate political behaviour. One should not work for things which, though they would help others, would make one suffer if they were obtained. The highest political motive was enlightened self interest.

To some extent the point is a semantic one, but it seemed to me then a liberating statement, and it still seems important to believe that socialist measures if achieved would actually benefit oneself. To live in a society with higher levels of education and culture, better housing and greater social and financial equality would be good for everyone, not simply 'the unfortunate'. Politics is a matter of working for particular goals from which one hopes to gain, not a form of higher social work. (All the same, when the Tories took one job from me in 1988 and another in 1992 I could not help but feel that it was a form of grim justice, that political wickedness should not redound only on the working class.)

I also remember two stories told by David and his friend Sheila. The first was that David was determined to be a conscientious objector to military service. Conscription was ending in Britain in the mid-1950s now that the Labour government had been replaced by a Conservative government with less need to prove its anti-Communist credentials to the Americans, and after David replied to his call-up papers saying that he would not serve he heard nothing further. He said ever after that the way not to do one's national service was to write a polite letter of refusal. (I didn't try it, but I doubt that it would have worked for me.)

We were discussing at one point the author Claud Cockburn, whose name Sheila pronounced as spelt. When Shirley or I pointed out to her that it was usual to say 'Co'burn', she replied: 'I can't keep up with how the upper classes mispronounce their names', a bon mot which I have never forgotten and often repeated or adapted.

I suppose that I should say that my two years at LSE were the most productive of my life thus far. So they were if I list the milestones which I passed, though they were all overtaken by subsequent events. I managed the overflowing Lab-Soc bookstall, which made large sums of money principally by selling the Foreign Languages Publishing House (Moscow) edition of the *Communist Manifesto* at 6d. a time. I was then elected chairman (in the parlance of the time) of the Labour Society. I was elected a vice-president of the Students' Union. I obtained a PhD and began a job. And I married Shirley Livingstone.

Even at the time my acceptance in student circles astonished me. This was, after all, the era par excellence of the Cold War and I could easily have been a CIA spy. (There was later reputed to have been one in our circle at the school and the allegation seems likely.) More prosaically, a voluble, naive, aggressive foreigner was not the obvious choice for election to the posts mentioned above. I put it down to English tolerance, but the longer my student days recede into the past the more curious my relative prominence at the school seems to me. (I should add that I was not the only American to be prominent in the Students' Union; another one was elected president, and when congratulated on his election he would reply: 'Thanks for your help', without knowing or caring for whom his interlocutor had worked or voted.)

I was a reasonably good speaker for those listeners not put off by an American accent, but I floundered amidst the wit and thrust of British debating techniques in which solemn Americans so often disappear without trace. John Hipkin, one of several highly talented young Conservatives in our Students' Union, could usually make mincemeat of me. But I was not the only loser. One young (English) woman pleaded with the assembly for tolerance, since she was making her maiden speech. The jeers were immediate and unceasing, and I think that was her last attendance at a union debate.

I did not then realise that successful debating in England (and no doubt in Britain) in privileged assemblies like the leading universities or the House of Commons was not only a question of putting a case as forcefully as one could but also of making the audience laugh. On one occasion the outside speakers at the union were Kingsley Martin, editor of the *New Statesman*, and the former socialist Malcolm Muggeridge. I was disgusted by Martin's failure to make a fighting socialist speech, but even I had to laugh as he or Muggeridge (who were close friends) described the typical English home on a Sunday morning, when a hand reached out, took in the milk and the newspaper, after which 'the door closed and stayed closed until opening time'.

I have had to develop a defensive kind of wit of my own in later years, but in order to debate with the natives on equal terms one has either to be a native oneself or to develop a verbal facility which is beyond me. However I greatly enjoyed the debates at LSE and sometimes seconded prominent political speakers; I remember once supporting Richard Crossman, the blunderbuss after the rapier.

The supervisor of my MSc(Econ) (later PhD) studies at LSE was Richard Greaves. He had been a student of Laski and was a notable political scientist, but he was not a successful supervisor. He was probably more shy than uninterested, but I was not at an age when I willingly gave much benefit of the doubt. (Perhaps I have never reached that age.) On one occasion he excused himself because his car was (illegally) parked in Houghton Street, which the school fronted. Possibly I did not wait long enough for him, but he certainly did not return while I was in his office.

Another of the staff at LSE was Reginald Bassett, who was notorious for his support for Ramsay MacDonald, whose behaviour in 1931 had led to the breakup of his Labour government. Bassett was to publish his influential defence of MacDonald (*1931: Political Crisis*) in 1958. But the tutor whom I knew best was Bob McKenzie, the jovial Canadian who had come to England as a soldier and had remained after the war. He had been a convinced socialist and was indeed one of the vice presidents of the Labour Society until he evidently decided that the position compromised his political and broadcasting independence.

He was the student of British political parties and his important book on the subject appeared during my LSE days. I reviewed it for the LSE student literary magazine. There was something anomalous about this Canadian tutor and his postgraduate group, most of whom were Americans, studying British political parties at the London School of Economics, but I imagine that all of McKenzie's former students remember his seminars as a richly rewarding experience. He was universally liked and respected, despite his personal retreat from left-wing politics. He was already a performer on the BBC, known to us as Bob 'BBC' McKenzie, and soon to be famous nation-wide for his 'swingometer' on general election nights. He would be surprised if he could see the electronic aids made possible by computers, but his death in 1981 put out a light for me and very many others.

When I decided eventually that I wished to move into university teaching myself I wrote to Greaves and McKenzie, saying that I hoped they remembered me and asking if they were willing to be referees. They replied characteristically. Greaves: 'Dear Rubinstein, Of course I remember you.' McKenzie: 'Dear David, Of course I remember you.' McKenzie then invited me to visit him at the school which I did without delay. He told me some of the latest political gossip, of which the only point I can remember is that Richard Crossman had threatened to curb criticism by the BBC in the event of a Labour government. (The government of 1964, in which Crossman was a minister, took office at about that time.) He mentioned that he had recently been made a professor, on which I congratulated him. Greaves (who had also been made a professor) would not have made a point of telling me so, but I am sure that I would have done.

LSE was different from Swarthmore, chalk and cheese. Nobody lived on site and very few lived in university accommodation at Passfield Hall which was within walking distance in Bloomsbury. The students were generally older and more experienced in every respect than those at Swarthmore. Instead of a little Quaker matchbox or fishbowl we were a much larger institution located at the heart of one of the greatest cities in the world, a stone's throw from almost everything that one wanted to do or see. It was a heady mixture and one which I was more than lucky to experience at an impressionable age.

I soon met Anne Bohm, who was born in Breslau (Wroclaw) in 1910, obtained her doctorate at the University of Berlin in 1935, came to Britain in 1938 and served for 37 years as secretary of the postgraduate (now called graduate) school. She was already indispensable to the functioning of LSE and has never ended her active association with it. Since shortly before the start of the 1980s when universities were subjected to deep cuts in their funding she has had a new role in liaison with former students, recruiter of new ones and as fundraiser, the school sensibly trading on her dedication and her unique place in the hearts of large numbers of old students. I liked and respected her enormously, as everyone did. She was much kinder to me than I deserved and gave me more of her time than I had any right to expect. I have, happily, been in intermittent touch with her over the subsequent decades; when last I saw her, in January 1998, her memory, her enthusiasm for the school and her appetite for travel remained astonishingly undimmed. I was also engaged to Margaret Anderson, one of her secretaries and a vivacious and charming young woman.

Margaret and I had little in common, but enough to understand in time that we were not suited to marry each other. I enjoyed my visits to her home in Bromley and going to Glasgow to visit her friends. Her parents were very kind to me and like most students I was glad to have a real home to visit. I met Margaret nearly ten years later when I was taking a school party through the Imperial War Museum and then, thirty years after that, she wrote to me when she saw a photograph of my son Paul who was then working in Durham, in her local paper. We caused each other to suffer at the time, but I hope and believe that she now thinks of me affectionately, as I do of her.

As chairman of the Labour Society at LSE I invited the leading Labour politicians to the school, and memory says that apart from Aneurin Bevan they all accepted. Bevan did come to the school to address a public meeting and spoke on the National Health Service which he had created a few years before; he talked about the advantages of state-organised medicine and added: 'Perhaps one day even the United States will be able to afford a national health service.' Perhaps it will.

I had some good moments in the Labour Society. I introduced John Strachey at one meeting. Two of us struggled to help him on with his enormous coat; the other student nudged me, pointing out by mime that the label was Burton's. We decided that if ordinary mortals removed a Burton's label and put in one from Savile Row, with Labour politicians the process was reversed.

It was either at this or at a subsequent meeting that I took the chair with a large and plainly visible hole in my sock. But it was certainly John Strachey whom I introduced as one of the most prominent of younger Labour politicians. When he pointed out that he had not been introduced in that way for some years I came back to the chair to say that anyone in politics under the age of fifty was young. Strachey benevolently replied that he entirely agreed but that he had by that time left his fiftieth birthday some years behind.

I also introduced Jim Griffiths, the former minister for Social Security who sat for Llanelly. I had been coached on how to pronounce the name of his constituency and brought it out with casual proficiency, as I thought, decades later in talking to my friend Jackie Tucker, who is of Welsh origin. 'Your pronunciation is *terrible*', she said. 'But', I replied, 'Jim Griffiths said that he had never heard the name of his constituency pronounced correctly in England before.' 'Don't you believe it', she replied. 'He must have said that wherever and whenever he was introduced in England.'

Not all meetings were disasters for the chairman, but the worst moment in my two years at LSE came at the formal dinner held by the Labour Society in January 1956 at which the guest speaker was

Hugh Dalton. Our vice presidents were there, including Frida Laski, Harold's widow with whom I was to be on close terms until her death in her early nineties in 1977. She later visited Shirley and me in Hull on several occasions and gave me many books, among them the limited edition of Shaw's works which Shaw had given to Harold Laski. The gift had been made by Shaw in apology for upsetting Laski by saying flippantly at a Fabian Society dinner in 1933 that Hitler should treat the German people, including the Jews, as he wished.

Another of our vice presidents was R.H. Tawney, then in his mid-seventies, whose works I had read at Swarthmore. He was a demi-god to most socialists, even though he himself was situated on the right of the Labour Party. It is difficult to explain now what an exalted position he held on the political left and how inspiring a figure he was. A note from Tawney and an inscribed copy of his *Equality* are among my prized possessions. A third vice president was Ralph Miliband, the then youthful politics lecturer, who had refused an offer of making a short speech before the main speaker at the dinner.

Dalton, who was wearing evening dress, made a good speech, studded with the kind of good-natured self-praise to which he was prone in later life. It was the self-satisfied speech of the ex-minister whose political career was over and who had seen great changes in his life. It was self-indulgent but, even to a convinced left-winger and Bevanite like myself, entirely acceptable on such an occasion.

When he had finished speaking a woman student rose and said that she would like to know what Ralph Miliband had to say in response to Dalton. (Was this planted?) I, a well brought-up American boy, thought the request and Miliband's subsequent rabble-rousing denunciation of Dalton's complacency totally out of order, but I had as much chance of stopping him as General Custer did of stopping the Indians. Miliband was cheered to the echo. (This was the first but by no means the last time that I learned that the English played to win; 'playing the game' was a convenient fiction to impress foreigners.)

What was worse was that when the evening was over all the fellow-students to whom I spoke thought that Miliband had spoken superbly and his speech entirely justified. I had never felt so isolated. I wrote to Dalton to apologise and received a friendly reply:

71

'I...enjoyed my evening very much. It was not even seriously disturbed by the Bellyache in Vacuo at the end.' (2 February 1956) But the incident remains green in my mind as one of those in my whole life which I would most have wished to avoid. Would I have cheered Miliband too if I had not been in the chair?

I heard both R.A. Butler and Hugh Gaitskell speak, wrote to both and had interesting replies from both, specially Gaitskell, who wrote on 2 November 1954 that 'the vast majority of Labour supporters...are moderate, sensible people, interested in practical results, but equally accepting the ideals of social equality...'. (How new is New Labour?) A friend told me that I had a manuscript letter from the next Prime Minister, and nobody would then have believed that neither Butler nor Gaitskell was to reach that office. (When Macmillan replaced Eden early in 1957 astonishment was almost universal.)

One of the most enjoyable events in my early months in London before I moved away from Highgate was a Sunday morning pint at the Flask Inn, a pub still popular with a fashionable set. That Sunday morning drink at the Flask was a well-known resort of the Labour Party left-wing intelligentsia. I forget some of the people whom I met there, but apart from Ian Aitken, the most prominent was Barbara Castle, the glamorous MP for Blackburn. It was at one of these gatherings that Ian declared that if he were French or Italian he would be a member of the Communist Party. It was no more than a statement of the obvious, but to a young American it was an astonishing and unforgettable declaration.

Ian Aitken put me in touch with his colleagues at *Tribune*, particularly Bob Edwards, the editor, and Peggy Duff, the dedicated and popular business manager who later became a mainstay of the Campaign for Nuclear Disarmament. They encouraged me to attend the Labour Party conference held in September 1954 at Scarborough. It was the German rearmament conference; the party's right-wing majority following its customary pro-American line supported German rearmament, while the left, strengthened by support from many others within the party, was passionately in opposition.

It was all hugely exciting, and heady for a young foreigner to realise how easy it was to come into at least intermittent and nodding contact with some of the leaders of the Labour Party. I have wearied Ann by pointing many times to the spot where Mrs Attlee reversed her baby Austin car away from the Scarborough Spa, the former Prime Minister in the passenger seat while I watched agog. Herbert Morrison, whom we had also had as a visitor to the Labour Society at the school, took the principal role at the conference in defence of German rearmament, support for which was secured by the narrowest of majorities. Did he really win over the last few votes by referring to the mover of the hostile motion, R.W. Casasola of the Union of Foundry Workers as 'Casanova'? The official record is silent on the point, but the then *Manchester Guardian* reported: '[T]he delegates burst into laughter and the mood...suddenly changed...Mr Morrison handled it beautifully' (29 September 1954).

I also remember from that 1954 party conference the *Tribune* rally, always one of the high points of postwar conferences. Thanks to my *Tribune* connections I was a steward. The star speaker was of course Aneurin Bevan, the idol of the left, who was then the subject of vitriolic and sustained attack within his own party and in the press (including the *Manchester Guardian*), as only Tony Benn was to be in later years. (At the time and long afterwards Benn was the youthful-looking centrist MP for Bristol West.)

As far as the outsider knew Bevan revelled in the role of bête noire of everyone to his political right. He called attention in his speech to the fact that Ernest Jones, President of the National Union of Mineworkers (then a prominent right-wing union) had recently attacked the opponents of German rearmament as Communist-inspired: 'I say frankly to my friend Ernest Jones, drop it.' The applause was thunderous. Then came one of the lines for which he is most remembered. 'I know that the right kind of leader for the Labour Party is a desiccated calculating machine who must not in any way permit himself to be swayed by indignation.' Was he referring to Attlee? to Gaitskell? Or defending the passion with which he proclaimed his socialist convictions with no ad hominem intention as he himself declared? (Michael Foot, *Aneurin Bevan*, vol. 2, 1973, pp. 450, 452) Nobody knows. But everyone present at the crowded rally knew that s/he had been privileged to hear one of the greatest speeches of one of the greatest of twentieth-century British orators.

Everything at that 1954 conference fascinated me, particularly the fringe meetings which are often more interesting than the conference itself. At one of them Bob Edwards of the Chemical Workers' Union, a Spanish Civil War veteran and soon to be a Labour MP, attacked the high cost of living under the Conservatives, using lino as an example. As a young American, knowing only 'linoleum', I was forced to turn to my neighbour to ask for an explanation of the word.

It was at this party conference in 1954 that I first met John Parker, with whom I was to be on close terms until his 'early death', as I think of it, in 1987 at the age of 81. John Parker had been MP, first for Romford and then for Dagenham since 1935 and he was to remain an MP until 1983, when he retired as Father of the House. He adopted me as a stepson or more properly as a younger brother.

My debt to John Parker was and remains enormous. It was he who introduced me to historical architecture, the subject which interested him more than perhaps any other and which has greatly enriched my own life. We went to the theatre together. I went regularly with him to Beatrice Webb House, the socialist centre near Dorking, where I engaged in gardening at his direction, a much needed distraction from the urban life which normally surrounded me. Even babysitting for John and his wife Zena gave me a meal and a congenial, warm flat, which I did not have to pay to heat. (Young and indifferent to comfort as I was, I knew the difference between student digs and a comfortable flat in the Temple.) And their lively son Michael was an added bonus.

John Parker gave me advice on innumerable matters, political, historical, personal. I joined a party which he led on a punting and camping weekend on the Thames, one of the most enjoyable weekends of my life in those years. He invited me to his annual bottle parties, where there were many prominent political personalities and the highlight of the evening was the singing of 'Cosher Bailey' in a light tenor voice by his old friend Michael Stewart, the future Foreign Secretary. John later came to the schools where I taught and spoke to my pupils. He also came to the University of Hull and spoke to the students too, and he was a great success. I remember him saying in Hull: 'In 1918, everyone wanted to go back to the prewar world; in 1945, nobody did.' Like all such apothegms this one needs qualification, but it contains an important element of truth.

David, John Parker, John's cousin Alan Montgomery on Thames journey, June 1955.

Though first elected to Parliament at the age of 29 when there were few young middle-class MPs on the Labour benches (he had attended Marlborough and St John's, Oxford), his political career was not a success. He had been sacked from his post as Undersecretary at the Dominions Office under Attlee in May 1946, on a point of political principle he said, due to incompetence said others. Whatever the truth of the matter he remained a back-bencher, but he had been influential in reviving the Fabian Society in the 1930s and had suggested to constituency Labour Parties the names of many young hopefuls in 1945 who, once elected, showed him little gratitude.

He remained active among Fabians, visited Eastern Europe and elsewhere (I joined one such Fabian delegation to Hungary in 1970) and assisted Lincolns-Prager, a small publishing company run by his friend Eugene Prager. He constantly encouraged young people in their chosen careers, as Hugh Dalton had done in his own and many other cases. I wish that he had been alive so that I could have seen him regularly after I began to live again in London in 1990; I

75

wish that he were alive now to read these words and to know the place which he retains in my memory and affection.

He invited me to visit South-West Norfolk ('Can't you get 'East' in there somewhere?', Bob Gaebler asked) with him during the general election campaign of May 1955. His friend Sidney Dye, who had lost his seat (held since 1945) by 442 votes in 1951 was standing again and John (and I) spoke at meetings throughout the constituency on his behalf. South-West Norfolk was then a maverick constituency, and Sidney Dye won his seat back by 193 votes in an otherwise disappointing election. This was one of my few experiences of small election meetings held by local candidates with little outside assistance in villages and small towns as had been done for so many years until they were suddenly and apparently irrevocably ended by the advent of television. John explained the result to me in terms of the large numbers of agricultural labourers and Nonconformists in that part of Norfolk. Now both categories are much reduced and even in the Labour landslide year of 1997 South-West Norfolk (no doubt with different boundaries from 1955) was held for the Conservatives by Gillian Shephard with a majority of about 2,500.

One last word about John Parker. He was not known for his sympathy with the Roman Catholic Church. (When I was appointed to Hull he congratulated me on having secured a post in a northern city with few Catholics, an inaccurate as well as a prejudiced comment.) I say this not because I want to denigrate John – quite the contrary – but in order to repeat a joke he once told me. He had worked as a young man in the early 1930s on the social survey of Merseyside carried out by a team led by David Caradog Jones. The enemy of progressives in the city at the time, according to John, was the Roman Catholic (Arch)Bishop of Liverpool, whose name was Longbottom. (Alas, I fear that there was no archbishop of that name and that his very existence may be apocryphal but the story is too good to lose.) The bishop died suddenly and unexpectedly. His erstwhile opponents hugged themselves and chortled: 'Arse longa, vita brevis.'

In between times I worked on my thesis. I was fortunate in a number of respects. I had no idea of how to write a doctoral thesis and for all his qualities as a scholar Richard Greaves did not provide much help. My friend Philip Bagwell who finished his PhD thesis at LSE six years before I wrote mine recently told me that when writing his thesis he too had had little idea of the expected standard. LSE's postgraduate school in the 1950s was largely foreign. The postwar expansion of British universities had hardly begun and British students did not then have to write a doctoral thesis to begin an academic career. Postgraduate supervision must not have loomed large in the lives of university lecturers. One imagines that the failure rate amongst candidates who completed their theses must have been small.

By the time I had become a university lecturer myself in 1965 the PhD thesis had become standardised and had reached a level of attainment which could not be reached except in rare cases within the regulation three years by new graduates who had written nothing other than undergraduate essays and, latterly, ten thousand-word dissertations. This was particularly true since postgraduates were by then expected simultaneously to do some undergraduate teaching, which I did not do. (This process provided cheap labour for the universities and essential experience for the postgraduates, but it fatally distracted their mental energies.)

My own PhD was to be absolutely essential to my later career at Hull and in France, but it was inevitably sloppy and inadequate (and completed in two years) even given the fact that the serious study of modern social and political history was then in its infancy. It was fortunate for me that it was so. But the low quality of the finished product was one of several reasons why I have always disliked being called 'Dr Rubinstein.'

My subject was what I claimed to be 'The Decline of the Liberal Party, 1880-1900'. If it was shoddy, it can at least be said that it contained a lot of pages. (I offer freely this hostage to fortune to friends and acquaintances on the look-out for stereotypical American observations.) My argument was that the historical mission of the Liberal Party had been to move the country towards political democracy. The assertion ignored the fact that none of the women and not much more than half the men (in their case mainly because of arcane registration laws) enjoyed the parliamentary vote by 1900. The Liberal Party, I argued, was good for political reform; its domination by the upper-middle class prevented it from passing the necessary social reforms. Its great election victory in 1906 was accidental, because of the divisions amongst Unionists (that is, in the main, Conservatives) over free trade and other issues. Labour, which had an electoral pact with the Liberals in 1906, had been bound to overtake the Liberals in the longer term and the 1906 victory hid the reality that the Liberals were a Victorian party unable to cope with the class-framed world of the twentieth century.

I seem to have spent all my life in considering this question, which subsequently engaged the attention of many historians who have studied the subject far more closely than I did. The fact that the Great War burst upon a startled world in 1914 and that the Liberal Party's two principal leaders quarrelled irrevocably in 1916 (a quarrel which was only nominally patched up in later years) means that there can never be a definitive explanation of the Liberal decline; history cannot be rerun. Most historians who have studied the question have been, like me, supporters of the Labour Party, and most have concluded that, as Henry Pelling wrote of the Edwardian years, 'a sort of undogmatic 'Labourism' was establishing itself, which consisted in little more than the opinion that the Labour Party, and not the Liberal, was the party for working men to belong to.' (*Popular Politics and Society in Late Victorian Britain*, 1968, p. 118)

The arguments are so good on both sides that I tend to agree with the last historian I have read, though it is difficult to think that the small Labour Party of 1914 could have burst the bonds of pressure group status or that except for the Great War the Liberals would not have tried harder to transform themselves rather than suffer oblivion. On the other hand, could Britain have been the only European country without a powerful labour-socialist party in the second and third quarters of the twentieth century? It seems unlikely. What is clear is the fact that the Liberal-Labour split, however inevitable, condemned the British people to endure the first 97 years of the twentieth century with only 13 years of what it is now fashionable to call centre-left (working) majority government (1906-10 Liberal, 1945-50 and 1966-70 Labour).

The emphasis of my thesis, however, was not on the years 1900-14 which have rightly fascinated Labour historians, but, as I have said, the late Victorian period. Wading through the material concerning Gladstone, Rosebery, Chamberlain and others was not the obvious choice for a socialist, but I was still in some ways a liberal in outlook, much like the Labour Party itself in its early years. I was also, after all, trying to explain the origins of Labour's later success. I enlisted the assistance of four veteran Liberal figures, two of whom had in later life been active on the political left, to support my case. I was, I suppose, one of the pioneers of oral history without knowing it, though in later life I have been sceptical of the genre.

Lord Samuel (1870-1958) greeted me at his home in West London in December 1955 and gave me forty minutes. What I remember best of my meeting with him was the fact that I asked him a question which I thought unaswerable, to be met with the reply: 'Well, Mr Rubinstein, if I can do anything further to help you, please don't hesitate to ask me.' Gilbert Murray (1866-1957), also a lifelong Liberal, lived in North Oxford, where I cycled to visit him in January 1956, enjoying the swooping vistas of the Chilterns in the happy days long before the M40. He gave me his recollections of the simultaneous Radical programmes of the 1880s, led by Chamberlain in Britain and Clemenceau in France. It had all happened seventy years previously.

The most interesting visit was to Bertrand Russell (1872-1970), then living in an upstairs flat in Richmond, and, when I went to see him on a snowy February day in 1956, aged nearly 84. He was far more vigorous than either Samuel or Murray and I recall my interview with him much more clearly. I remember him bobbing up and down to pour me more tea, to give me more light and coming downstairs and outside when I left him, since he was surprised that I had travelled by bicycle on such an inclement day.

He told me that Gladstone would never have adopted Home Rule in 1886 if he had not needed the votes of Irish nationalists, which seemed a revelation to me then but which is unlikely to surprise anyone who analyses the election returns. He reminisced about Gladstone and told me stories which later appeared in his autobiography. It was a stimulating and exciting experience, and judging by his vigour and enthusiasm I should not have been at all surprised that Russell lived for a further fourteen years. I could not know of his future role in the peace movement and how he would become in later years even more of a hero to many of us than he already was.

The most useful of my four contacts proved to be Sir Charles Trevelyan (1870-1958), formerly a Liberal MP and later a Labour MP and cabinet minister. My mother offered to pay for me to visit his home at Wallington in Northumberland, a beautiful property now in the possession of the National Trust, to interview him. I cannot remember why I did not take advantage of the offer, but the documentation which Trevelyan sent me was much more useful than an interview. (I was able to visit Wallington after his death and hear his daughter Patricia Jennings playing the Northumbrian pipes.)

I thought, in view of his own political journey, that he would provide support for my main argument, which was that the Liberals were in reality finished as a major political force before the land-slide election of 1906, and bound to be overtaken by Labour. In fact, he wrote me a long and helpful letter on Christmas Eve 1955 arguing exactly the opposite. In 1906 he was the newly elected MP for Elland, a working-class constituency near Halifax. He wrote that it was ridiculous to say that the Liberals were moribund 'in face of the biggest political victory there has ever been in 1906'. (This was true in terms of seats, but the Conservatives or Unionists had 43.6 per cent of the vote against the Liberal 49.0 per cent.) 'I had the whole of my Yorkshire working class behind me in a typical Yorkshire radical constituency, for what we should now call a Welfare State programme. What smashed the Liberal Party was the war, their blundering into it and not knowing how to blunder out of it.' (reprinted in thesis, pp. 573-4)

I took some consolation from the fact that a book which Trevelyan wrote in 1921 and sent me in 1955 called *From Liberal to Labour* took a similar if less clear-cut line to my own; that the pre-1914 Liberals were incapable of reforming themselves to meet the working-class challenge and that their decline was inevitable: 'Even without the war it is more than doubtful whether the mass of Radical voters would not have transferred their allegiance to Labour within a very few years.' (p. 22) We are all entitled to second thoughts. In any event I used Trevelyan's letter and book to illus-trate the varying points of view on the controversy with students until the end of my academic career.

Why did these elderly celebrities take time and trouble to assist the young scholar? Only Emrys Hughes MP refused to see me, telling me that he had said in his short book on his father-in-law Keir Hardie (1950) all he could say on the subject. (He was presumably already writing his longer book on Hardie, which was published in 1956.) Perhaps, apart from Russell, they were less busy than the practising politician; perhaps even in those years Hughes had had enough of enquiries from young Americans. Whatever the truth, I finished the thesis in the summer of 1956, went with much apprehension to Richard Greaves's flat in Mayfair to defend it, and was told that I had just squeaked through. Inadequate though I have always felt it to be I have never ceased to be pleased that I obtained the doctorate.

Part of the reason that I had come to live in England had been that I had felt programmed to be a university lecturer and did not want to be one. But what did I want to do? I had no idea. By 1956 I knew that I did not want to return to the United States, though I had no real answer to the friend who pointed out to me somewhat maliciously that socialists were even more required there than here.

I was walking across Waterloo Bridge one day, probably early in 1956, when I suddenly realised what I did want to be – a teacher in one of the new comprehensive secondary schools then springing up in London and elsewhere. I know now, both as a former teacher and as an historian of comprehensive education in England and Wales, much more about the subject than I knew in the mid-1950s. Even then, however, I knew that before 1944 secondary education had been limited to a minority who attended what by the 1950s were called grammar schools and that secondary education for all had only been introduced, in some places no more than nominally, under the stimulus of wartime enthusiasms.

I knew that all the prestige and a disproportionate share of resources were devoted to the grammar schools, and that both psychological and sociological research were beginning to show that selection for secondary schools at 11+ was both inaccurate and unfair. I knew also that as Britain emerged from the war and the dire years of postwar shortages and reconstruction, large new schools were being built which dazzled their many visitors. Kidbrooke, a girls' school, opened near Eltham almost immediately after my arrival as a student in London. It was the first purpose-built comprehensive school in London and among the first in any urban area. Newspapers and visitors were fascinated by its six science labs, nine housecraft centres, five gyms and 16½ acres of playing fields. The *News Chronicle* called it 'Britain's great new palace of educational varieties...a blaze of colour – crimson, yellow and blue' (29 June 1954).

Such an encomium from the liberal-left was not universal, and support for grammar schools has never died, particularly in some parts of (mainly southern) England. It is astonishing how widespread the idea was and remained that 'good' (that is, selective and mostly middle-class) schools should not be amalgamated with schools catering for other pupils; it should have been obvious to everyone that 'opportunity' for the top 20 per cent of the age group as measured by tests of ability and attainment at age ten meant relegation for 80 per cent.

The grammar school retained partisans among members of the Labour leadership; working-class members were proud of its achievements in helping working-class boys (sic) to climb out of their class and public school-educated members usually understood little of what was at stake. The whole of the leadership was wary of the grammar school's prestige with the electorate. In May 1963 I was to attend a meeting held at the headquarters of the National Union of Teachers addressed by Harold Wilson as party leader. He was asked whether he would abolish the grammar schools and replied disingenously: 'Over my dead body'. (He later denied having said this (Ben Pimlott, *Harold Wilson*, 1992, p. 512), but it was reported in the NUT paper *The Teacher*, 7 June 1963, p. 2 and widely discussed in the politico-educational world. Wilson added that local authorities should have freedom of choice on the issue.)

But I had decided that I wanted to play my part in the new educational system then taking root. One major problem was the fact that my two years' national service in the American army hung over me. I did not want to do my national service. I was a partisan neither of the Cold War nor of American foreign policy, but I was sure that I would not be allowed to remain in Britain in defiance of my call-up and I had no desire or intention to flee to Eastern Europe as at least one young American in a similar plight had done. As far as I knew, conscientious objection to American military service on political grounds was punished by two years in prison.

Having established myself in London and begun to dig roots in Britain, the last thing I wanted at that stage was to leave the country for two years. But though another year as a student would have taken me over the maximum age (then 26) for call-up, I had been a student for six years and was sick of it. I wanted to do something active even if the 'something' was soon followed by the army. But how could I in honour apply for a job knowing that I was likely to be called up before long? And, in less American terms, what chance would I have of finding a second job if I left the first one within weeks or months for expected but undisclosed military service?

I was sitting in a House of Commons bar one evening with John Parker discussing these perplexities when Margaret Cole, the prominent author and alderman of the London County Council hove into view. It was the LCC which was the most important local education authority in advocating and building comprehensive schools. Margaret's husband, G.D.H. Cole, was an even better-known (indeed, celebrated) author and they had collaborated on a number of works. 'Damn', said John, 'here comes Margaret, that means a double whisky.' She joined us, asked for a double whisky, recognised me and asked what I was doing now. 'Looking for a job with the LCC', I replied, 'but I doubt that I'll get one.'

Margaret arranged for me to be interviewed by an Assistant Education Officer of the LCC, which was to be replaced by the Greater London Council and the Inner London Education Authority in 1965 and in turn abolished twenty-odd years later. He gave me a form to fill in and I noticed at the bottom the comment that any attempt to canvas or solicit appointment would disqualify the applicant for employment with the LCC. 'Now, where shall we send you?' the officer mused. He suggested the name of a school in South London. 'No', he said, 'I think it should be Woodberry Down.' This school was in North London and he may have suggested it because, as he told me, he had a 'paternal interest' in it, having been involved in planning its development. In any event, he could not have made a better suggestion.

The early summer of 1956 was a turning point in my life. On 4 June I married Shirley Livingstone at Kensington Register Office. On 9 July I began 'real life' as a history teacher at Woodberry Down. I was appointed for a single term in the first instance, but both the American conscription authorities and the London County Council allowed me to remain at Woodberry Down for a full year.

CHAPTER 4

Marriage, work, the army: 1956-9

SHIRLEY, THOUGH born in Birmingham, was a Londoner and a student who moved in the same circles as I did at LSE. She was also a member of the Socialist Society, which was the apparent cause of considerable grief to us a year after we married. Our marriage was not a success. Although we were both heavily involved with left-wing politics our personalities and interests were quite different. She enjoyed all the kind of social functions at which I felt a fish out of water. 'I lack the social graces', one of my Labour Party colleagues later said to me. (As he was soon thereafter elected an MP perhaps he learnt them.) He could have been speaking of me. I had no small talk and little to offer any young woman who wanted to enjoy life without taking it too seriously.

Shirley and I lived together until 1971, though our marriage was not formally dissolved until the end of 1973. I felt later that she deserved a medal for putting up with me for so long. Both of us tried to make the marriage work but she certainly was right to decide (before I did) that we would do better to try again, separately. We quarrelled frequently, even on our honeymoon, to the embarrassment of anyone who happened to be around at the time.

I sometimes think that Shirley wanted a light affair, but was landed with a deadly serious young pursuer and did not know how to extricate herself. There were, however, two things to be said for the marriage. One is that it lasted longer than many others of that and especially later periods. The other is the fact that we had three sons, who and whose families have given both of us much pleasure and happiness.

It should not be imagined that the marriage was a failure from Day One. It was fun to set up housekeeping together. There was still London to explore, often by bicycle. We had many friends and made new ones, particularly at Woodberry Down, where I began to teach a month after our marriage. Our close, joint political involvement lasted at least till we went to Hull in 1965. One can dwell on the good things, and as Shirley and I have both gone on to much more successful marriages, our years together can be regarded as apprenticeships for future happiness. But it is impossible for me to think of our years together without sadness and pain. A failed relationship is the worst thing that can happen to two people and I am profoundly grateful to have found happiness in my second marriage.

A French friend told Ann and me a few years ago of her sense of frustration in her marriage shortly before it broke up. 'He never even let me buy my own car', she said. Shirley and I never had more than one car and I had little interest in driving it, but she undoubtedly felt that her own marriage had been marked by a similar feeling of frustration and confinement.

The first dinner guests to our furnished flat in north Islington were Arthur and Grazella Shepherd, who had a delightful home at the top of the hill overlooking Cleveland from the east. Arthur Shepherd (1880-1958) was a well-known composer and retired professor of music; by a startling coincidence he and his wife had also been my parents' first dinner guests. The Shepherds were nice and interesting people, but I have never forgotten a blunt question posed by Mrs Shepherd. 'Why are you living here?' she asked. 'Haven't you got any friends in the United States?'

We also entertained G.D.H. and Margaret Cole, ostensibly to thank Margaret for helping me to find employment, but equally to meet the great G.D.H. The evening was incredibly sticky and difficult. What had we done wrong? I should have remembered John Parker and the double whisky. I told a friend afterwards about the evening, and he admonished me for not having given the Coles alcoholic drink from start to finish. He told me of a young acquaintance without political, social or any other cachet who had visited Fabian Society friends and been plied with aperitifs and wine throughout the evening. Unbelievable as it may seem over forty years later, neither Shirley nor I had thought of providing drink. I

85

wonder whether any young people of our social class and age (I was just 24, she was 21) could possibly be so innocent now?

I remember G.D.H. Cole looking at my shelves and observing with pleasure: 'You have some of my books.' As he was a prolific author I would have thought that he would have taken for granted the fact that any young socialist would have owned a shelf of works by Cole. I took some consolation in the thought that of the three renowned British socialist thinkers of the second quarter of the twentieth century, I was growing close to Harold Laski's widow Frida and had met Tawney and Cole. He died in 1959 but Margaret lived until 1980 and I learned much from further contacts with her.

On 29 June to 1 July 1956 Shirley and I went to a Fabian Society weekend school for 'under 30s'. It was held at Wilton House, a country house in Sussex used by the Foreign Office for meetings and conferences. The school was led by Hugh Dalton, who took us for a walk to Chanctonbury Ring (he was a famous walker) and reminisced about his political life. For a weekend at least he was an ideal companion.

The weekend was particularly memorable for me because I made within 48 hours two friendships which were to last for decades. Peter Jackson, then a postgraduate student at Liverpool University, and I dominated the weekend by being more persistent and aggressive than anyone else. He was another young left-winger, entirely absorbed with politics and determined on a parliamentary career. He was to be elected for High Peak ten years later, but unfortunately for him served only a single term. He was one of those people who, lacking a sense of humour, made up for it by energy, enthusiasm and boyish charm which he has never lost. I remember him saying to me in the early days: 'We [the Labour Party left] will win over this union and that one and we'll have their votes at party conference, and so we'll have socialism when next there is a Labour government.' It was not to be quite like that.

The other friends were Clive and Masha Davies. Clive, who came from a Welsh family, at that point managed the Fabian Bookshop, where I had worked briefly the previous year, and was reading for the bar. He eventually became an academic sociologist at the University of Liverpool before retiring to Kent. Masha was the descendant of Russian aristocrats and would herself have been one in the absence of the revolution; I remember listening

Peter Jackson, parliamentary candidate (High Peak), March 1966.

(Left to right) Clive Davies, Ann, Masha Davies, David; Kerzenstüberl Restaurant, London, January 1996.

enraptured to her explaining that her grandmother had not known where the kitchen was. After the revolution of 1917 her family emigrated to Germany and were in Dresden when it was bombed by the British and Americans early in 1945. They had then gone to Sweden, and Masha had met Clive when she came to Britain on a working visit.

They were married a year or so before Shirley and me. Clive was full of fun and excitement, sparkling with ideas and imagination. I found him an immensely stimulating and enjoyable companion. Masha was instantly lovable, a beacon of good sense and stability. During the first year of our marriage when we all lived in London we and the Davieses saw a great deal of each other. I retain a vivid memory of a number of events in that year, notably of Clive and Masha sailing at top speed on their bicycles past our Islington home and our having to rush out to tell them where we lived.

Peter Jackson became one of my closest friends and I owe him a enormous amount, both personally and in helping to shape my political ideas. Shirley and I saw the Davieses regularly even after we had, between us, six children, when they lived in Birkenhead and we were in Hull. Ann and I later saw them fairly regularly after they moved to Kent to be near their daughters. It was lucky for me that Shirley and I decided to attend that Young Fabian school.

A few days later I Began Life by teaching history for the final few weeks of the summer term at Woodberry Down, in North London. It was the first mixed, purpose-built comprehensive school in North London and I taught there in (though at the very end of) its first year. I have never stopped being proud of having done so. I cycled to Woodberry Down, past an enormous sign on a cycle shop reading: 'Get off that bus, it will never be yours.' We did not realise in 1956 how completely British life was to be dominated by the motor car; I am glad that I did not know.

I had no idea what to expect when I began to teach. What I found was friendship and assistance at almost every turn. Harriet Chetwynd, the headmistress of Woodberry Down, was then married to the Labour MP for Stockton, George Chetwynd. She was one of very few, perhaps the only woman head of a mixed comprehensive school at the time. She was unfailingly kind to me and gave me advice on things to do and see in London, including the Euston Arch and the Coal Exchange, both of them fine Victorian buildings torn down soon thereafter by the vandals allowed to reshape postwar London. She was not an inspiring head, but I have a happy memory of her.

The great person in my life at Woodberry Down was Sam Fisher (1914-92), my head of department. Robert Samuel Fisher was a Scot by birth, known I believe as 'Bobby' at home. When he went to Cambridge his contemporaries thought Samuel such a comic name that he was dubbed Sam and remained Sam for the rest of his life. He was one of the Communist intellectuals of the 1930s generation which had such a marked influence on British intellectual life after the war, and whose names are household words to professional historians and the reading public: Eric Hobsbawm, John Saville, Rodney Hilton, Christopher Hill, Brian Simon and others. Sam was, with George Rudé, one of the few members of that group who was a secondary school teacher, and he and George had devised a common syllabus for their history teaching. He had taught at Latymer Upper grammar school and moved to Woodberry Down in order to teach in a comprehensive school.

Sam Fisher, probably in the 1970s.

I hero-worshipped Sam Fisher, the only person of whom I can say that, and even after his death I still do. I can think of three outstanding qualities which attracted him to me. The first is that he was a decent, kindly man with no sense of rank or his own importance. (This sense of proportion was a quality which I found sadly lacking when I became a university teacher.) I could take advice or reproof from him without anger. He had a fertile and happy wit; he was funny without being hurtful.

Secondly, Sam was the complete history teacher. I once went into his room and saw a beautiful, detailed coloured map of the medieval manor on the board. It lasted for only a single lesson, was rubbed off but could be reproduced at will. He knew everything. A colleague was to be married on the tenth of August: 'le dix août' said Sam, at once referring to the revolutionary day in 1792 which marked the fall of the French monarchy. He told me, no doubt quite accurately, that he could have taught to O level in any subject. In any case he could certainly have taught any historical subject to anyone.

I realised when I came to teach history how little I knew and, like all new teachers, I learned far more than my pupils. Learning what I had to teach, however, was not accomplished without much weeping, wailing and gnashing of teeth. One colleague, trying to be helpful, said to me: 'After all, even Mr Fisher has chinks in his armour.' I didn't believe that then and I don't believe it now. On his history syllabus appeared Types of Church Architecture; Norman, EE, Dec and Perp. How was the young American who had studied modern British political and labour history to know about that? I didn't and told Sam as much. 'Well, you'd better learn, hadn't you?' said Sam. I did, and found church architecture even more fascinating than the secular architecture which mainly interested John Parker. I might even have ended up knowing more about it than Sam Fisher.

I went to him one day and asked how I could punish certain children. 'They do just what I did when I was a child', I said. 'It isn't a question of punishment', said Sam: 'it's a question of survival.' The comment may have been obvious, but it was enormously helpful when I needed help.

The third quality which I admired in Sam Fisher was his Communism, or perhaps I should say his political commitment. I had known a few Communists at LSE whom I had not much cared for. Strongly opposed as I was to American foreign policy I may still have imagined that the typical Communist was a bloody, unkempt revolutionary with a knife between his teeth. (This image, first used by the political right as a poster in the French legislative elections of 1919, was frequently reproduced. It did not resemble Sam Fisher.) Sam was not only a Communist but as another colleague once suggested, a member of the outer circle of the inner circle of the party. (In the National Union of Teachers he was very much more than that. He lived to become its president and, far from being a bogeyman to the political right, became a hate figure to the young Trotskyist teachers of the next generation.)

I didn't become a Communist but I learned much about Marxism and Marxist attitudes from Sam. I never found a member of the Labour Party whose attitude to politics was as sympathetic as his. Talking to me of a recent movement of popular unrest in East Germany he said that it had taken place because the people had not wanted Communism, especially the version which they were then undergoing; they felt that it had been forced on them. I could hardly believe that a Communist was saying this. Everything he said about politics or society was worth listening to and pondering carefully.

Sam did not leave the CP in 1956 at the time of the Hungarian rising. I respected him for this. The last time I saw him he told me that he believed that a Marxist party was necessary to British politics. So did I and so do I, and Marxists in the Labour Party all found sooner or later that they were wasting their time. Whether Communists, a (partly unjustly) reviled and tiny minority, were doing the same, is an open question.

I only spent a year at Woodberry Down, but in that time I learned from Sam Fisher most of what I know about teaching. Knowing him was a rare and happy privilege and his death was a great shock.

Sam was not the only friend I made at Woodberry Down. I was close to Geraldine Murray, a colleague in the English Department, who lived on the Woodberry Down estate with her husband Mike and their two small girls. Mike was a science teacher at a South London comprehensive school. Of New Zealand origin they were also Communists, and we had many a discussion/argument about politics over the years. By the eighties, however, they had turned away from close interest in the subject, as many on the left did then or earlier. I remember once asking their inseparable friend Jimmy Joyce if he believed in a free press. 'Not if it includes the Beaverbrook papers', growled Jimmy. Perhaps he was right after all. It is hard to explain to an apolitical generation how the political process dominated our lives in those days, when we still believed that a fairer society could be created by political will and that capitalist society could be transformed into something more efficient and much fairer.

I was also friendly with Dorothy Gardner, also in the English Department, who later became a deputy head in Newcastle and a headmistress in Essex, and whom Ann and I saw regularly after we moved back to London in 1990. Peter Caldwell was a bearded and popular mathematician, who was a good friend to me in my year at Woodberry Down. He and his wife Winifred (known, unfortunately, as Pooh; many of my colleagues were children when the A.A. Milne stories were still quite new, as indeed I was) invited us to a party at their Finchley, North London home less than three weeks after I began teaching at Woodberry Down, once Peter found that I was returning to the school the following September. The following summer they were involved in an horrific car crash returning to London from holiday, and so far as I know Peter never walked again.

I was at Woodberry Down for too short a time to follow its progress in detail, but it was a happy school with a dedicated staff, both of which were factors more important than (though they contributed to) good examination results. It was of course very helpful that many staff had actively wanted to teach in a comprehensive school and were conscious of the fact that the new system was on trial. In any event in a new school with equipment far more lavish than had previously been available to the children of a working-class area like Woodberry Down steady progress was expected and achieved.

There was naturally a certain amount of unease, though I would not say hostility, between at least some of the teachers whose experience had been in the earlier, divided forms of secondary schools. Only a few, like myself, were at the start of their careers and had not previously taught in a tripartite secondary school, and I was perhaps the only one who had attended a comprehensive secondary school (though in a prosperous area) as a pupil. Teachers from grammar schools tended to think, probably correctly, that all children could achieve what had previously been possible only to a few. Their colleagues from secondary moderns felt in some cases at least that the former grammar school teachers, specially Sam Fisher with his Cambridge education and his political perspective, could not understand 'these children' who had failed the 11-plus and would otherwise have ended up in the sec-mod. I must add that I heard once or twice comments I would have preferred not to hear in a school which was, though not multi-cultural, multi-religious. Remarks about 'Jewish children' and 'English children', as if the categories were mutually exclusive, caused me distress, though they were made without malevolent intention.

Shirley was still a student in 1956-7, so we continued to see a good deal of our LSE friends. Although our marriage had its ups and downs, that year was the happiest one of my first marriage. I was one of the youngest members of staff at Woodberry Down, and was treated with a good deal of forbearance and patience by my colleagues. I took part in the Debating Society and formed a cycling club, taking the members (or perhaps they took me) into Hertfordshire to Rye House and Theobalds to which Christopher Wren's Temple Bar of 1672 had been removed, and in Essex to Greensted, the Saxon church whose nave, built soon after the year 1000, consists of divided oak logs.

Shirley and I were childless so we were responsible only for ourselves. We went two or three times to Devon and Cornwall, once (in April 1957) as far as the Scilly Isles, which were the first piece of the British Isles I had spotted from the *Liberté* in 1952. A woman restaurateur said to us: 'You'll come back, they always do.' I believed her and she turned out to be correct, but I did not know that her prophecy would not be be fulfilled until September 1996.

David in sub-tropical gardens, Tresco, Isles of Scilly, April 1957.

David in sub-tropical gardens, Tresco, Isles of Scilly, September 1996.

93

By this time I had visited the Peak District, especially Castleton and Edale, more than once. I had been on repeated visits to south-western England. I had visited a friend in Louth, Lincolnshire, with its magnificent church and also the Cotswolds. I had my 1952 trip to look back on, when I had been as far north as Inverness. I felt that I was becoming embedded in British life. And I had to give it all up to go into the army to defend a cause in which I did not believe.

What made it worse was that Shirley had belonged to the wrong society at LSE. Although she had never been a member of the Communist Society, her membership of the Socialist Society was evidently suspect. The American consulate appeared to know all about this; perhaps they really did have a spy amongst the left-wing students at the school. If so, it would have been consistent enough with their actions in other spheres.

I was told that I should expect my call-up notice at the end of August 1957. Shirley had not been refused a visa to enter the United States, but a decision was not to be made about whether or not to admit her until after I had left Britain and started my basic training. Richard Crossman, whom I had met on several occasions, made enquiries on my behalf, from which he concluded as he wrote to me on 21 August 1957: 'I am sure you are quite right in your view that, if you stay here and fail to fulfil your military obligations, you can by no means rely on the Home Office giving you permanent residence.' I had, obviously, only one option – to undertake my national service and hope for the best.

We went to Hampton Court on 24 August, a lovely Saturday afternoon, and bought a bunch of grapes from the famous old grapevine for six shillings; I kept the receipt for decades. On Sunday 25 August I went to Heathrow, all available pockets stuffed with books so as to evade the weight allowance, on Monday I was in Cleveland, on Tuesday in the army.

My mother was as sympathetic as she could be, but the double blow of leaving England for the army and leaving Shirley behind was almost too much to bear. One of the books I took with me was *Here's England* by Ruth McKinney and Richard Bransten, an affectionate account of an English journey by a pair of amusing American writers with illustrations by Osbert Lancaster. (It dated from 1951; this was the new edition of 1955.) It was a delightful book from which I derived much solace and satisfaction. It was given to Shirley and me by Clive and Masha Davies to mark '[our] departure from these shores'.

I should perhaps add that conscription had loomed large in my life during the whole of the Woodberry Down year and our friends and other contacts were doubtless sick of hearing about it. Nor were they especially sympathetic about my undergoing an ordeal which most of our male friends had already experienced, in war or peace. It is always easier to feel sorry for oneself than for others.

Someone suggested to me that I should volunteer for the British army as a means of remaining in Britain and a short-cut to British nationality. It is a suggestion which I am glad I did not follow. I would have had to volunteer for the British army for three years against two as a American conscript. I would have been paid much less and had inferior conditions. (In fact, my army salary as a private was higher than my salary as a teacher at Woodberry Down, which was £60.12.9 gross a month.) And the British army is not an institution I would have cared to join.

The American army was, in my day at least, basically a civilian organisation in uniform, in which graduates and other middle-class conscripts were to be found at all levels. (Preference for killing large numbers of enemy civilians by the use of massive, superior technology, rather than their own servicemen has been a consequent and marked feature of the American armed forces, even after the end of conscription. It is an unattractive characteristic but it makes life relatively comfortable for the American serviceman. The Vietnamese war with its huge commitment of personnel was an aberration which, as everyone knows, deeply scarred the American psyche.) The British armed forces on the other hand are the most obviously undemocratic element in the national life, and were doubtless far more so in the 1950s. On the other hand I would have had the opportunity to meet young men from social backgrounds different from most of the British people with whom I had previously mixed.

I went to the recruiting station in Cleveland on Tuesday 27 August 1957, almost forty years to the day before first writing these words. There I found that my destination was Fort Knox, Kentucky, not far in American terms since Kentucky is the next state to Ohio. It was, however, a very long way in terms of the life which I had previously known. Fort Knox, as used to be well known, is 'where they keep the gold', but the site was strictly off bounds to conscripts. We were taken to our barracks and had almost all our hair cut off, presumably to lower our morale and make us reluctant to return to civilian life even had the option been available. We were shown the barracks and given bunk beds and lockers.

We were told emphatically that 'there [was] no such creature in the American army as a sarge', whatever we had read in newspaper comic strips such as Beetle Bailey. The soldier in charge of us was a sergeant and was to be addressed by that term. (Some, by the way, were of Latin American origin, others black.) We were given our serial numbers, which did not replace or precede our names as in the British army, but were nonetheless crucial and not to be forgotten. The only person we ever gave our numbers to were sergeants, so that I think of my serial number as 'US 52 443 973, sergeant'. The 'US' was a precious prefix; it meant that those who had it were conscripts, not regular soldiers. In basic training, however, volunteers and conscripts were in the same platoons and barracks.

We were taken to see the army chaplain of our choice. At the time I thought of myself as an agnostic, though my friend Nick Tucker was to persuade me not long afterwards that I was an atheist, and I kept that designation for thirty years. So while everyone went to see a chaplain I remained alone outside all the chaplaincies. It seems to me sometimes that I have stood outside institutions all my life, a posture which induces both loneliness and an unwarranted feeling of rectitude and self-satisfaction.

We lined up early in the morning for roll call and the sergeant called out our surnames. We had to reply with our first name and initial (if any), even if we were actually known by another name. So for the eight weeks of basic training the sergeant would shout 'Rubinstein', and I would shout back 'Beryl D., sergeant.' This is the only time in my life that my first name has been used and even then only in the context of the roll call. I used to enjoy that; I have a loud voice and could rival most of the sergeants in this respect.

As we got used to army life it gradually got less worse. I enjoyed marching, the first time (apart from briefly in the Boy Scouts) that I had ever done any walking, which was to become so important a part of my life less than a decade later. I was happy to carry the pack, apart from the occasion when I managed to put it on upside down and was verbally abused by the sergeant in front of the platoon. (I was later asked how I managed to keep a deadpan countenance during this process.) I was treated more gently, however, than my later army friend Dan Payne, who was cleaning his rifle one day on his bed (a forbidden procedure) when a sergeant came by and screamed: 'Whaddayadoing Payne?' What could Dan say? He replied 'making a peanut butter sandwich, sergeant', and was promptly assigned the repugnant task of cleaning the kitchen grease trap.

I felt at the time that my life was virtually saved during these early weeks by Charles Dickens. After lights out I read *Pickwick Papers* under the covers by the light of an electric torch. I have never enjoyed a book so much. Of course I appreciated the humour and the other qualities which make the book a classic, but I also felt that there really was an England and English life; it was not a mirage. (In later years I read the book to Ann in bed over several weeks. She was less appreciative than I had been and kept asking when the plot would start. I found this view curious.) This brief, blissful forgetfulness of army life and of the fact that my wife was 4,000 miles away and visa-less was interrupted one night by the sergeant who passed through the barracks and found me reading. He took away the book. A day or two I asked for its return and he gave it to me. (Would this have happened in the British army?) I was lucky enough not to be caught subsequently. I was also able, either in basic training or later, to put the *New Statesman* up my trouser leg, since the trouser was tucked in or fastened on to my boot. Off parade or at any other moment of leisure I could take it out within a second or two. I believe that at the time the readership of the *New Statesman* among privates in the American army was small.

As I was called up at the end of August basic training went on until late October. I was lucky that I had not been posted to Fort Benning, Georgia, where one or two new recruits, I was later told, actually died of the heat. Even so, the cold nights and warm days posed a problem of what to wear. If I put on the long underwear known as long johns early in the morning I could be sure that I would swelter in the hot afternoon southern sun. If I did not put them on I would freeze in the morning.

97

Life was stringent in the army but given the nature of the institution my fellow soldiers were decent men. Our own platoon sergeant, Sergeant Ramos, was universally liked. My fellow soldiers were congenial; I recall no bullying or unpleasantness. One of my fellow soldiers, a volunteer from Kentucky or Tennessee, had little education but a very nice wit which constantly kept us amused. I recall one of his best *mots*: 'I'll give you three guesses and the first two don't count.' I have never stopped using this line, usually with acknowledgements.

And so I went to see my commanding officer about the fact that my wife had not been given a visa and asked if he could help. I was amused to find that he treated the State Department which had withheld the visa as the common enemy, rather than Shirley as an enemy of the American way of life, as the State Department evidently thought. He arranged, to my everlasting gratitude, that when my basic and specialised training ended I should be posted abroad. Not long thereafter the visa at last came through. It was strictly forbidden for soldiers to leave camp during basic training, but I was allowed by the same commanding officer to go to New York to meet Shirley's plane and spend the weekend with her. (I uncharacteristically developed 'flu as soon as I left the camp and was not much use to her or myself during much of the weekend.) She then had a short period with my mother in Cleveland before coming down to Fort Knox to spend the second period of training with me. It should have been eight weeks, but in order to fit it in to the available time before Christmas, when Fort Knox emptied, it was reduced to seven.

We found a small bungalow some distance from the camp and I was able to join her on four of the seven nights; twice during the week, Saturday and Sunday. I was given a lift to and fro by two soldiers who went home to Louisville, a large town some thirty miles distant from Fort Knox which contained some precious features of civilian life. If they accepted any money at all for this service, which I don't think they did, it was the very smallest pittance. Of course it was a vast improvement for me to sleep in barracks for only three nights a week, but life was grim for Shirley. She was only 22, she had not been to the United States since the end of her wartime evacuation there in 1944 and she knew nobody but me. The little house, hardly more than a shack which we had rented, was insubstantial and she knew nothing of the neighbourhood or the people there. She was, however, somewhat cheered by the milkman who, discovering that she was English, bid her farewell daily by saying 'TTFN'; he had been a Tommy Handley fan when in Britain during the war. Still, she must have thought often enough that married life was surely meant to be less gruelling than this.

The seven week period of training, while I was at clerical school, was brightened by two features. The first was the fact that clerical school attracted the intellectual elite, such as it was, of the recruits. It is a sombre reflection on army life that pounding a typewriter should attract an elite. The soldiers with whom I was serving were good companions and I enjoyed the course because of them; there was even an Englishman named Neville. He had not volunteered for the American army to advance his case for citizenship; rather, the American practice was to recruit compulsorily all young men from friendly nations resident within its borders. He too helped to remind me of the happier days in London. There was also Dan Payne, the above-mentioned teller of droll stories and a budding actor, and Jim Agenbroad with whom I kept in touch for some years and who visited us a little later in France. I was delighted when in about 1993 Jim telephoned out of the blue while visiting London. I didn't remember his face when we met at Euston Station but we had a very enjoyable time with him and his wife.

The second factor was that Bob Gaebler's mother had moved to Cincinnati (I think that his father was working elsewhere) and she invited Shirley and me to spend the Thanksgiving weekend at the end of November with her. (I later found that my favourite journalist, Alexander Werth, had been in Cincinnati at the same time.) I don't remember much about the visit but I do remember that it was the happiest I had had for a long time. Apart from the brief visit to New York to collect Shirley it was the first period of time I had had away from Fort Knox for three months and it was enormously enjoyable. I had always liked Bob's mother but never so much as then.

And so, Christmas, spent in Cleveland Heights with my mother for the last time. My fear of flying was increased by our trip to Cleveland. We managed to leave Fort Knox somewhat before we had expected but we had no tickets for the earlier date. Louisville airport was a madhouse with soldiers frantic to go home but we got the last seats on a plane leaving Louisville for Cleveland; the weather was rough and the plane lurched and plunged. Two passengers had to leave the plane at an intermediate stop to reduce the weight of the aircraft and we, the last on board, were the two. I have never been so glad to be back on terra firma. We spent the night in a hotel and took a half-empty plane to Cleveland the next morning. After Christmas we went to New York and once again I set sail, this time however not on a transatlantic liner but the troopship *Geiger*. Shirley and I dined one night in a small restaurant in Greenwich Village. I was about to go abroad and I had no civilian clothes. The feelings of hostility towards me from my fellow American diners (whom I was after all protecting against the menace of Communism; otherwise, why had I been called up?) were palpable. I must have wanted to be a soldier as little or less than any young man in the room; still, I would probably have bridled too if I had been a civilian and some other unfortunate in the middle of a disrupted life had come into the restaurant.

The *Geiger* was notably unlike the transatlatic liners. We did not sleep in hammocks, as Ann's father had done when he went to India towards the end of the war, but bunk beds were not much fun. There was nowhere inside the boat for recreation or reading apart from the bunks and it was lucky that January 1958 was exceptionally mild, so that it was possible to be on deck a good deal of the time. I took messages on occasion to the first-class deck, where there were officers and their wives, and I noticed that their facilities *were* like those available on an ocean liner.

In any event, the ship landed after a voyage of ten days or so at Bremerhaven, and the troops (American soldiers were no longer known as 'GIs' and I much resented being referred to once as such by an officer's wife, even though she said 'serve this GI first') went to their destinations overland. I went to Verdun, where Shirley joined me soon afterwards. (The family story, no doubt true, was that the crack Golden Arrow train was held up at Victoria Station while she rushed to join it.) I could not then know that, apart from many or most of my holidays, I would live and work in France for five of the next forty years, while spending well under six months in my native United States.

Life was by this time looking up considerably. Nearly a quarter of my nominal army service lay behind me. I spent only the first couple of weeks in Verdun in barracks. I was far closer to England than I had been at Fort Knox. I had a new part of France to explore and Germany, Luxembourg and Belgium were all close at hand. The soldiers at Verdun were on the whole an agreeable lot. There was virtually no real army life, other than guard duty and visits to the firing range.

As to the last-mentioned, we were told that the French allowed visits to the range only once a year. So in the sixteen months that I lived in Verdun, I visited the range only once or twice. I was awarded a badge as an expert shot but lost it in one of my many moves, much to my chagrin. Guard duty was less fun. It came round every six to eight weeks. We patrolled the camp but were not allowed to carry live ammunition. We escorted the camp prisoners to breakfast before we could sign off. Guard duty was especially onerous in the winter rain and guards often tried to hide in army vehicles if they could do so without being spotted by the duty sergeant.

There were 'alerts' when the barracks had to be emptied within a matter of seconds, but living away from the camp (Caserne Maginot) I was unconcerned by the call in the early hours. I remember morning parade (though that term is not an American one) and the sergeant saying to us: 'smoke 'em if you've got 'em', before we were dismissed. I remember Tom Benson, a fellow-conscript and private, telling me that one would waste a huge sum of money (I think that the figure he picked was $50,000) in a lifetime, so if one spent money foolishly or unnecessarily one should shrug one's shoulders and think of it as part of the $50,000. Whatever allowance one should make for inflation I have certainly thrown away my $50,000+ and Tom's dictum has stood me in good stead.

It was surprising to find that many of the sergeants were extremely pleasant. Sergeant Courtney sold me a pram for $8 or so and then presented me with two of the dollars as a gift. 'Kickback', he said. My particular favourite was Sgt Bob Kiesewetter, as decent and kindly an individual as one could hope to find in any walk of life. I got to know slightly Lieutenant Aune, pronounced, in the American fashion 'Awny'. There was no question of calling him by his first name, but I did pluck up courage to ask him how an intelligent man like him could be in the army by choice. (I don't think that any conscript was either a sergeant or an officer.)

101

'I have four children', he said, 'and when the second was born my wife had a long labour. I was then a civilian and it was an expensive procedure. Medical care in the army is free to soldiers and dependants; I returned to the army.' 'But what', I asked, 'happens in civilian life if you haven't got the money to pay the bills?' 'They wait', he replied, as chilling a phrase as any I have heard. It seems inconceivable that, forty years later, Americans still have no proper health service, and even more inconceivable that the British seem (perhaps I should optimistically write 'seemed till 1 May 1997') poised to follow the same path. I was also told, on a slightly less elevated level, that free access to the Class VI store was in itself justification for remaining in the army. The Class VI store sold spirituous liquors cheaply.

My fellow-privates were a mixed bag; I should add that I had been promoted to private first-class (Pfc), the equivalent in rank of a lance-corporal but not a non-commissioned officer. (I was later to become a Specialist 4th class, equivalent to corporal, a new rank designed to indicate its non-fighting nature.) I never had any problems with any of them, perhaps partly because I went home at the end of the working day. However little we had in common, we got along well enough. I remember Jim Meche (pronounced by the Americans 'meechy'; he said in wonder that only the French pronounced his name correctly) from the southern state of Arkansas. I thought then that he was the least intelligent graduate I had ever met. Shirley and I went to the Brussels World's Fair in 1958 with Jim and his wife. The pavilion of the Soviet Union was a formidable affair, as proficient and modern as anything the Americans put forward. (I still have a Russian tea caddy purchased at the fair.) It was Jim's view that the Russians had produced only one of each item on display. It seemed ridiculous at the time; in view of later revelations perhaps we should not have laughed.

What did I do as a soldier in my sixteen months in Verdun? (Ann asked a friend 25 years later in Tours what Barclays Bank was doing there. 'Not much', he replied.) My first main job was attached to such educational facilities as were provided for the troops, which were limited mainly to the provision of literature. I do not remember any actual classes. Here I made the acquaintance of Mr Sullivan and Mr Snell, Americans with French wives who had remained in Europe since 1945, living on an American income in France. If

102

they felt resentment or envy of a Pfc with a doctorate they did not show it.

I then moved to the section which dealt with the formalities of American civilians, mostly wives who had come to join their husbands in France. Once a week I took their passports to Bar-le-Duc to be processed by the departmental authorities. While they were being dealt with I visited the local churches and other architectural features. (This was unusual for an American soldier in uniform and my visits did not pass unnoticed.) This life was on the whole more congenial than working for Mr Sullivan, and the more attractive Mr Snell was in a different office. On the other hand Mr Sullivan did not have to be called 'sir' unlike the young lieutenant in the passport office. (One of my Cleveland contemporaries told me that he surmounted the 'sir' problem by calling his officer 'captain', but I recall no such option.) In at least one of my offices if not all of them we were given no headed stationery and typing had to be perfect. We were not allowed to use correcting fluid and word processors had not yet been heard of. It must be said that there was a strong tendency to mistype 'US Forces' (I don't know why it was not 'US Army'; perhaps as an attempt to unify the different services), by changing the 'o' in the second word to an 'a'.

Most of my life, in short, was that of someone who was living abroad doing a very dull but by no means wholly uncongenial civilian job. I would not say that I greatly improved my French, but I was able to chat without difficulty to the many French civilians employed on the base. (Chatting to a clerk as I paid for my purchases with a queue waiting behind me did little for my popularity.) On one occasion I even acted as interpreter for an American soldier who had committed an offence for which he was being tried in a French court. The trouble with my French was not that it was bad but rather that it has never improved significantly, even though I have obviously become more fluent during my periods of residence in France.

Real army life, I repeat, seldom impinged. I was deeply concerned that President Eisenhower, who had had a couple of heart attacks, might die during my period of service. I dreaded the formalities and ceremonies which would have resulted, but he obligingly lived on until 1969. The working day ended at 4.30 or 5.0, when there was a ceremony as the American flag was lowered. All 'other ranks' made a point of not being caught outside when this happened, because if we were we would have to remain at attention, saluting, until the ceremony ended. I was skulking inside on one occasion when a major appeared from nowhere, telling me to 'go outside, soldier; salute and salute proudly!'. I don't think that I was ever caught that way again. In fact I prided myself on not being a good or smart soldier, but being good enough not to get in trouble.

Shirley and I had two homes in Verdun. The first was chez Bouvy, an electrical goods shop near the centre of Verdun. (I remember Mme Bouvy picking up the 'phone and saying 'j'écoute', an expression which I have always wished that I had the nerve to copy.) The address was 60, rue de Rû, a difficult combination of words for Anglo-Saxon (to use the French expression) tongues. The flat was certainly convenient, near the market and the theatre, and in spite of its tragic history Verdun was a nice little town with much to admire, notably its cathedral on a hill and the roadside Tour Chaussée. Peter Ustinov's *L'Amour des Quatre Colonels* played at the theatre and we attended it; I don't think that I caught a single word. (The French theatre has always been difficult for me.)

We had a meal every now and then at a Routier restaurant, then cheap and cheerful but now generally of a higher status. The set meal cost a set 350 francs, which is now 3.5 francs, and forty years later the cheapest equivalent meal other than at a self-service restaurant is about 80 francs. My mother visited us while we were still chez Bouvy, though she stayed in an hotel; we had but a single, largish, well-lit room. She came to see the flat, having lived all her life in large detached houses. We opened the door and waited for her reaction: 'How lovely!', she exclaimed. I think that that moment must have been the high point of Shirley's affection for her, but we were to be together all too rarely in the five remaining years of her life.

The only snag about living off-base in the army was getting to work. Caserne Maginot was just outside Verdun and one really needed a car to get there. I applied to my mother and was sent the £500 or so needed to purchase a lefthand-drive Morris Minor. I remember vividly Ken Bannon, a nice young conscript of my own grade saying: 'And how did you get the money for a car, Pfc

Rubinstein?' I do not remember my reply as clearly as I remember his question, because I was naturally covered in confusion.

I had two tremendous assets in the army which most other private soldiers did not have. The first was living away from the barracks, to which I have already referred. The second was that I had a passport, whereas almost no other conscript had ever been abroad before. (The fact that I was past my 25th birthday when called up should be borne in mind; most of my comrades were somewhat younger than I was.) Being married and living in my own flat transformed my life as a soldier. And having a passport meant that I could come and go as I pleased. The American soldiers travelled on a leave paper or a 72-hour pass. I needed none of that, and always arranged my leave so that I could have a weekend before and sometimes after it, which gave me a maximum of four extra days. A faithful friend, Pete Malcolm, arranged to send me a telegram if I was on guard duty the weekend after leave (and hence had to return promptly) but that happened only once.

Shirley and I took full advantage of our passports and our car. I was desperate to be in England as much as I possibly could, and all our leaves but one were spent there. As none of the people we visited expected us till the leave was actually due to begin we used our extra 48 hours to tour east Kent. I remember visiting Dover Castle, the Roman fort at Richborough (though I had totally forgotten it when I visited it again 39 years later) and the Nicolson home and garden at Sissinghurst. We and the other visitors were greeted by Harold Nicolson and Vita Sackville-West, and they expressed concern when they saw Shirley, who was then pregnant with a bandaged leg, the result of a fall in Dover.

We visited Luxembourg, Belgium to see the World's Fair of 1958 and the principal cities as well as Liège and Namur on their cliffs above the river Meuse (or Maas), the Joan of Arc home and basilica at Domrémy, Alsace, Paris of course more than once, and the cathedrals at Chartres and Amiens. During our one leave spent in France we drove by slow stages to Montpellier, the perched village of Les Baux, along the Côte d'Azur into Italy, over the Alps to Annecy (the most beautiful place in the world to my thinking) and home to Verdun. We lived in the town where the flower of French youth had died in 1916 and lost no opportunity to visit and take our visitors to see the forts and monuments outside the town.

(I was appalled to find that the town's postal frank read: 'Verdun; ses glorieux souvenirs', and I hope that it has been changed subsequently.)

On our drives to and from the coast we visited other Great War sites and discovered for the first time how overwhelmingly moving are the British war cemeteries. Those visits took place about midway between the tragic events they commemorate and our own time, and like almost every visitor I remain impressed and grateful that the cemeteries remain so beautifully maintained. We also visited an area near Ypres where the lines of British and German trenches remained clearly visible and terrifyingly close to each other after forty years. Our guide, a Mr Bekaert I was told many years later, said that he had never been to England. He had learned his fluent, Cockney English from the British troops in 1914-18.

Those sixteen months in 1958-9 resulted in the Great War becoming one of my permanent obsessions, though I made no attempt to read more than the better-known war literature. Like others of my generation I am the product of the Great War, though I was born fourteen years after its end. No Great War would have meant no Hitler, no Russian Revolution, no Second World War, no Cold War and almost certainly no move on my part to England. Ann and I visited Great War sites, above all the Somme more systematically in 1997, and I remain like so many others shocked and horrified by what the people of that generation were willing to do to each other at such an horrific price to their own and later generations.

Shirley and I both liked France (my love for it came later) and we tried to behave like good guests. We chatted in French in the shops, read a French newspaper and gave lifts to French servicemen, whose salaries were much inferior to mine, when we had the chance to do so (there was a French garrison in Verdun, between whom and the Americans there was no fraternisation; I was also told, I am sure correctly, that white and black American soldiers frequented different bars). Unlike most of the other Americans I had no feeling that 'the land of the big PX' (the army shop), as one of my comrades put it graphically, was superior to France.

But I blush to admit that we also did what we could to subvert the French economy. We could change our army dollars for about 350 francs to the dollar (and in addition could buy petrol at a reduced price), but at that point the French economy was under pressure, and in Luxembourg one could get up to 420 francs or even more to the dollar. A weekend in Luxembourg could thus almost pay for itself once money was changed.

The year 1958 was a stirring one in France, indeed one of the most exciting in modern French history. It was the year that the Algerian war came to a climax and General de Gaulle came to power after a semi-coup. Nothing much happened in Verdun, but the radio and the French and British press were wholly absorbing and Shirley and I tried to pose as experts when in England on leave.

In my view the high wages of American soldiers and, as one might expect, American incomprehension of everything French were alone enough reason to push out the American forces as de Gaulle was to do in 1967. This was the only occasion since the war that a European country has had the courage to tell its American occupiers to leave. (And if the Americans were not needed to protect the French against the Russians in the 1960s, why are they still stationed in European countries over thirty years later?) They must have done something for the local economy if not (see above) much for the national one, but they could not have been liked. My car was cared for by MM Taboga and Mabille, two extremely nice *garagistes*; one of them walked with a limp as the result of a wartime wound. They told me that during the war German soldiers would come into a shop or garage, remove their caps, address the staff politely, often in French, and generally behave in a civilised manner. Americans, on the other hand, never removed their caps, and shouted in English at shopkeepers. They were more disliked than the Germans had been fifteen years earlier. Readers may say that the *garagistes* were having fun at the expense of the innocent abroad, 'winding me up' in ugly modern parlance. I don't believe it.

Shirley found that she was pregnant in spring 1958 and the Bouvy flat was clearly going to be too small for three. We moved to 72, rue St-Victor, on the way to the Great War sites north-east of Verdun. The house where we lived was built round a central well, like many of its age, so light came through from two sides. There were four or five flats and we were the only Anglo-Saxon family. The proprietors were Pierre and Fernande Moignard, a dignified couple in their sixties, who showed Shirley and me enormous kindness during the year or so we were with them. M. Moignard had fought in the Great War and had little faith in mankind's ability to stay out of war. 'Un peu de tambour, un peu de trompette, et tout le monde suit', he said.

Life was now even more like a boring civilian job in congenial surroundings. We had a nice flat in which we could put up visitors, but I cannot now remember how we had enough room for Geraldine and Mike Murray and their two girls who came to spend Christmas 1958 with us. We had our Christmas turkey cooked for us by the baker, just like a real French family. I can still sing some of the non-sense songs from records which we gave the girls that Christmas.

We had a central, closed coal stove which kept us warm and snug. My mother and our friends wrote to us, at our request, at rue St-Victor, not at the caserne, so our mail was independent of the army. We had a radio which picked up the BBC and we listened faithfully to 'Life with the Lyons', with the British-based American comedians Bebe Daniels and Ben Lyon. We were even more faithful to Jimmy Edwards, Dick Bentley and June Whitfield in 'Take it from here'. My affection for Jimmy Edwards even survived his standing for parliament as a Conservative in 1964. We subscribed to the *Manchester Guardian* daily and it arrived within a day or two. (Those were the blissful days of slim newspapers.) We continued to take the *New Statesman*. We borrowed *The Messiah* from the caserne library, with Malcolm Sargent conducting the Huddersfield Choral Society. It, with *Pickwick Papers*, was the cultural highlight of my army life. I thought that Isobel Baillie singing 'I know that my redeemer liveth' was a voice from heaven and mine was the common view; her *Dictionary of National Biography* (1981-5) entry was to comment that her rendition of the aria was 'acclaimed by all who heard her'. I have never heard *The Messiah* sung more movingly subsequently. I suppose, looking back, that this was one of the best periods of my first marriage. It is sad that it did not seem so at the time.

Peter was born on 2 November 1958. Shirley had been in hospital for a day or two when, early in the morning, Madame Moignard knocked on the door with the unforgettable words: 'M. Rubinstein! Vous avez un fils!' (We had no telephone and the hospital had arranged to phone the only flat in the building which had one.) Peter was, I believe, the first baby to be born in the new Hopital Desandrouins, recently built for the American forces outside Verdun. (I wonder what became of it after the Americans were booted out?)

I felt at the time and still feel that with a surname like mine, first names should be as short, classless and international as possible (though it must be acknowledged that 'Peter' has unfortunate connotations in French). I was also not keen on naming innocent children either after family or friends. And I have never liked middle names or the American habit of middle initials. (Harry Truman had a middle initial, S, which referred to no actual name. He was president when I began my career at Swarthmore and John Purnell used to call him 'Harry S-for-nothing Truman'.) Shirley accepted these views and we settled on Peter. (I should add that neither of my sons who became fathers took the same line. Nor did they have the same free hand that I had.) We sent a telegram announcing the birth to Geraldine and Mike Murray and received one from them: 'Congratulations. Another victory for socialism.'

We were sorry that Peter did not acquire French nationality at birth, even though it would have made him liable for French national service in later life. But we were outraged to find that he was not British either. If his father had been British and his mother American he would automatically have become British at birth, but the person who actually gave him birth could not pass on her own nationality to her foreign-born son. This was of course well before the days of modern feminism and it infuriated us. We wrote to a well-known woman Labour MP, thinking that it was the kind of subject which might interest her but we received an offhand and unhelpful reply. Peter remained American until I was naturalised shortly before his sixth birthday, when he also acquired British nationality. The law remained unchanged until the rights of father and mother were made equal under section 2 of the British Nationality Act, passed by the Conservative government in 1981. (See 997 *HC Deb.*, 5s., 28 January 1981, col. 938.) By the time it became law Peter was just short of his twenty-third birthday.

Mr Snell had said, when he found that Shirley and I were to have a baby, 'that will change your lives', and as every parent discovers, he was of course right. In a good relationship children are a strengthening influence; they tend to make a shaky one shakier. In any event, Peter lived in France for his first seven months. Our travels did not end, because a baby fits nicely into a carrycot, and our long trip to Montpellier and the Côte d'Azur was made with Peter, who was quite a star with onlookers. It is a shame that babies cannot remember their early experiences.

I have kept many mementoes of my early life but I regret the loss or disappearance of a few. One such was a card which French soldiers bought to indicate the passage of their army service day by day. Each day one changed the number to indicate how many days' service remained. Mine had a cartoon in which one private said to another: 'Doucement! J'entends le pas du Caporal Duchêne!' They had rigged up a contraption which ensured that a container of water would fall on the head of the unfortunate corporal when he entered the room. In fact, it was a high-ranking general who was about to come in. I gave my card to the American soldier who followed us at 72, rue St-Victor, and have always regretted it. Such cards no longer seem to be available in the shops of French garrison towns.

There had never been any question of our returning to the United States after my military service was over. It is possible that if I had remained in London without being called up I would eventually have become bored and wanted to leave England, but my wife was British and I had adored life at Woodberry Down so I doubt that I would have returned in any conceivable circumstances. But I had spent 21 months eating out my heart to return to London, and visits there on leave had only strengthened my desire to return. I think that in fact I was keener to return to London than Shirley was. As before I did not consider my mother's sentiments.

There was no vacancy at Woodberry Down, much to my regret, but it was perhaps time to move on in any case. On one leave, perhaps in March 1959, I had read an advertisement for a post teaching history at Forest Hill School in South London. With a flagrant failure to check my references unforgivable in an historian I telephoned not Forest Hill but Tulse Hill, another comprehensive school in South London between the working-class area of Brixton and the more comfortable suburb of Streatham. This was the era when secondary education was expanding all over the country and there was a desperate teacher shortage. Married women, who had been generally banned from teaching until 1939, were begged to return to the classroom in large newspaper advertisements. Tulse Hill was designed for over two thousand boys (I heard the head one day tell parents that the school register contained 2,222 names) and was one of the largest schools in the country. One history teacher more or less would hardly be noticed.

In any event the head invited me to visit the school, although there was no official vacancy. Later I had to make a special trip from Verdun to London for a formal interview and was offered the post. There was a provision in the American army to suspend the final three months of military service if the affected soldier would otherwise lose the offer of a civilian job. I persuaded Tulse Hill to write a letter offering me the job on 1 June 1959 and no other date, which allowed me to leave the army on 26 May, exactly three months before my service was due to end. This was an odd date to start teaching (though I had begun at Woodberry Down on 9 July), especially to Americans, for whom school would have normally ended by the end of May. But the army authorities were satisfied and I was allowed to go.

It was a wrench to leave our home and especially M. and Mme Moignard, both for us and for them. We had really not appreciated how much we liked and respected them and how happy we had been in Verdun until we were due to leave it. But we were young and thoughtless and in any event would have left Verdun three months later. And so we returned to London, visiting Bayeux to see the tapestry en route. I did not know that I would only make two brief visits to France in the next thirteen years (in 1963 to visit the Moignards and introduce them to our children; in 1970 to go walking with Nick Tucker in lower Normandy), nor that from 1972 I would be in France virtually every year.

CHAPTER 5

Six Years at the Chalk Face: 1959-65

THE YEARS 1959-65 were crucial to my life. By the end of the period I was no longer young, if I had been when I started teaching again in 1959 (even then I was by no longer the baby of the staffroom). I was no longer either an American or a school teacher. My mother had died and I was the father of three sons.

When I first left the army Shirley, Peter and I lived in Muswell Hill, North London, in a private hotel run by friends we had made in the Peak District before we were married. We then moved into a furnished flat in Streatham, then another near the Crystal Palace. The move to South London was momentous. I had lived for nearly a year in Stockwell in my student days, unaware of the social rule which prescribed that anyone with social or intellectual pretensions must live north of the river. Now we were to have six years of life in South London and north-west Kent.

Crystal Palace was interesting, though the area had changed drastically since Camille Pissarro had painted there in the early 1870s. What I remember best about it, apart from steep hills up and down which we had to push Peter in his pram (I took him out once in the winter without mittens and when his hands were cold he howled till I could get him home), is how in an area which had remained middle class throughout the decades the houses had become smaller in each successive period as domestic help became less and less available. It was an object lesson in one phase of modern middle-class history. We then returned to Streatham and in spring 1960, nine or ten months after starting at Tulse Hill and nearly four years after our marriage, we at last had our own home. It was an unfurnished, two-bedroom, centrally heated flat in Streatham

Hill, easy to run and within a few minutes' walking distance of the school.

The block of flats, called Corner Fielde (sic), had been built as a luxury block between the wars. It was based immediately next to a London Transport garage, where eight buses began or finished their run. As we no longer had a car and the tube was distant the proximity of the garage was very useful. We were glad to have our own furniture to our own taste after so many years of living in homes which had been furnished by other people. It was an interesting area with its own theatre (the Streatham Hill), at which top West End stars like Sybil Thorndike and Lewis Casson performed. There was also common land to explore. At this stage Peter, at the age of two or so, was fascinated by trains, especially steam trains. I would wheel him in his pram to Tooting Bec Common where he could watch the trains thunder past on a viaduct, an occasional steam train adding zest to the proceedings.

The first of June was not a good time to begin teaching. I had been demobbed but the pupils were also demob happy. Despite my year at Woodberry Down I found it difficult to control them and I was forced to appeal for assistance to my head of department, Fred Dwyer. He appeared in my classroom, resplendent in suit and gown, swishing a cane and threatening the boys. After that I had no more trouble. It was a salutary and highly embarrassing incident for someone who disapproved of corporal punishment.

I was not happy at Tulse Hill. I did not like the all-male environment or the school itself which was built on nine floors with pilotis on the architectural principles of Le Corbusier. (It was the tallest school built by the London County Council.) I did not care for the headmaster, Mr Thomas, who had been a master at Dulwich College, the public school not far away, and who seemed to be mainly concerned with the appearance of his pupils outside school (wearing caps, not eating ice cream in the streets). The deputy head, Mr Loveless, complained that he was 'the highest paid office boy in the the LCC [London County Council]', being occupied mainly by the timetable and finding replacements for teachers who were absent. He claimed to be descended from the Tolpuddle Martyrs of 1834, two of whom were named Loveless.

I also did not make friends as easily as I had done at Woodberry Down or as I was to do at my next school, Abbey Wood. There was no Sam Fisher, no figure on whom to model myself and in any case Fred Dwyer soon left for another post. One colleague to whom I suggested that we use each other's christian names told me that he preferred surnames. He was a former public schoolboy and 1959, before the takeover of British society and culture by television and Americanisation, was a different world. Our friend Michael Gordon-Bates, an active member of our CND group, complained bitterly to me that he had received a letter from an unknown correspondent in New York addressed to 'dear Michael'; he pretended in jest to hold me personally accountable for this unacceptable breach of good manners. Before 1988 when I left academic life it had become standard operating procedure in contemporary Britain to be addressed in this manner by people one had not met; I object to it as much as Michael did.

However, all was not lost in the personal sphere. When school began again in September 1959 Nick Tucker joined the staff of the English department. It is somewhat of a shock to realise that I was just 27 and that he was not yet 23. He was the son of Archie Tucker, professor of African languages at the School of Oriental and African Studies (University of London), and was himself a product of King's College Cambridge. I liked Nick at once and immensely and have never seen any reason to change my mind. It is not easy to say what attracts one to another person, though we were both young, with intellectual interests and general left-wing views. He was as he has remained, attractive to look at, entertaining and witty, and bubbling over with ideas and zest. Early in our friendship we marched together the full distance in the 1960 Aldermaston March to London to protest against nuclear weapons.

Nick and I remain in close contact after nearly forty years' friendship. For two people who are opinionated and self-centred, determined to force their own views on other people (or at least on each other), this is no mean feat. We both became university lecturers in due course, Nick at Sussex after a spell as an educational psychologist for the new Inner London Education Authority (he had a joint degree in English and Psychology), I at Hull. He also branched out actively into journalism and broadcasting, specialising (as he did also in his work at Sussex) in the development of children, notably their reading. He has published a number of books in this field and also on the mass media.

114

Nick Tucker, probably mid-1970s.

In the summer of 1960 he and I took a school journey with a colleague, no further than Sussex. Our own forms were all in the lowest streams and it was only to be expected that there would be a certain amount of good-natured but boisterous behaviour on the part of the boys, specially in the youth hostels where we stayed. The headmaster chose to interpret my frank report on the journey as meaning that in reality it had been chaos from start to finish, which was exactly the opposite of the truth. We felt that few other teachers could have given such a good time to underprivileged children. Never mind, Nick and I said to each other. It is the school's loss, not ours. We went on our own to spend a few extremely enjoyable days in Shropshire.

This was the start of a remarkable series of annual journeys; certainly I have never known of anything like it (the only parallel which occurs to me is those colleagues both in London and in Hull who spent their evenings in the pub while their wives minded the baby). We have had many shorter walks, and missed longer ones in 1963 and 1964, but otherwise we have gone away every year

115

without a break for a long weekend or several days, in all some 37 times. We have been to Austria, Spain, France, Wales, Scotland, Northern Ireland and the Republic, and over twenty times to different parts of England.

The friendship has not always been easy; someone, usually myself, gets irritated (or even furious) with the other. The fact that our political views, while both remaining in broad supportive of the Labour Party, have diverged sharply since 1959 has not made for harmony. But Nick has given me endless intellectual stimulus and emotional support over the decades, and the relationship has been a fortunate one for me. It alone would have made worthwhile an otherwise not very happy two years at Tulse Hill.

The years 1959-65 were the most politically active ones in my life, though I was a British citizen for only the last few months. Though we belonged to the Labour Party and had good friends in it, our activity in 1959-61 was poured into the Campaign for Nuclear Disarmament. I marched all the way from Aldermaston to London in both 1960 and 1961, in a state of excitement and dedication. 'They'll *have* to listen to us now', somebody said as we reached Trafalgar Square on one of the marches. We had yet to learn that 'they' listen only to voices they want to hear, at least in Britain; with the media and the leadership of the Labour Party on the same side as the Conservative government there was little for the powers-that-be to worry about. The British government could afford to ignore the noise we made, the fact that millions of British people wanted to end Britain's nuclear deterrent, and that a smaller but substantial number felt that we would have been much safer without the American alliance formalised in Nato. There was, after all, no danger of industrial action or civil turmoil over the issue. There is probably no western country whose middle class is more vocal and active over minority political issues; there is also no country in which public agitation has so little effect on public policy. If the governing class was worried by us it certainly had little reason to be – so at least says hindsight.

This fact was certainly apparent to Bertrand Russell and his friends who moved from CND marches to direct action through the Committee of 100. I joined their earliest protest in February 1961 when we sat down in front of the Ministry of Defence, despite the vigorous protests of Peter Jackson who visualised me being deported on the next plane to Cleveland. No action was taken against participants on that protest and I did not continue to take militant, provocative action. Russell, however, did, and at the age of nearly 90 he was sent to Brixton Prison (where he had already served a sentence for anti-war activity in 1918) for a week in September 1961. The *New Statesman* rightly called the prosecution an 'inspired blend of stupidity and panic' (15 September 1961, p.329). I heard Russell speak in Trafalgar Square on more than one occasion. Many thousands of us were there; listening to such a man speaking for a cause in which we all believed so passionately was a thrill which few participants are likely to have forgotten.

It was also during the Tulse Hill years that I took part in an all-night vigil outside South Africa House to protest against apartheid and I think against the Sharpeville massacre of 1960. I joined the vigil from about midnight until 3.0 a.m., returning home by all-night bus. These were years of passionate political activity and I am happy to have been a participant. I have not the slightest inclination to mock at my political activies in youth; my only regret is that so little of what we wanted so urgently has come to pass, that society should remain fundamentally unjust, protest mitigated by the collapse of the organised working-class movement and the growth of consumer durables. The end of apartheid, however, was finally achieved, even if, as in other cases, it turned out 'not to be what they meant, and other men have to fight for what they meant under another name' (William Morris, *A Dream of John Ball*, 1st ed. 1888, ch. 4)

Shirley and I took a full part in the general election of 1959, Peter becoming a live (and lively) rosette in his yellow and red costume. I canvassed actively before the election and was rather puzzled when one voter said, rather grumpily that yes, he would be voting Labour. One of my colleagues asked me what reaction I had had at that house and I reported that I had been received less than gladly. 'You do know that the voter is Harry Nicholas, the treasurer of the Labour Party?', he said. No, I had not known that previously but I did now. It was perhaps as well that before the next election I had moved to areas where such exalted personalities were unlikely to live.

John Parker and I went together to the Labour Party conference in November 1959. It was held at a weekend in Blackpool, since the holding of the general election in October had prevented the usual week-long event from taking place. It was the conference when Hugh Gaitskell urged on delegates, after three successive election defeats, the need to reform the Labour Party, drop the Clause 4 commitment to sweeping public ownership and base the Labour Party's socialism on ethical rather than economic criteria. John and I arrived too late to hear Gaitskell, but I remember vividly the contributions from the floor of the young Shirley Williams and Michael Foot.

Shirley Williams's speech in defence of moderation and practical measures was a masterpiece of its kind. It was not to my taste but she spoke eloquently. Michael Foot is, I think, the finest orator I have ever heard, and his speech on behalf of public ownership and traditional socialist values expressed exactly what I felt. '[I]n order to win an election we have to change the mood of the people in this country, to open their eyes to what an evil and disgraceful and rotten society it is.' He was cheered to the echo by the majority of delegates and almost all of the visitors; it was one of the most exciting moments of my life and Michael Foot remained my political hero for many years to come. (I was staying with my friend David Smith in the later 1960s; he met me in a bookshop by prearrangement and I said to him: 'shake my hand, David!' He looked surprised but complied, and I said: 'The last person who shook my hand was Michael Foot.' I remember hearing Foot speak on the radio in the early 1980s, by which time he had lost some of his magnetism as a speaker. Typically quoting Shelley (*The Mask of Anarchy*) he shouted: 'Rise like Lions after slumber...Ye are many – they are few.' It was an electric moment even to a listener hundreds of miles away. I understood how great demagogues could move crowds in any way they wished.)

Aneurin Bevan replied to the debate and though his speech was not heroic he drew the delegates together as nobody else could have done. He pointed out that both Gaitskell and Barbara Castle, who chaired the conference and made her own left-wing sentiments clear, had quoted his dictum on public ownership of the commanding heights of the economy. 'Barbara and Hugh quoted me. If Euclid's deduction is correct they are both equal to me and therefore must be equal to each other', he declared a trifle heavy-handedly but effectively (*Report of the Fifty-Eighth Annual Conference of*

118

the Labour Party, 1959, pp. 122, 144, 151),). The party was badly divided, but thanks to Bevan it was possible at least to leave Blackpool with the semblance of unity.

It was the last time I heard Bevan speak; seven months later he was dead at the age of 63. Although he had been moving to the political centre for several years, his death was a shattering blow to the whole political left in Britain. It is impossible in a non-political age to understand just how great a a blow it was. It was as if a close family member had died as well as a political leader of tremendous charisma and appeal. I rang up a Labour Party friend and asked if she had heard the news. She had and I rang off; there was nothing one could say. It seems impossible now to think that there was such an outpouring of grief for a politician, but so it was.

★   ★   ★

The years at Tulse Hill were, I suppose, the end of my youth. Our son John was born at our flat on 30 January 1961 and when Shirley went into labour I was the only person in support. I have never been so terrified in my life, unlike modern fathers for whom childbirth is a great moment (or so I am told, though I cannot believe that the race of cowards is dead). The midwife arrived after what seemed like hours and, wakened by all the turmoil, Peter began to cry. I fled to console him and this ended my active part in proceedings to my enormous relief. Johnny (as he quickly became and remained in childhood) was our only child actually born in London, though Paul's birthplace subsequently became part of London after the boundary changes of 1965. It was obvious that our flat would soon be too small and by now I had had enough of Tulse Hill.

These were the days when teachers left London schools for £50 and £100 annual salary increases. Nick Tucker had left Tulse Hill even before me. Salaries were of course far lower in those days, but people were desperate for promotion and those of us with experience of comprehensive education in the early days were in a strong position to secure it. I applied for the post of head of the History department at Abbey Wood School, built with its adjoining council estate on the Plumstead marshes east of Woolwich in south-east London. To my surprise I was appointed and moved in September 1961 to an environment very different from the all-male, sub-public school atmosphere of Tulse Hill. I was aged 29 and I had had a

119

little over three years' teaching experience. I might not have been appointed had the school not only been in its third year, building itself up year by year. I thus began to teach in a school with only three different age groups.

The headmistress of Abbey Wood was Yvonne Giuseppi, a very different sort of character from Mr Thomas. Although small and round and jovial, she was no soft touch; she said to one heads of department meeting: 'I am asked if I am a democratic head. I try to be; I have listened to what you have said.' (She sent round notes signed 'YBG'; one of my friends, cross on one occasion, referred to her as 'BYG or whatever she calls herself'.) Presumably the status of listening autocrat is not only accepted but advocated in our own day by schools inspectors who think that a school rises and falls by its head alone, class teachers being putty to be moulded by the will of the leader. Yvonne was, however, an excellent choice as head, responsive, hard-working and, so far as her position allowed, affectionate to her staff. She contributed a good deal to making the school a happy place. Her deputy, Albert (Bert) Porter, was a somewhat isolated person as deputies often are, but one could not have wanted a nicer, kinder man even if he seemed sometimes rather more formal or awkward than he needed to be.

I made friends at once; this was no school filled with former public schoolboys who wanted to be called by their surnames. It had a large number of members of staff who went on from the classroom to higher things. They included the following: Michael Marland, head of English, who became a well-known headmaster and a prolific writer on matters educational (including an attack on my own published views in at least one book); Laurie Norcross, also in the English department, a former Communist, then a Labour Party member and later a prominent and controversial Conservative headmaster (he was a passionate cricket fan and I gave him my *Spy* caricature of W.G. Grace, which he framed and gave pride of place in his home); Brenda Wilkins, head of languages who became a headmistress in Sussex; Ray Bolam, then in the English department, later a prominent educationist at Bristol University; and David Smith, who taught languages and ended up as chief adviser to the county of Cheshire. Others went into colleges of education or the inspectorate.

Most of the staff were aged between 25 and 35 and it was a place which fizzed with ideas and fun. Being elected first chairman of the Common Room was a great honour which I still think of with pride. We organised discussions with or without outside speakers and social activities. I think that taking everything together Abbey Wood was the most united and happiest group of people, both children and staff, that I have known in my working life. Personal relationships were reminiscent of the casual intimacy of student life. We were different from each other but most of us were dedicated to the job.

I remember with particular sympathy Jack Watson, a former missionary who joined with gusto in Debating Society meetings and was my tennis partner. He had more long-term influence than he realised on my religious views. Dan Dingle, the sports master, was another lively personality, though I never quite forgave him for saying once that I thought nobody was worth talking to who did not have a PhD (Had that been so, I would have had a lonely time of it). Peter Wareham, an English teacher, was never a close friend but his warmth and generosity were typical of the ambience of Abbey Wood. When Shirley and I went with Nick Tucker and his wife Jackie to a dance at Petworth, the National Trust great house in Sussex, Peter spontaneously lent me his evening dress.

The Debating Society was my creation. With the assistance of Jack Watson and others we had good debates on such perennial topics as religion, and patriotism (one pupil once accused me of 'spiking our [anti-patriotic] guns with Hadrian's Wall'). I also organised the History Society and took pupils out on Saturday trips all round London and beyond. One popular journey was to Old Sarum, Salisbury and Stonehenge, long before the last-mentioned became a battleground between hippies and police. We also went to Canterbury and other sites within a day's reach of London.

I never saw much point in taking school children abroad, particularly in term-time, so that they could grumble about the food or make trouble; I thought that they could find out about 'abroad' when they were older and could travel in smaller numbers. (Other staff, however, organised successful foreign trips.) But I took one party on a tour of East Anglia which Nick Tucker joined, though now teaching at another London school. I took another to the Cotswolds, a third to the Lake District and the most successful one to the magic territory between Edinburgh and Newcastle, including the Scottish border country with its houses and abbeys, Hadrian's Wall, a walk along the Scottish-English boundary in the Cheviots, a Northumberland coal mine and so on. The journeys needed a lot of organising but they were all successful and much enjoyed, at least by me. Indeed, the Northumberland journey was so successful that Shirley and I took two family holidays to the Cheviots, one in the company of the Norcross family.

Miss Giuseppi seemed quite elderly to those of us aged 30 or less. She certainly seemed unlikely to marry or even think of marriage. More then was the surprise when she suddenly announced her engagement to the school secretary, Ron Zackerwich, who was her junior by some years. (The large London comprehensive schools had administrative secretaries, often men.) The story ran that one unfortunate, noticing that the head was wearing an engagement ring, said to Ron: 'Who's the lucky man? You? Ha, ha, ha.' He received the reply: 'Yes, it's me, ha, ha, ha.' If the story was true it is nice to think that I am not alone in suffering regularly from foot-in-mouth disease.

The intellectual level at Abbey Wood was high; the people I knew best were certainly more alert than the average among the staff when I became a university lecturer. Nonetheless, we gossiped about the Giuseppi-Zackerwich marriage like a lot of...what can I say in an age of political correctness? The gossip was unending, not only in our school but also, we were told, across the London education service. Why should we have gossiped when there was every reason to congratulate a somewhat unorthodox but very happy couple and no reason to do anything else? But for a period it was hard to concentrate on other matters in the staffroom.

Came the wedding, and the officers of the Common Room were invited as well as some of the staff who were Ron's cricketing cronies. The best man met the situation head on. 'We have all heard of the boss marrying the beautiful secretary', he declared, 'but this is a new twist.' We all roared with laughter, none more than the bride and groom. I still exchange Christmas cards with the Zackerwiches, who have invited me to a number of celebratory functions over the years which, because of Yorkshire or French residence, I have been unable to accept. It would certainly be forgivable if the Zackerwiches had asked 'who's laughing now?' as their marriage reached 20, 25 and more than 30 years and their younger friends and colleagues proceeded to divorce.

The school was not quite a matchbox, but romance blossomed amongst its youthful staff. The English department in particular was prone to love affairs, but one would hardly have expected otherwise in a school full of healthy young, often single adults. There was thus fairly regular opportunity for tongues to wag.

My modest journalistic and broadcasting career began in Abbey Wood days. I talked on educational matters on Radio 4 and wrote occasionally for educational and other journals. I wrote a piece with Michael Marland for *New Society* ('Fourth form sociologists') on 19 September 1963 which was later the subject of a television programme. (This may have been the start of Michael's media career.) I wrote a forthright article called 'What can we learn from American schools?' for *Where* (Winter 1964, pp. 12-14). The journal's publicity machine was excellent and I had a number of press enquiries about the piece. It was perhaps as well that when the story broke I was on one of my Saturday educational outings with my pupils, so that if I was a nonconformist at least I was a hard-working one. But some typically rash replies to the press led to unwelcome though brief notoriety and several pained letters. I was officially reprimanded by the LCC for unauthorised press comment in the form of a letter in the *Listener*, 1 October 1964. It was a reasoned and unsensational defence of the comprehensive school, but the council's educational hierarchy was terrified of any public discussion of its staffing policies and priorities.

Meanwhile Shirley, Peter, Johnny and I had moved to Albany Road, Upper Belvedere, then in the north-west Kent borough of Erith and now in the London Borough of Bexley. (I had caused some shock by asking the committee which appointed me to my post at Abbey Wood if I could rent a council house on the estate which supplied most of our children; the answer was that the committee was in no position to do so and Miss Giuseppi, who drove me back to Streatham after the interview, assured me gravely that I would not want to live there.) The house was small and new, having been built only in 1955, six years before we moved in. Peter Jackson, who visited us there frequently, lost no opportunity to tell us then and afterwards how much he disliked it, but it suited us admirably.

It was two or three miles from home to the school but there was a steep hill on the way and I normally travelled by no. 99 bus. By this time we again owned a car but I had no wish to use it to get to work. (When Shirley and I divorced I pointed out that she had had sole daytime use of our car, but she replied that as I had not wanted to use it anyway no credit accrued to me. This was logical, I admit.) I walked the last half mile or so from the bus to the school but frequently was given lifts by sharp-eyed colleagues, especially Tom Palmer, the craft master.

In the cold, foggy winter of 1962-3 I walked to or at least home from school. A parent had arranged to see me (I think that she was one of the school cleaners) but, because of the bad weather, school ended soon after lunch. She asked me if I wanted to postpone our meeting and I replied recklessly that I did not. It was an exciting experience to walk home that evening. There was no traffic, which meant no buses, and I had little idea of where I was. I crossed the main Woolwich Road without knowing that I had done so. It took me a long time to get home, but I was never seriously lost and it was a good story to tell my friends. Due to the inauguration of smokeless fuel and then the abandonment of the open coal fire this was almost the last London 'peasouper'; such events had been famous since the days of Dickens and the image of foggy London is hard to eradicate from the minds of many foreigners.

Abbey Wood and Belvedere, together with the wider area of Woolwich and Greenwich, were a fascinating area. Lesnes Abbey, not far from the school, had been founded by Richard de Lucy, a high official at the court of Henry II who was excommunicated by Thomas à Becket in 1169, the year before Becket's death. There are still scanty remains of the abbey to be seen. I used to take my own children to the edge of the river to gaze at the giant power station and the equally giant Ford factory at Dagenham on the opposite side. Woolwich and Greenwich teemed with parks, history and fascinating buildings; I draw at random on buildings associated with or designed by Thomas More, Hugh May, Wren and Vanbrugh. There was a medieval hall at Eltham, a Jacobean house at Charlton. Exciting days!

Paul was born in a nursing home (not at our own home, to my great relief) in Bexley. The date was 2 July 1963. He was called Paul Geoffrey, despite my antipathy to two first names, in the hope that this would please my mother, who was now nearly at the end of her life. I was distressed to learn that, having suffered a stroke in 1962 and being confused, she thought that my Uncle Geoff's son would not in consequence be able to name his own son after his father (which in fact he did). But Paul seems not to have suffered.

I visited the United States four times in the six-year period included in this chapter. (I went there twice in the 34 years which followed; the second visit was at the end of 1973.) In the summer of 1960 we went with Peter to visit my mother and also to arrange to take charge of the money which my father had left me and which my mother had administered at some cost in time and trouble to herself; I had been legally entitled to the capital when I turned 25 in 1957. It was, I think, on this trip that I met in Philadelphia my 'wicked uncle' Percy, who had disappeared from the sight of his family many years before, having committed unspecified enormities. He told me that his wife had been chasing him and he thought disappearance his best course. I did not warm to him, but I was amused by his reaction to what he chose to think was my 'English accent'. Referring to his own southern drawl he said: 'You can take the boy away from Jaw-gia but you can't take Jaw-gia away from the boy.' (He neglected to tell me that he had been born in Sheffield, a fact discovered by my sister Ellen decades later.) He told me that he was looking for someone to whom he could leave his money and I invited him to consider anyone other than myself. I said this without thinking as usual, but I have no regret at not having grasped at the unknown wealth of this unknown old man. We had no further contact.

I went alone to the United States in 1962 after my mother had suffered a stroke in California, while visiting her sister Helen. I went with Peter soon after Paul's birth in 1963 for a final visit to my mother, who now had six grandchildren but was clearly not going to live much longer. I returned home from school on 10 October 1963 to be told by Shirley that Ellen had phoned with the news that my mother had died. Her death was expected but it was nonetheless a heart-rending shock.

I did not cross the Atlantic for the funeral and I do not regret not having done so. It is not my absence from the funeral but from my mother's life since 1954 which weighs on my conscience. Ellen told me that the third chapter of *Ecclesiastes* ('To every thing there is a season, and a time to every purpose under the heaven') was read. It then seemed appropriate to me (I wonder if I had known previously of its existence) but it now seems bitterly misplaced. My mother was a lovely, intelligent, cultured woman, who in 1952 had a beloved husband, two children, many friends and a prominent place in the local community. By 1963 she had had eleven years of widowhood, increasing illness, her daughter in Missouri until nearly the end of my mother's life, her son in England. But despite these years of sadness she still had a very lively interest in things around her (she had for instance taken part in campaigning for Adlai Stevenson, the Democratic candidate for the American presidency, in 1956) and an enormous amount to give and receive. She was still under sixty. As transatlantic travel became more commonplace the miles between us could have been more easily and regularly surmounted. How could it possibly have been 'a time to die'?

We went again to the United States in 1964, chiefly to agree with Ellen on the sale to her of my half of my mother's house, and to take a few of my parents' possessions, mainly books, back to London. We went by ship, the Holland-America line's *Amsterdam*, for the last time. Peter took part in a children's concert, singing 'The big ship sailed on the alley, alley-oo', and was a great success. It is sad to think that that marvellous way of crossing an ocean is now a privilege mainly of eccentrically and nostalgically wealthy Americans. We had the unforgettable experience of sailing into New York Harbour and waving at the hundreds of workers finishing the magnificent Verrazano Narrows Bridge as the ship majestically completed its journey.

I inherited about £60,000 in dollars from my mother, considerably more than from my father. It was a lot of money in those days. I remember telling my friend Brenda Wilkins about it when she was driving me home from school; she stopped her car in stunned amazement. I converted the money into sterling, but I bore a grudge against Harold Wilson and James Callaghan after I had done so. If they had devalued as soon as the Labour government was formed in October 1964 rather than waiting until November 1967 I would have received considerably more sterling, for it took a year or so to pay me the money and convert it; they were advised to devalue at once (and blame the Tories) and I was advised against conversion. Sterling is now worth little more than half what it was against the dollar in October 1964, but never mind. My mother also left me a share in her house and in other property.

It was at this time that I became a British subject. I was eager to do so and have never felt sentimental about losing my American nationality. To me the real break was the initial decision to leave my country, not the legal fact of nationality. I had come to Britain in large part for political reasons and had been involved in politics to the hilt from the moment that I disembarked from the *Queen Mary*, always with some apprehension that I might be penalised in some way. Besides, it is ethically dubious for a national of one country to become involved in the internal affairs of another, though of course the American government then and since has had no scruples about doing so all over the world. I felt no special wish to be an American (though, equally, no particular desire to lose my American nationality) and, after several years' residence, I was sure that I wanted to spend the rest of my life in Britain. Much later, residence in France shook this conviction from time to time, but I have never had any inclination to return to live in the United States. To become a British national was only common sense. It was not my fault that the American government did not then allow dual nationality.

So I applied for British citizenship at the earliest possible opportunity, in 1962. John Parker was one of my referees, but his support was not enough. I was told, to my dismay but not surprise, that the Home Office was not prepared to make a decision in my case and that I would have to wait for another two years and then apply again. It was not the only penalty I have paid in my life for being 'too political'. I applied again in 1964 and this time was successful. On 26 October I went to the American consulate in Grosvenor Square to vote for Lyndon Johnson for president, little realising that I was voting for the expansion of the nascent war in Vietnam. I then went at once to a Commissioner of Oaths in Hanover Square and affirmed my allegiance to the Queen and her heirs and successors; republicanism was incompatible with the status of naturalised Briton. (So too, I was told officially, was Communism.) I was now a British subject. Not long thereafter my American passport was withdrawn by the United States consulate and my brief period of dual nationality ended.

On 6 April 1965 the *Guardian* published my article on my attempts to become British, the delays and difficulties to which I had been subjected and my resistance to swearing allegiance by an Almighty God in whom I did not believe. The article was followed by snide comment in the 'Peter Simple' column in the *Daily Telegraph* (15 April), accusing me of thinking that I had conferred a 'supreme favour' on the United Kingdom by condescending to apply for its nationality.

I am well aware that I came to Britain largely because I was a socialist and have remained here while the British population disengaged itself more and more from political ideology. Socialism as I knew it in the fifties and sixties has almost disappeared from the political scene. The notion that I was coming to a country with a socialist future turned out to be one of history's jokes about which there is no point in repining. I have noted wryly other Americans settling in Britain in later years without the slightest political motivation and reflected that we are all the creatures of our time. But equally I have seen no reason to change my own political convictions.

I cannot now remember whether I was surprised to find that in the eyes of the world, or rather the eyes of some of my friends, I remained an American. People I meet casually have no trouble in accepting me as a fellow-citizen. It is only some of my closer contacts who point out (in effect) 'of course you don't really belong here'. One colleague at the University of Hull told me so often that I might be British but I could never be English that I had to tell him that the point was taken and need not be repeated yet again. Another was overjoyed when I inadvertently used an Americanism. In 1977 I gave a party to celebrate the 25th anniversary of my first arrival in England. Ann said, not without reason, that it was being held so that my friends could 'ask me how I liked it here and when I was going home'. Being told I am not really British is far from being a daily or even monthly occurrence, but it happens often enough to irritate. On the other hand, no historian would be foolish enough to ignore origins, let alone the first third of a subject's life, and I have not the slightest desire to claim that my whole life has not been heavily influenced by my American origins – nor indeed to regret them.

One further paragraph on this subject. There are Americans who live in Britain, firmly American and equally firmly at home in Britain. Or so they say. Good luck to them, but I found that I had to make a choice whether to take my native country with me or leave it behind. I chose the latter, with the consequence that, as said above, I visited the United States for three weeks twice in the 34 years after 1964. I have of course paid a price for this choice, part of which may have been taking an unfairly prejudiced view of the United States and American foreign policy, but I have never regretted my lifelong immersion in British life, town and country-side, history and politics.

I was more active in the Labour Party between 1961 and 1965 than I had ever been before or have been since. CND had faded away (it was to revive later) and party politics were exciting. Our constituency was Erith and Crayford, the names of a borough and an urban district in Kent, both swept away in 1965 to become part of the London Borough of Bexley. The constituency had a Labour MP, Norman Dodds, an eccentric character best known for his championship of gipsies and their rights. He had also secured notoriety for alleging that workmen on a building site he had been watching did too little work and drank too much tea.

Both Shirley and I were active in Belvedere Ward, attending meetings, helping to pick council candidates and collecting subscriptions on a Sunday morning. We were both delegates to what was then called the General Management Committee; I was the delegate from the GMC to the Labour Group of Erith Borough Council (and once got in hot water for reporting to the GMC what individual councillors and aldermen had said) and, in December 1964, delegate to the national Labour Party conference. These latter nominations were partly the result of the fact that there was always room for somebody prepared to work, but another example of the surprising ease with which I was accepted in Labour student and party circles. At the time I was chosen a delegate to party conference I could at most have been British for a matter of days; by the time of the conference I had held British nationality for two months.

The Erith and Crayford Labour Party was full of interest and, as it is now probably a middle-class organisation like most local Labour parties, the type of body we are unlikely to see again. The membership consisted almost exclusively of men and women from the higher levels of the working class and the lower middle class, between whom it was not easy to distinguish. As Charles Booth had found in his massive study of life and labour in late Victorian London, these classes, 'the central mass of the English people, consort together in a free and friendly way', with similar tastes and outlooks (*Life and Labour. Volume I: East London*, 1889, p. 99). My Abbey Wood friend Brenda Wilkins was a GMC member from Crayford and there may have been other graduates, but certainly very few. We noticed somewhat to our surprise that even in the early 1960s many of our fellow members, including the working-class ones, were house-owners. We had paid less than £2000 for our own house, but a mortgage for this sum was a considerable burden for many families.

I was still relatively young and extremely enthusiastic, and I had little time for the politics of Hugh Gaitskell. I was always moving resolutions advocating this or deploring that. One member said in exasperation: 'Policy should be left to Mr Gaitskell', while the ordinary membership recruited new members, canvassed and organised social functions. It was a salutary lesson and a point of view which was no mystery to the party leadership. They knew that what the rank and file of the membership wanted and still want is a Labour government: 'Policy should be left to Mr Blair'; left-wing views are unrepresentative, often not of the zealots but certainly of the Labour-voting public. In any case it was a right-wing local party; several of the more prominent members including the MP, by that time the affable Jim Wellbeloved, were to join the SDP long after our departure from the area.

But my years in the Erith and Crayford party were happy ones. I remember vividly one meeting which was held to select a candidate for council elections. It was not easy for Shirley and me to go out in the evenings with our three small sons (I recruited assistance as babysitters from my pupils), and getting away was often a last-minute job. On this occasion we got to the meeting just in time, carrying our fish and chips with us. There was a scandalised hush in the room, broken by Jim Wellbeloved who guffawed and said: 'You can't join the working class just by eating fish and chips out of a newspaper!' This broke the ice and everyone joined the general merriment, but the transgression against the norms of working-class respectability had been entirely innocent on our part.

Gaitskell's death in 1963 came as a great shock. He was even younger than Bevan at the time of his death and his death was even more sudden. I could not then and cannot now account for the fact that I was so shocked and upset. I had been at the Labour Party conference in Margate in 1955 when Gaitskell made his great profession of socialist faith and, comically, was disturbed to find myself as a Bevanite moved by the eloquence with which from his position on the right of the party he said: 'I am a Socialist and have been for some 30 years...[A]t a very early age I came to hate and loathe social injustice...I became a Socialist because I hated poverty and squalor' (*Report of the Fifty-Fourth Annual Conference of the Labour Party*, 1955, p. 175).

I can only explain my reaction to his death by pointing out that everyone felt that Gaitskell was about as honest as it was possible for a politician to be. Despite his Winchester and Oxford background he was a passionate believer in a more just society and this attitude came across to the public, certainly to party members. He was a revisionist and the hammer of the Bevanites and nuclear disarmers, thin-skinned and too ready to think that those who opposed him were crypto-Communists, but he was a man of stature.

The party conference of 1964 at which I represented Erith and Crayford was the high point of my Labour political activity. The conference, like that in 1959, was restricted to a weekend (12 and 13 December), since it too followed a general election, this one finally won by Labour with a miniscule majority after three consecutive Conservative victories. (Shirley and I had worked unceasingly in the election, my special contribution being to damage the sump of our car in ferrying voters to the polls. I was always a rotten driver.)

I was lucky enough to catch the eye of the chair and spoke on education. (I hope that if I had written my speech rather than delivered it off the cuff it would now look rather more literate on the printed page.) I attacked the dominance of the public schools on the country at large, called for grammar schools to be incorporated into comprehensive schools and questioned the value of 'some of the grammar school influences'. I also pointed out that comprehensive schools should not be limited to council estates, as they tended to be at that time. 'Until we get comprehensive schools away from council estates and above all...until we have housing estates which represent all classes in society, until our schools are socially as well as intellectually comprehensive, they are not being properly comprehensive.' (*Report of the Sixty-Third Annual Conference of the Labour Party*, 1964, pp. 125-6) I enjoyed the conference, which, with its male preponderance and trade union block votes epitomised a Labour Party of an earlier epoch but no greater radicalism than today's.

I was also present when the members of the Erith and Crayford Labour Party, finding (in some cases reluctantly) that they had become part of Greater London ('I don't want to have to move to London', one constituent was reported as saying) met with others in Bexley to pick candidates for the GLC. This body came into existence in 1965 and incorporated not only the old County of London but also the whole of Middlesex and the metropolitan parts of Kent, Essex, Hertfordshire and Surrey. It was an enormous change in local government and few people in the London education service were enthusiastic about it. There was hostility to amalgamating boroughs (was Abbey Wood's new borough to be 'Green-wool' or 'Wool-green'? we asked. The answer was the London Borough of Greenwich; Woolwich was abolished as a political entity) and to the setting up of an ad hoc education authority for Inner London.

There was in short a good deal of reservation, scepticism and hostility to the creation of Greater London, especially as there was no doubt that a principal reason for the Conservative decision to do so was to abolish the LCC which had been Labour since 1934 and create a Conservative London by adding Conservative-dominated outer-London boroughs. (When the GLC went the same political way as the LCC it too was abolished.) My experience in the London education service was limited to the LCC and I am happy that this was so, though the GLC and the Inner London Education Authority achieved great things and built up a good deal of loyalty in their short lives. I think that it is at best an open question whether the greater efficiency involved in larger boroughs compensated for breaking the loyalty of local people to smaller authorities like Erith and Crayford.

I worked hard at school and for the Labour Party, and I spent a lot of time with my children. On one occasion in 1962, on a school holiday, I looked after the boys while Shirley went to Brighton to hear Gaitskell attack British participation in the Common Market at the party conference. In another holiday period she went to the Three Choirs Festival in (I think) Hereford, while I saw no adult for several days apart from Clive and Masha Davies, who took pity and invited the boys and me to their home in Fawkham, further south-east in Kent; I greatly appreciated this gesture.

Nonetheless I still had time on my hands, partly because when I left Abbey Wood in 1965 it had still only grown to the first-year Sixth Form, and that was very small; the fully comprehensive forms coming up behind produced many more Sixth Formers. So I set out to write about the comprehensive school, partly history, partly surveys of other schools, their intakes and examination results, partly an account of my own experiences. I sent my typescript, quite unbidden, to Sam Fisher's old friend Brian Simon, who taught educational history at the University of Leicester. This was the start of a long relationship, mostly by correspondence, from which I have gained greatly.

Brian Simon was another 1930s Communist, the son of Ernest and Shena Simon, Manchester business people, authors and leading social reformers. Even by the early 1960s Brian had a long and effective history as champion of the comprehensive school. He sent me a glowing letter about my manuscript and we became friends at once. My manuscript was not published but it was useful preparation for other work which I was to do on the comprehensive school, some of it in collaboration with him. It was an encouraging start for a would-be author whose productions until that time had been limited to occasional articles in the educational and general press and even rarer talks on the radio.

The years from 1959 to 1965 were an exciting period in the London theatre, and Shirley and I saw many of the productions of the time, not least at the new Mermaid Theatre. I also went regularly to the theatre with John Parker. The British theatre had finally freed itself from comedies and murder in drawing rooms, and was presenting plays about the working class, Ireland, women's lives, homosexuality and other subjects drawn from the lives of the authors and their society. Accents became more realistic and working-class characters were no longer cast simply as comic relief or villains.

We were bowled over by *Roots*, Arnold Wesker's celebration of human emancipation which we saw with the young Joan Plowright in the lead soon after I left the army. (I saw it again in March 1998 and wept at the defeat of Wesker's (and my) youthful political hopes.) Wesker was briefly the leading voice of the theatrical left but was already at war with the critics. He replied in August 1959 to the letter of congratulation which I sent him by saying that my understanding of *Roots* was expressed 'in terms that I intended. You did not call my characters mean or squalid for instance, which is what some critics have said...'

At the head of the new trend was Joan Littlewood's Theatre Workshop in Stratford, East. Nick Tucker took Shirley and me to a performance of *Oh, What a Lovely War* soon after it opened in March 1963. It is hard to imagine now the impact which it had, however much it may in turn have been influenced by the musical-satirical-political plays of Bertolt Brecht. Leonard Woolf says in his autobiography that the plays of Ibsen in the late nineteenth century said 'Bosh!' to a 'vast system of cant and hypocrisy' (*Sowing*, 1960, pp. 163-4), and Joan Littlewood and her brilliant cast did the same thing for the 1960s. Bertrand Russell, who saw the play on his ninety-first birthday, wrote of how 'moving...true and important' it was and expressed surprise that it had been 'allowed on a London stage' (*Observer*, 23 June 1963). Later productions and a muddied and muddled film, together with the passage of time, have blurred the way it cut through our society in the 1960s like a knife through butter. (The National Theatre production in spring 1998, however, packed some of the punch of the original.)

The futility and horror of the First World War, the endurance of the ordinary soldiers and the ambitions of the generals ('I ask thee for victory, Lord – before the Americans arrive') and politicians were explored and condemned as no other form of production could have done. It was a welcome shock for us to hear the soldiers of 1914 singing that they didn't 'give a fuck for old von Kluck' (the general who led the first German army) and to realise the ease and insouciance with which British leaders in particular had joined the war because they felt if there was to be a European conflict Britain should not be left out. For someone like me who had spent sixteen months in Verdun and was already convinced of the enormous and disastrous importance of the Great War the play had a special resonance. I can still remember nothing like it in the theatre. I should add that having learned a good deal more about that war in later years I still endorse wholly Theatre Workshop's interpretation of it. As A.J.P. Taylor said at the time, combining on this occasion verve with accuracy, the play's explanation of the war had done 'what the historians have failed to do' (*The Times*, 31 May 1963).

I attended *Oh, What a Lovely War* three times. Ray Bolam and I took some of our school children after careful preparation. He tackled the nature of satire and I explained some of the history of the war itself. By now the play was in the West End and perhaps slightly toned down, but it was a huge success with the public and, notably, with our pupils. I thought that Richard Senner, one of the most engaging of them, would die laughing when the Tommies sang at the onset of the Christmas truce of 1914 that 'the bold bad sultan...gazed on his marble halls, saying "What do you want for Christmas boys?" and the eunuchs answered – "Tidings of comfort and joy..."' I don't suppose that he has forgotten that moment either.

The reaction of the Erith and Crayford Labour Party to an outing we organised to the play was strikingly and instructively different. Nobody liked it, even the few old enough to remember the songs from the first time round. The language and above all the central message of the play shocked them; that the lives of the working class had been thrown away to satisfy the ambitions and incompetence of their social betters. If it was British and patriotic, they seemed to feel, it had to be supported, and how could one enjoy anything which made fun of British patriotism? It was interesting that the school children, even more working class than the Labour Party members, were not encumbered with that kind of loyalty to the established order.

Very different but also influential on the lives of my generation were Michael Flanders and Donald Swann. Each had an independent performing life, but they will always be remembered for the musical shows which they put on together, *At the Drop of a Hat* (1957) and *At the Drop of Another Hat* (1963). The shows were witty, relevant and understated. Ageing persons still go around saying to each other: 'It was on a Monday morning that the gas man came to call', or 'They practise beforehand, which ruins the fun', or profess confusion about how many of the letters are pronounced in 'gnu'. I remember saying to Paula Yates, formerly a student at Hull and leader of Maidstone Borough Council in the early '90s, that my name had been mis-spelt in the proof of a book. 'They called me Mr Sanderson', I said to her, and we chanted to each other, 'which isn't quite me name'. Flanders and Swann wrecked the last movement of a Mozart horn concerto with their 'lost that horn, lost that horn, found that horn – gorn!', but it was in a good cause. What can one say of a pair who could get a whole crowded theatre to sing 'mud, mud, glorious mud', and then burst into ecstatic, jubilant applause? In the Quaker phrase (and Swann was a Quaker), they spoke to our condition.

Flanders and Swann were in a sense the British counterpart of Tom Lehrer, though unlike Lehrer they were not overtly political. Lehrer did much to persuade us in the dark days of the Cold War that good things really could and did come out of the United States, that the 'American way' had its absurd (as well as sinister) aspects and that not everyone in that country really thought 'just the same'. Flanders and Swann more subtly burst the balloon of official pomposity and gave an enormous amount of pleasure to a great many people. While we saw many other performances of all kinds in that period, these were the high points. Members of the generation which saw Joan Littlewood plain and to whom Flanders and Swann spoke have a special bond of sympathy with each other.

All good things had to end. Michael Marland left Abbey Wood after three years and the itch for promotion and new horizons affected many of us at Abbey Wood. What was I going to do next? I had already decided that I did not want to be a head, much less a downtrodden deputy. Part of the reason was that I had stayed away from school assembly on grounds of atheism, a decision which now seems to me mistaken and sad, in view of all the hymns which I could have learned. I could hardly, I felt, lead a religious service in which I did not believe. (This point of view did not appeal to Sam Fisher, who was to become a successful head.) But there were other reasons too. I did not believe that I could inspire teachers more successfully than their own professional zeal and consciences. It was more satisfying to do than to try to motivate others.

But while I was sure that I did not want to be a head, I was not clear about what I did want. I had recoiled at Swarthmore from being processed into the assembly line of school-university-university teacher, and in consequence I had spent nine years, including my period of military service, in the classroom since my LSE days. But I now felt ready for what I supposed to be more of an intellectual challenge. Before I became British I wanted desperately to be a Labour MP, but by the time I had been a party member for ten years that ambition was waning. I did apply to be head of research at party headquarters, then at Transport House, and to my surprise was shortlisted, perhaps because John Parker was a referee. I had no real qualifications for the post, however, and was not appointed.

My other applications were all for positions in higher education; colleges of education, polytechnics, universities. I applied for a history lectureship at the University of Sussex, was interviewed by Asa Briggs and was not appointed. (He and his colleagues thought that if I wanted to be a university teacher I should not have spent all my spare time working for the Labour Party. I disagreed.) I was interviewed by the new Lancaster University for a lectureship in politics on 25 January 1965, the day after the death of Winston Churchill, and was asked: 'You are really an historian, aren't you?' 'I suppose I am', I replied. (I noticed a shop in the town boasting that it had been founded in 1875, 'the year that income tax was 2d. in the £', and was so astonished to see in the local museum the menu of the extraordinarily lavish breakfast served to Queen Victoria by the London and North Western Railway at Castle Station, Lancaster, in 1867 that I wrote to request a copy; it was duly typed out and sent to me.) Applications to Manchester Polytechnic, where I was shocked by the virtual absence of a library, and Brighton College of Education also failed. It was all rather dispiriting.

Peter Jackson came to my rescue, telling me of a social history post at the University of Hull, where he himself was based, and telling John Saville, the chief economic and social historian at Hull, that I was qualified to fill it. (I should emphasise that even in those days when academic jobs chased applicants I would not have been considered for these posts in higher education without my PhD, despite its inadequacies.) I shall write about John later but here I will only say that he rang me one Sunday when I was out collecting membership subscriptions for the Labour Party, to give me advice about the interview and ask what he was not to ask. (What research I would be undertaking, I said.)

So I was interviewed by him, by Stuart Wilson, head of the department of Economics and Commerce into which economic and social history then fell, and by the Vice Chancellor, the chemist Brynmor Jones. Only three of us were interviewed and I imagine that what made John Saville plump for me was not only Peter Jackson's recommendation but the feeling that I would be politically congenial. The Vice Chancellor asked me to summarise my thesis in thirty seconds (he had been interviewing all day, he pointed out). During the course of a supplementary reply I made him laugh by telling him that one of Gladstone's backbenchers had said that he didn't mind the old man having a card up his sleeve but he wished that he wouldn't insinuate that the Almighty had placed it there. He then asked why I had settled in England. 'Shall I answer that in thirty seconds too?' I asked. He laughed again and I was appointed.

I remember feeling absolutely dreadful on the train on the way back to London. What had I done? I had committed myself to leaving an occupation I loved and which I could do well, moving 200 miles from London to enter a new occupation, aged 33 (and hence handicapped as compared to younger lecturers) and with no assurance that I could carry out the new post successfully. Geraldine Murray said, 'oh, well, at least you are not going really far, like Manchester', which did little for my morale as Hull was further from London than Manchester. If I had known that my marriage would end in six years and that I would remain in Hull altogether for 23, I would have thought that I had some reason to feel sombre.

Everyone was very complimentary, however. I had asked not to have money collected on my behalf for a leaving present at Abbey Wood as it had been so often collected (one always gave half a crown) for others. So my colleagues arranged for somebody (I never knew who it was) to make a substantial earthenware statuette (Shirley called it Queen Victoria) in commemoration of my school teaching days. I assumed that the sculptor was a talented pupil and was not paid. Mrs Zackerwich referred in her speech to the fact that I had devoted my youth to the classroom, and I thought: 'This is it, I really am leaving teaching, life will never be the same again'. It was a momentous occasion. I was to find, unsurprisingly, that anyone who had actually faced a classroom of children for a substantial period as I had done was never the same again, and I was always to be influenced by my early years as a secondary school teacher. I have continued to feel proud and happy about those years.

I went to Hull soon afterwards, staying with Peter Jackson and his wife Christine, to talk to John Saville about my teaching load. Shirley went later to find us a house and when school ended in summer 1965 I took the boys (then aged 6, 4 and 2) to Scarborough, aided by two of my pupils from Abbey Wood, to stay in a guest house while Shirley supervised the removal from Belvedere to Hull. We moved to Cottingham, one of the principal suburbs of Hull and near the university, which was based on Cottingham Road. Our house in Belvedere with its three small bedrooms, had been sold for over £4000. For only a little more we bought a house with seven bedrooms and a box room, a living room, a dining room, a play-room for the boys and a large garden. My gross annual salary to finance the new home and growing family rose from £1542.10.0 under the London County Council in March 1965 (subsequently adding £30 or so as annual increment) to £1740 at the university in October of that year.

On 7 August 1965, my 33rd birthday, the boys and I came down to Cottingham on the railway line from Scarborough (I don't think that I had seen the new house previously) and the Hull adventure began. A few years later I was to play a part in keeping that railway line open for myself and others.

CHAPTER 6

Early Years at Hull: 1965-70

I WAS APPREHENSIVE about starting a new career at Hull, uncertain whether I had the intellectual stamina required of a lecturer in higher education. I was to find the university and the city of Hull both attractive and disappointing. The impact of both was enormous. As with many other people who have lived in Hull I have not emancipated myself from its spell. I feel little loyalty to Cleveland but I feel about Hull the way my Uncle Percy felt about 'Jaw-gia'; its effect is permanent. In February 1998 Ann and I spent a weekend in Hull with our friend Margaret Palfreman. It was the longest period we had spent there for nearly ten years and the nostalgic pull was far stronger than we had anticipated.

I was to find that there were both pros and cons of academic life. I took to scholarly research like a duck to water in terms of the appeal it made to me. Oddly, perhaps, given my previous career, I had neither interest in nor ability to write history for a wide audience, though I have dabbled in journalism (mostly non-remunerative) over the years. What attracted me was crawling along the frontiers of my particular field of knowledge with a hand lens. I was not an ideal researcher in terms of my own career. I was unable to follow the prescription of a colleague in the Geography department, who advised that one should publish an article every six months and a book every two years. Within the broad field of British social and labour history I generally chose topics which were new to me, so I had no intellectual capital on which to build the next project. My research was painstaking rather than speedy. I could spend a year researching and writing an article.

Hull's university library was a splendid institution for the social historian. This was due partly to the hard work of John Saville (specially in amassing manuscript collections), partly to the reputation and dedication of the librarian, the poet Philip Larkin, partly to the fact that under the national subject specialisation scheme Hull had an excellent collection on socialism, and partly because luck and beneficence had brought many precious publications to the library. *The Times* from the early nineteenth century until the present (or, at least, the recent past, when Larkin got his way and hard copies were replaced by microfilm) was on open shelves. I undoubtedly used it more in my 23 years at Hull than any other member of the university staff. There was also a large collection of nineteenth-century journals which were essential for the kind of research I undertook, including the *Nineteenth Century*, the *Contemporary* and *Fortnightly Reviews* and many others. These too were on open shelves and I had free run of them. There were other, less heavy journals, including a complete run of the *Strand Magazine*, from which Ann and I much later read the original Sherlock Holmes stories aloud to each other. A complete run of at least the first century of *Punch* was also of great value.

I enjoyed teaching and liked the students. After secondary schools university teaching was relatively easy, though it was not always a simple matter to motivate a seminar and persuade the students to take part in discussion. (It is difficult to have an intelligent opinion on historical topics without systematic reading; the same is not true of all academic subjects.) I also enjoyed preparation for lectures, delving deep into contemporary sources and spending ages to prepare my initial lectures, work which was subsequently to stand me in good stead. Like other university teachers, however, I was to find that it was not easy to balance the demands of teaching and research; one or the other tended to suffer, specially as the universities recruited new staff who added to the lists of publications.

It was not all gain. I had not wanted initially to be a university teacher, partly because of the ivory tower aspect inescapable from university life. Teaching the relative handful of 18 year-olds who were enough of an elite (specially in the early 1960s, when only one in twenty young people entered higher education; *Social Trends 1998*, p. 61) to have achieved a university place did much less good to society as a whole than the work of a school teacher concerned to raise intellectual and social standards of the population at large. I was asked at a dinner party at John Saville's home why I had initially entered school teaching. My reply was naive, idealistic and American. John Saville snorted and said, typically: 'If I weren't in my own home I'd spit!' I was the only person at the dinner table not to roar with laughter at this witty sally. I have grown something of a defensive shell since then. But I still think that, at least in the arts and social sciences, a good secondary school teacher is usually more useful to society than a good university teacher of the same subject.

I found plenty of scope for political activity, including work with socialist students and speeches in the Students' Union. This was very enjoyable. But I was disturbed by the competitive atmosphere of university life and the discovery that most university teachers as I experienced them had intellectual interests narrowly focused on their research specialisms and little in the way of broader culture. Many of my colleagues typified the male members of the Great British Public in showing little interest, outside their research, in other subjects than cars, sport, holidays and sex. It should in fairness be added that I had previously been a big fish and was now a small one, and I may have reacted against looking at a competitive environment from the bottom rather than from closer to the top of the pyramid.

I was at 33 perhaps too old to develop close friendships after I arrived at Hull. In any case the atmosphere was very unlike the relaxed and happy situation I had known at Abbey Wood. Peter Jackson was of course at Hull, but he was elected Labour MP for High Peak at the end of March 1966, less than a year after my arrival. Many of my friends were in the Sociology department (as Peter had been), including Ian Cunnison, the highly intelligent, cultured, shy professor of Social Anthropology. I loved Ian as did almost everyone who knew him and we had many happy lunches together over a twenty-year period.

I was later also friendly with Valdo Pons, the professor of Sociology who arrived from Warwick in the early 1970s. Ann and I watched five general elections on television in Valdo's company, our (relative) early pleasure in 1974 turning to disappointment and dread as the results arrived in the Thatcher years. ('I thought we were supposed to enjoy these occasions', Valdo observed in 1987.) Talal Asad and his wife Tanya were also good friends and both stood by me when I needed them most. Talal was of exotic, part-Arab origin, and I shared (from a somewhat different perspective) his opposition to Israel and his sympathy for the Palestinians. He was and is a man of high intellectual abilities, respected and admired by students and colleagues alike.

Another friend was Colin Stoneman, a highly political chemist who tried and eventually succeeded in escaping chemistry for the social sciences and research into African issues. Colin and his wife Patsy and I saw a great deal of each other, and Colin and I worked together on two books. They too stood by me when I needed them. But none of these friendships nor the other contacts I had in Hull continued on anything like the same terms after I left in 1988, to my regret.

John Saville was half the economic and social history staff at Hull until 1963 or 1964. At that point Janet Blackman, to whom I was close for a period, arrived to be followed by two others and

John Saville, Hull, 1979.

143

me in 1965. We became a department of our own a few years later and eventually reached a total of twelve or thirteen economic and social historians. John, who was born in 1916, was the third survivor I had met of the Communist student left of the 1930s, all of them characterised by outstanding brains, total political commitment and, in most cases, shrewd, well-aimed wit. I knew John longer than Sam Fisher and better than Brian Simon. He bestrode his world like a colossus and aroused strong passions. He was hospitable and affectionate, likeable and interested in other people. At the same time he was conscious of his own eminence and concerned that others should be conscious of it too.

Hence he would pull rank from time to time. ('Pull rank?!', exclaimed Sam Fisher. 'Pull rank? John pulled rank when he was a student!') His friends were often the butt of his wit, as already suggested, and continued intimacy with him was not always easy. But he made my life in Hull very much richer than it would otherwise have been and I was glad to co-edit his festschrift in 1979. He is one of those people who makes a permanent mark on the lives of anyone who knows him well, and he did me many good turns in my years at Hull, though I was not always as grateful to him as I should have been.

His devotion to economic and social history was inspiring and his dedication to and understanding of Marxism was impressive. He was clear sighted and vastly knowledgeable. His loyalty to the University of Hull and its library were total and the university was fortunate to have had him on its staff, though it was some time before the more timorous could see him as other than a red bogey. He was also a fine lecturer, much appreciated and well liked by his students. He was one of the few of my colleagues with a serious interest in culture and general learning, quite apart from politics, and relatively late in life he developed a serious interest in music. But it was sometimes easy to be exasperated by a man who, as one of his colleagues who knew him well put it, 'thinks he's a cross between Karl Marx and Machiavelli'.

I had never visited Hull before my interview in early 1965, but from August of that year it was to be nearly fifteen years before I spent more than three consecutive weeks away from it. The appearance of the town was not attractive. It had been badly damaged in the early 1940s by the Luftwaffe, indeed 'the town that suffered most' in the entire country according to Herbert Morrison who, as wartime Home Secretary, was in a position to know (*Herbert Morrison, An Autobiography*, 1960, p. 227). It was very flat; people learning to drive were forced to practise the starting-on-a-hill manoeuvre on bridges over railway lines. On the other hand, it was a good place for the cyclist and I (mainly) cycled to work from Cottingham during the six years before I moved to within walking distance of the university. It was easy to feel a sense of isolation from the rest of the country, a feeling encouraged by the fact that the railway connection with Doncaster, where it joined the East Coast main line, was and has long remained abysmal. Its status as Misery Line was not much affected by the appointment in 1997 of John Prescott, a student in my department in these early years and later a Hull MP, as Deputy Prime Minister with responsibility for transport matters.

What Reichsmarshal Goering and his Luftwaffe had not been able to finish in the early 1940s Hull City Council undertook by wanton destruction of old buildings, grossly insensitive new ones and new roads. (In all these respects it was typical of British urban rebuilding after the war.) The rejuvenation of Hull city centre which has made it a lively and attractive place and the movement of population back into the heart of the town lay far in the future. By the time it came new roads had cut the potentially beautiful Old Town in two. Yet I felt great loyalty to Hull and its hinterland as soon as I arrived there. The fact that Hull is geographically on a limb appears to have increased the mutual solidarity of its citizens. I have heard Hull people say over and over that they would not leave Hull or that they had done so, realised their mistake and returned. The attitude of outsiders to Hull, specially those who live in the south of England, tends to be contemptuous or indifferent. The consequence is ambiguous for the university teacher, who occupies an anomalous position as a resident of Hull or its area, who has usually come from elsewhere and may well be promoted to a post in another university before long. Some responded by largely ignoring the fact that they lived in Hull, while others, like me, took an active part in the city's political or social life. All, however, enjoyed at least subconsciously the fact that Hull was an area of low prices and relatively cheap houses.

For those who made the best of being in Hull there was much to do and see in the area. (William) Wilberforce House which contained a unique museum of slavery and the Transport and Archaeology Museum, subsequently considerably improved, indeed transformed, were both of abiding interest. Holy Trinity, the large church in the centre of Hull, was of outstanding quality and neighboured by the Old Grammar School, attended by Andrew Marvell (1621-78), the Hull poet. The King George Dock, from which large ships sailed to the Netherlands, and the Fish Dock, to which one took one's visitors at 6.0 a.m. to see the landings and buy fresh fish, were both fascinating. Hessle Road is the main artery of a working-class community which I never tired of visiting. Hull Garden Village, to those who know something of its history, is also full of interest; it is located in East Hull near the Reckitt works to which it was once ancillary, though East Hull is as socially undesirable to the conventional middle class as South London. It should be added that Hull has a paragon of a railway station; in fact Hull Paragon, which rouses hilarity in outsiders as did the morning newspaper with which I grew up, the *Cleveland Plain Dealer*. (In both cases locals fail to understand the reason for hilarity and think the names perfectly normal, as indeed they are.) To the south lay the wide skies, the unbridged immensity of the Humber estuary and the mysteries of Lincolnshire, as entrancing to every visitor to Hull as they were to Philip Larkin.

Cottingham itself, my home for six years, has not only a splendid Perpendicular church but many fine, mainly Georgian houses. Beverley, eight miles away, is one of the most appealing small towns in the whole country, with Beverley Minster, more splendid than many cathedrals, St Mary's, another magnificent Perpendicular church, many Georgian houses and the Westwood, one of the few open spaces in what was then (and is now again, with changed boundaries) the East Riding of Yorkshire. The Yorkshire coast has attractive resorts, specially Bridlington and Filey and, a little further afield, Scarborough, Robin Hood's Bay and Whitby. I was to appreciate greatly the glories of the quiet Yorkshire Wolds after the pressures on London's countryside, and I grew to love the North York Moors, probably England's least known national park. It is in fact far more varied and attractive than it appears from a casual drive across it though, in season, the most casual cannot fail to appreciate the purple glory of the heather moorland. Fine waterfalls, charming villages and dramatic landscape are among its attributes, to say nothing of the enthusiasts' railway from Pickering to

146

Grosmont, the longest such line in the country, which passes through splendid scenery. One can spend many happy days in the national park without twice visiting the same attraction.

The move to Hull took place at the same time as the beginning of a shift in my political activity. Harold Wilson's accession to power in 1964, with a majority of four, was hailed by Labour supporters, if not quite like the victory of 1997 (there was a thirteen-year period out of office in 1964, as opposed to eighteen in 1997, and nobody in the happy earlier period had heard of Margaret Thatcher). There was much talk of incomes policy before the election, which the Labour left decried as meaning that we would all become richer by 2 or 3 per cent a year; there would be no change in the distribution of income or capital. As with Tony Blair's Labour Party the leadership had searched for attractive-sounding policies which would offend no one; incomes policy and 'the white hot heat of the technological revolution' seemed to fit the bill.

Nonetheless, there was much hope and excitement when the new Labour government took power. In my case it took rather less than two years to wear off. The government refused to withdraw its support for the American war of aggression in Vietnam. The war itself and the British government attitude to it rightly roused great protest in Britain if, naturally, not on the scale of the demonstrations in the United States. It was typical of that and perhaps any Labour government that it was willing to alienate its own supporters, for the protestors were mostly Labour people, so long as it did not criticise openly the United States.

Wilson refused to crack down on the rebels in Rhodesia and he was evidently more concerned to avoid the use of force against white settlers than to end their rebellion. He also refused to ask for the assistance of the United Nations; that would mean inviting to Rhodesia the 'Red army in blue berets', he alleged (see *New Statesman*, 19 November 1965, p. 770). In the spring of 1966 a seamen's strike took place involving, among others, the young John Prescott. Wilson seemed more concerned to discredit the ringleaders than to resolve the strike. The 'select few' leaders behind the strike he alleged were Communists; they were, he said, 'this tightly knit group of politically motivated men' (730 *HC Deb.*, 5s., 20 June 1966, col. 42). Tony Topham, a colleague in Adult Education, was convinced that he was one of those being attacked, though he was not a Communist and was an eminence grise rather than a leader; he was not in fact named by Wilson. (I wonder when I think of these years how journalists and the public have allowed themselves to be so gulled as to accept the claim that there is a New Labour party. In my view the claim can only be accepted by those who know nothing of Labour history.)

When Shirley and I decided to move to Cottingham we did not take into account the fact that we were moving to a constituency which was so bourgeois that the Labour Party virtually did not count. (But my former colleague Norman O'Neill, another sociologist, was to come within just over 800 votes of winning it for Labour in 1997. I hope that those in the constituency who voted Liberal Democrat 'tactically' have learned their lesson.) Labour Party meetings were thinly attended and Labour won few seats even in local elections in the constituency, despite the fact that the Conservative MP was Patrick Wall, well known as a strong supporter of white South Africa (and dubbed by his opponents 'the member for Pretoria'). Had we moved half a mile away, to North Hull, I might have continued in the Labour Party and some of my subsequent life might have been different. CND, as I have already said, seemed to be moribund at the time.

In January 1966 a by-election took place in Hull North, where Labour had narrowly won the seat from the Conservatives at the general election of 1964. Richard Gott, a *Guardian* journalist, stood in the by-election as an independent opponent of the war in Vietnam. I thought it a mistake for him to stand but as he was going to do so in any case I did what I could to help him. It was an exciting and rowdy by-election, with the big Labour party guns visiting Hull North and Barbara Castle, the Transport Secretary, promising that the people of Hull 'would have their bridge.' ('Speeches went down well', she told her diary; *The Castle Diaries 1964-1976*, 1990 ed., p. 49). A bridge across the Humber had long been a symbol of Hull's aspiration to national recognition, though traffic was mainly to the west, not across the Humber to the south. Hull North was a constituency which was home to most of Hull's relatively small middle class, but which was growing more working class as new housing estates were built. Concern for the war in Vietnam, in which Britain was not an active participant, was minimal in the working-class electorate.

Moreover, Britain was not the United States. People here voted and vote for a party, not for a maverick individual. Gott had a great deal of publicity but only 253 votes, while Kevin McNamara won the seat for Labour with a much increased majority, over 5,000. He has been MP for the constituency, called Hull North or Central ever since, and his majorities have grown significantly over time. His assertion during the campaign that a way had to be found of 'getting the Americans off the hook', finding a way for them to withdraw from Vietnam without losing face, was perhaps more sensible than it appeared at the time.

But I had had enough of Harold Wilson's Labour Party. I left at the end of 1966 when my subscription ended, and apart from rejoining in 1968 under the influence of the branch membership secretary or treasurer, John Prescott (I still have my card, signed 'J. Prescott' and the indication that I had paid twelve shillings annual membership fee), I remained without party affiliation until I rejoined Labour when it needed friends in 1978. (By that time I had to pay £1.20.) Besides, by then Wilson had retired. Despite misgivings I have remained a member continuously since that date.

This disillusion with the Labour Party coincided with a new interest in the rambling (still known to many of the uninitiated as 'hiking') movement, with which my concern was both practical and political. Nick Tucker and I had begun walking together in the early 1960s and my school journeys in 1964 and 1965 had visited two of the finest walking areas in England, the Cheviots and the Lake District. My interest was also aroused by outside events. In April 1965 thanks initially to the inspiration and hard work of Tom Stephenson, a working-class autodidact and old socialist militant who by then was the secretary of the Ramblers' Association, the first long distance footpath in England and Wales was opened. This was the 250-mile Pennine Way. Though membership of the Ramblers' Association was only 4,662 on 30 September 1964 (and still only 32,000 ten years later as against about 125,000 as I write in late 1998) and its use of the media was still fairly rudimentary, the opening of the Pennine Way was one of the best publicity agents the association has ever had and I joined that summer.

Soon after I moved to Hull a dispute which had been brewing over common land at Millington Pastures, one of the most beautiful spots in the Yorkshire Wolds, came to a head. The pastures

149

had previously been open to public access but now they were being fenced and ploughed. This was in an area almost devoid of access land. I participated in a Ramblers' Association-organised protest walk on 21 November 1965, only weeks after my arrival in Hull, persuading Peter Jackson and other friends to take part as well. I met then or soon afterwards Bruce Riddell, a Scot who had up to that point spent most of his adult life in England, and with whom I soon became friendly. He was the secretary of the Ramblers' Association's East Riding Area and was one of the first people who helped to make the Area an energetic, publicity-seeking organisation. I joined the Area committee at its AGM early in 1966 and when Bruce left Hull for Scotland (to my great regret) in the spring of that year I uttered the fateful words 'I have a typewriter' when the committee sought a successor. I did not realise that I had entered a new world into which I was soon drawn ever more closely and from which I was to have neither desire nor ability to escape. Within the RA, as it was universally known, this was a common experience.

In April 1967 I went to Birmingham to represent the East Riding Area at the RA's National Council. A speaker criticised the East Riding for the militancy it had shown over Millington Pastures which, he claimed, seemed to have achieved little. I leaped to the defence of militancy and was surprised when Frank Head, a long-serving member of the National Executive, approached me and asked if I was willing to stand for election to the executive. (I later realised that EC members, including myself, were always on the lookout for new blood.) I rashly agreed and to my surprise was elected, despite the fact that before that National Council virtually the only RA members I had met outside the East Riding were Tom Stephenson himself and Andrew Dalby, his assistant. To my pleasure Bruce Riddell, now based in Ayrshire, was also elected.

That weekend in Birmingham and my earlier acceptance of the East Riding Area secretaryship changed my life. I had an activity which took the place of the Labour Party, an outlet from the isolation of university life and an opportunity to make friends outside the university. On the other hand, I later realised, I also had a commitment which would take time away from the academic's single-minded concentration on publication – and promotion. Whether in self defence or not, however, I have never regretted my participation in the RA.

The Ramblers' Association became a registered charity at about the same time that I joined its national executive. This fact did not prevent it from continuing its work of putting pressure on politicians, civil servants and local government officers. Tom Stephenson was fond of quoting Chuter Ede, the former Labour Home Secretary and former RA president, who had called the RA the most political non-political body he had ever known. The point was that the RA was non-party political, though at national level the leading spirits were mostly Labour voters. As for me I never lost my interest in a wide variety of subjects, mostly party political, and I felt in some respects out of place in an organisation in which members' interests, bookshelves and leisure were devoted almost exclusively to the out of doors. I also was more sceptical than most ramblers, not about my commitment to the cause but about its importance in the global scheme of things. I felt initially and continued to feel a rambler amongst academics, an academic amongst ramblers. (However, it must be added that the flexibility and relative freedom of the academic's life gave me essential opportunities to pursue the work of the RA.)

I was, however, a typical rambler in two respects. I had grown to love walking in the countryside, the recreational passion of the intellectual (as of course of so many others) par excellence. The English, Welsh and Scottish countryside had the same magic effect, the same magnetism on me that they have had on thousands of others. And I believed passionately in the RA's aims. These included safeguarding the integrity of the ten national parks in England and Wales, achieving access by foot to uncultivated mountains and moorland, and ensuring that the system of access by footpath throughout the country was signposted and waymarked and free from obstruction or ploughing. The RA was also concerned to protect the beauty of the countryside outside national parks and designated areas of natural beauty.

RA members were divided into Areas (mainly counties) and Groups (mainly towns and suburbs). We in the East Riding Area realised at the Millington rally that the media were interested in our activities (the more militant the better so far as they were concerned) and that ramblers were photogenic; publicity was ours for the asking. Membership and aims overlapped with the YHA, the Council for the Preservation (later Protection) of Rural England

151

and the National Trust, but there were important differences. Members of the YHA were mainly concerned with finding somewhere to sleep and eat, while the top level of both the CPRE and National Trust were often too genteel to involve themselves in hard political lobbying and infighting. Besides, they could be seen as the wealthy wanting to preserve land and great houses for the good of themselves and their class.

It was mostly the middle class which joined the RA and provided the bulk of its volunteers, but it was rare to find a titled or really wealthy member among the activists. We thus appeared before the public as ordinary people, concerned not for our own selfish advantage (though I have been accused of exactly this by those who enjoy motorcycling in the countryside) but to preserve our (in my case, as with W.S. Gilbert's Major-General Stanley, acquired) heritage and to extend it to future generations. We certainly wanted to walk in unspoilt and quiet countryside, but those who joined the RA were often sufficiently knowledgeable to be able to read maps and find their own walking routes. Our concern was not primarily for ourselves but for the general public. We were in no doubt that we were the activist, even 'left' wing of the countryside movement and I took pride in the fact that the RA East Riding was and remained the most active and prominent amenity organisation in the county. I should add that those few of us in the RA locally and nationally who were graduates and intellectuals and who talked for a living enjoyed considerable advantages; the RA is (as said above) much larger now and it is less easy to rise to national leadership on the basis of the odd effective speech at National (now General) Council.

I was the RA Area Secretary from 1966 until 1972 when, after the collapse of my marriage to Shirley, I felt too bereft to spend the long isolated hours which the work of the secretary demanded. Later I held many other Area offices. I was a member of the National Executive from 1967 to 1975 and, after a break, again from 1978 to 1988. I spent much time and energy on the work of the RA in the later 60s. I used to say to my university colleagues that while they talked about the class war I actually practised it, for the RA frequently, in a heavily rural county, locked horns with farmers and landowners. 'Mr Rubinstein' was not a name in much favour with many of them.

University people often commented in a surprised manner on my rambling activities. I decided that my colleagues supposed that as one of the minority of university staff with intellectual interests I would not want to spend my spare time discussing countryside issues, typing minutes and associating with people of less extensive formal education. Still less did they think that I would wish to take part in organised rambles. (I observed to two ramblers at an unguarded moment on a Sunday walk through idyllic Wolds landscape that in 24 hours' time I would be reading the *Star* newspaper for 1888 at the British Museum Newspaper Library. I have never forgotten their genuine bewilderment that I should wish to do this and that I was paid for doing it.) The university types could not have been more wrong, for though (unlike some of my rambling friends) I never wanted to take up the countryside as a full-time paid occupation I certainly could (and can) think of no better leisure activity. I also enjoyed enormously organised rambles, far more than I had anticipated. In addition I had taken part extensively in outside interests since my student days and, being disillusioned by party politics I naturally sought another form of activism. And for me, as for Chuter Ede, work for the RA was most certainly political activity.

Though we were an association of ramblers the RA in the East Riding before my time did not organise walks for members, this activity being left to the walking clubs well represented on our executive. We promptly ended this abdication of function and though in my time as secretary the walks programme was thin compared with its later flowering, we did walk regularly and attracted new members by doing so. Footpath law and public footpath inquiries were meat and drink to many activists, but I was always more interested in amenity (countryside) questions, which had the added advantage of attracting greater media interest. (Our secretary Chris Hall, who succeeded Tom Stephenson in 1969, taught us that there was little point in doing things if the media were not informed and we consequently enjoyed no publicity for our activities. But he was and remained a footpath man through and through.)

One of my activities as Area Secretary was to take a leading part in a campaign to prevent part of Farndale, the celebrated daffodil valley in the North York Moors National Park, from being drowned by a reservoir. We got up a petition and secured wide publicity on the subject. Taking my three small sons (Peter, the eldest, would then have been no more than about ten) with me encouraged interest and signatures. Opposition to a proposal to create a yachting marina close to the Flamborough Head Heritage Coast (with the attendant traffic and congestion) was another ultimately successful project. A third success for the local ramblers was the defeat of the planned closure of the Hull-Scarborough railway, proposed by British Rail in 1968-9. The East Riding RA and others stimulated and organised opposition by local communities and commuters, and in the end 3,444 objections to the proposal were received. It was then and may still be the largest number of objections ever received to a railway closure proposal. (See Rubinstein and Speakman, *Leisure, Transport and the Countryside*, 1969, p. 24). I make no apology for the fact that our successes were often the result of combating other people's destructive plans. Indeed I am proud that I was once rung up by someone in Hull who wanted assistance in opposing a plan, I think, to close a pedestrian bridge over a railway. He had heard that I was 'a man who likes things to stay as they are'.

A particularly long-running affair was the attempt to secure a right of way through Welton Dale, the most beautiful of the valleys between which the Wolds come down to the Humber. This was a complicated saga. I had first walked through the lovely, isolated dale with Bruce Riddell one snowy day in early 1966, when we were spotted throwing snowballs (the 'neiges d'antan' indeed) at the Raikes Mausoleum, a late Georgian (1818) landmark near the footpath. After Bruce's departure for Scotland I walked through the dale several times, defying the gamekeeper and his 'beware Alsations' (sic) notice. I took, or tried to take a television crew through the dale on another occasion when we were met and barred by legal representatives. Finally, I was served with a writ to prevent me from walking through the dale, but perseverance and good luck won in the end, and Welton Dale is now not only freely open to the public but part of the national long-distance path the Wolds Way.

This seventy-mile walking route from the Humber to the North Sea at Filey Brig was the brainchild of the RA East Riding Committee. We were astonished at the immediate and favourable publicity which our sketchy initial proposals for a Wolds Way generated when we published them in 1968. Putting forward the

Tom Stephenson addressing a Wolds Way rally near Millington, East Yorkshire, October 1968 (David, in anorak, seated behind Tom).

plan was one thing but seeing it through to a triumphant conclusion was quite another; it took fourteen years. There was farmer and landowner opposition and we were urged by National Farmers' Union members at one meeting to agree to a route entirely on minor roads open to motor traffic. One major hurdle lay above the attractive village of Thixendale where the route went through the land of Lord Middleton, who was a member of the Council of the University of Hull. The relevant footpath was eventually proved to be a right of way but Lord Middleton was determined to ensure that the Wolds Way would not follow this route, which passed the fascinating remains of the deserted village and ruined church at Wharram Percy. This was another titanic struggle for a group of volunteers working in their spare time against a wealthy landowner with a full panoply of legal support.

Putting the case for the Wolds Way over the years did give the East Riding Ramblers many opportunities for publicity. We had more than one rally and several walks over parts of the route. Tom Stephenson, then a youthful 75, came to speak to a rally in the

155

Millington Pastures area in October 1968. We had a good contingent from West Riding Area and one of the party captured the scene in a photograph many times re-used in our publicity. I gaze ruefully at the side view of myself thirty years ago, my hair less sparse and darker than it is now.

We prepared for that or another Wolds Way event by a 'recce' of ramblers from East and West Ridings. We stopped for tea at a garden in Thixendale, whose owner showed us the trap door in her living-room ceiling through which coffins could be lowered. It was an idyllic day and the good fellowship was almost palpable. One of us bought jam from our hostess: 'money for jam', somebody observed, and we laughed as if the joke had only just been invented. That day and that incident remain among my permanent moments. We in the RA had a special affection for Thixendale, and were glad to be involved in the discussions for converting the village hall into a Youth Hostel.

In National Footpath Week in 1970 we persuaded Miss Hull, the local beauty queen, to join us on part of a walk from Hull to Beverley, to popularise an intended walking route. We publicised a scheme for country parks which included one at Danes' Dyke, near Bridlington, and persuaded a representative of the Danish Embassy to join us at an event. Richard Wood, the local (Conservative) MP was also with us and used a photograph of the occasion in his election literature that year. (Another Conservative MP who helped us by taking on the honorary role of president was Patrick Wall; his name was put forward by the socialist Area secretary.) We also established groups of the RA in York, Driffield and Scarborough, in conformity with the national drive to strengthen the RA's third, grassroots tier, and I was pleased to join in October 1998 one of three rambles held to celebrate the thirtieth anniversary of the founding of York Group. In short we had a good deal of fun, made feathers fly and publicised the case for walking and preserving rural beauty in East Yorkshire as nobody had done before us. We felt that we were at the forefront of the work of the national RA.

I did not always find the work of the RA as much fun as on that day in Thixendale. It is no easy matter to coax a group of volunteers to carry out specific tasks, nor to end a meeting at 11.0 p.m. or even midnight, and then make a list of the consequent work which has to be carried out before going to bed. As my friend Colin Speakman put it later: 'Overload a volunteer and he or she will simply quit. That is the golden rule of any voluntary body.' (Ann Holt (ed.), *Making Tracks: a celebration of fifty years of the Ramblers' Association*, 1985, p. 67). Such considerations applied to all my colleagues, but totally committed to the RA as I was, not to myself. I had to try to treat other EC members with tact, but friction could arise and my impatience was often the cause. On the whole, however, the local committee worked harmoniously to the common end.

My service on the national executive was full of interest and the topics with which it dealt were numerous and varied. In summer its meetings were held in Buxton, the beautiful Peak District town which at nearly a thousand feet is a claimant to be the highest town in England. In winter we met in London. When I went to Buxton for my first EC I changed trains in Manchester, missing my connection and arriving, mortified, at the meeting half an hour or so after its start. Fortunately for me, I was greeted in friendly and forgiving fashion.

The executive then had several members who had been active in the access movement since the founding of the RA in 1935 or even before; Frank Head, Wally Smith, Walter Tysoe, Arthur Roberts and Vic Morecroft were chief among them. Though the office was in London the association's heartland was in the north; Tom Stephenson himself was a Lancastrian though he had long lived in the south. There was then more emphasis on access to open country and less on footpaths than there was to be later, after Tom retired and the southern membership predominance began to assert itself.

I went to different parts of the country, especially different parts of England, to address AGMs and other meetings. It was always interesting to visit ramblers in their homes and elsewhere and it was moving to see how much hard work was done at local level by people without hope of other reward than to fulfil the aims of the movement. I attended conferences staged by the National Trust, Countryside Commission, national park committees and others to represent the RA.

I continued to see a good deal of Bruce Riddell since we both served on the RA national executive for nearly a decade. He was

Speakers on Latrigg, above Keswick, at mass protest against the proposed Keswick bypass through the Lake District National Park, October 1973. (Left to right) David, Colin Speakman, Roland Wade (Friends of the Lake District), Gerald Haythornthwaite (national park and countryside campaigner), Geoffrey Berry (Friends of the Lake District), Graham Watson (Lake District Planning Board). One of the high points (1203 feet) of my speaking career.

one rambler with interests wider than the cause and we enjoyed many stimulating discussions; I remember one in particular after the Soviet repression of the Prague spring in 1968. I was always sorry that Bruce, who had missed the opportunity for higher education in youth but who in his Hull years had close contacts with the university's sociology department, was never able to take a degree. A family of small daughters meant that he could not afford to exchange his salary in Customs and Excise for a mature student's grant.

I have already mentioned that Andrew Dalby was assistant to Tom Stephenson at national office. Andrew was another Lancastrian, a former school teacher and passionate about both cricket and football as well as rambling. After a break to return to school teaching (during which time he worked for the RA in a voluntary capacity and rose to become national chairman) he returned to national office, in whose employ he worked off and (mostly) on over a period of 33 years. Andrew and I became friendly as soon as we met and I have had many happy hours with him over the years, both in England and on his visits to us in France, though it is in some respects a friendship of opposites, since he is as cautious, reflective and conservative as I am rash, impulsive and radical. It is fortunate for me that he is calm and tolerant, seldom allowing himself to say anything which he might regret later. I was glad and grateful to be a speaker at one of his farewell functions in October 1998, soon after his retirement.

Colin Speakman was when I first met him at National Council a Leeds school teacher, moving by way of college lecturing to work for the Yorkshire Dales National Park and eventually to setting up his own consultancy, specialising in 'green tourism'. 'We thought he would last [as a consultant] for six weeks', a common friend once observed. Colin was a pioneer in his field and has been highly successful for more than twice six years. His long and committed service to the environment was recognised in 1997 by the award of an honorary doctorate by the University of Bradford.

Colin and I wrote together a pamphlet for the Fabian Society on *Leisure, Transport and the Countryside* (1969), in which we argued the case for more public and less private, motorised transport in rural areas. The pamphlet made a considerable splash and we were gratified to be the object of adverse comment in Allan Patmore's study of *Land and Leisure* (1970). (Later Patmore, an agreeable and kindly man, was to become my colleague at the University of Hull.) If we could not agree with the academic geographer's anaemic (as we thought) conclusions we were delighted to be the object of his criticism as 'the preservationists' who thought that complicated issues were clear cut and who sought access for ramblers to what we called 'our precious, shrinking countryside' but opposed unfettered access by motorists. He pointed out: 'The whole theme of the car in the countryside is perhaps the most critical and hotly debated of all aspects of outdoor recreation, and one where opinions are most entrenched and violently opposed.' (pp. 251, 253) Time has not resolved the controversy but Colin and I can claim to be amongst the first to warn of the dangers of unrestricted car use in sensitive countryside.

159

Gerald McGuire was not primarily an RA man, though he was to be our president in the mid-1970s. We became friends initially in 1969 over our common opposition to potash mining in the North Yorkshire Moors National Park, he representing at a public inquiry the YHA, of which he ended up as Deputy Secretary, I the RA. At that time he lived in Hemel Hempstead, and I stayed with him and his wife Peggy on more than one university research visit to London. The McGuires moved to Malton, where they had earlier been based, when Gerald retired in 1982 and our friendship has remained close. I was heavily indebted for the advice which he gave me from his lengthy experience of personalities and issues in the amenity movement.

I did not get to know Alan Howard well until somewhat later, since he was not elected to the RA executive till the mid-1970s. He worked for the North West Regional Health Authority, mostly undertaking their art and design. Alan was one of the wittiest people I have known, and he could be guaranteed 'to set the table [i.e., National Council] on a roar' once if not repeatedly every year. A verse of his on the esoteric question of whether to say 'AsONB' or

Peggy and Gerald McGuire with a grandchild, Wigton, Cumberland, summer 1973.

'AONBs' (for Areas of Outstanding National Beauty) resolved the question once for all with gaiety and elegance (his reference to 'JsP and MsP' was unforgettable; reprinted in *Rucksack*, Autumn 1978, p. 10). At one point we combined to demand an end to smoking at EC meetings; later we worked together in defence of public transport and in opposition to motorways, a cause as dear to him (and to me) as to Colin Speakman.

Chris Hall, who replaced Tom Stephenson as RA secretary in 1969 and remained in that post until moving to become CPRE director in 1974, was the closest friend I made in the RA, one of the closest I have ever made. Everyone who knew Chris appreciated his many talents. He was a professional journalist, a persuasive, hard-hitting and effective writer. He was an outstanding speaker. Having written for several national newspapers, been information officer to Barbara Castle at the Overseas Development and Transport ministries and secretary of the highly successful amenity group the Chiltern Society, he was ideally suited to take over from Tom Stephenson. Indeed, Tom was largely responsible for Chris's appointment, since he lived in the Chilterns and had

Tom Stephenson with his successor Chris Hall in the Ramblers' Association office, autumn 1968.

161

grown to appreciate the work of this dynamic younger man nearly forty years his junior.

Under Chris, with his flair for publicity, the RA was to move to new heights. He was later to serve the association in elected roles as executive committee member, chairman and president; although he was secretary for only five years his connection with the association has never ended. He will be on everyone's list of the two or three people to whom the RA in its sixty-odd year history is most indebted.

I have said that I was not a natural rambler and I had much to learn. Either through culpable negligence or because the interview was arranged at the last moment I had not appreciated that Chris was to be interviewed formally by the executive before the beginning of an EC meeting. It was held, exceptionally, at Hope in the Peak District. I left the train at an earlier station, walked happily over the hills and arrived at the CHA guesthouse where the meeting was held. When I arrived I found the interview actually taking place; I was wearing my boots and eating an iced lolly. Chris's later tactful comment was that he was pleased to know that the executive contained at least one real rambler, but it will be easily understood how humiliating the occasion was for me. It was not mitigated by the fact that Walter Tysoe, then chairman, and another EC member took me aside to explain that boots inside the guesthouse, the iced lolly and bursting into the interview were unacceptable behaviour. I of course had no answer but an apology.

Chris and I were close during his period as secretary and long afterwards. We were of almost identical age, similar political and intellectual outlooks, and if I lacked a long background in the rambling past I was sympathetic to the reforms which he wanted to carry out and about which some of the older EC members were sceptical. It was in some ways surprising that we remained close friends over the next 25 years, for we were both touchy and opinionated, convinced of the correctness of our facts and views. Many aspects of life changed for both Chris and me over that period but I gained tremendously from his friendship and loyalty, and while he was RA secretary I felt that our views on matters relating to the countryside were close to identical.

These were the people to whom I was closest on the national amenity scene. But there were many others. There was Donald Lee of Manchester, a footpath fanatic who announced to a group of us late at night at one National Council that his parliamentary vote would be cast for whichever party would promise to maintain and improve the footpath network. There was the much loved Harry Smith of West Riding Area, whose rhyming votes of thanks at the end of National Council were universally acclaimed. ('It gets worse every year', Walter Tysoe commented sadly from the chair, as the roars of laughter subsided.) There was Ian Campbell, secretary of the Commons, Open Spaces and Footpaths Preservation Society, a man who was as moderate in manner and dedicated in policy as Chris Hall was aggressive and dedicated. Tom Stephenson himself was very approachable and told many fascinating anecdotes of the political and rambling past. One of my first scholarly publications was an edited interview with him about his early life, political experiences and work for public access. (As well as being a (by then) somewhat nominal socialist he was a convinced atheist. When in hospital in the late 1960s the chaplain came to his bedside. 'I'm a cantankerous old man', said Tom, 'bugger off.') These personalities and others added greatly to my enjoyment of working for the RA in these and later years.

Meanwhile my political commitment outside the amenity movement had not come to an end. I was no longer a Labour Party member, but I took part in the left-wing activities of the period, above all opposition to the American war in Vietnam. There were demonstrations and meetings, not only during the Gott campaign but long afterwards. I was a moving spirit in the weekly discussions and occasional conferences held by the (university) Staff Socialist Group.

I attended faithfully the Socialist Teachers' Group (almost all Hull and district schoolteachers apart from me) and served on its committee. I was responsible in that role for inviting Sam Fisher and other London friends to speak. It was through the STG that I met Margaret Palfreman, who was to become one of my closest Hull friends. She was a Hull woman, the mother of four children, who was cruelly widowed while still young. She and her husband Bill had been members of the Communist Party in Hull and she was close to John Saville and other local Communists of that generation. In later life she became a Quaker and this was to be an additional bond when Ann and I too joined the Friends. Her

David, Margaret Palfreman, Ann; near Poitiers, June 1984.

friendship meant a great deal to me, especially during the period when my first marriage came to an end, but also both before and after that time. Ann and I were glad to be able to attend her eightieth birthday party in August 1994. Typically, Margaret prepared a speech for the occasion in which she had something nice to say about every one of the large number of friends and family who attended. (I have previously mentioned our nostalgic visit to Hull as her guests in February 1998.)

I was also involved on the fringes of the movement for workers' control which was led by my colleague Tony Topham and Ken Coates, then of the University of Nottingham and later a controversial MEP. I was always, however, too convinced of the importance of the vanguard political party and too sceptical of how much control the workers really wanted to be very enthusiastic about this cause.

I was moderately active during these years in opposing the policies of the state of Israel, sometimes in collaboration with my Hull colleague Talal Asad. I spoke to meetings in the Hull University

Students' Union, once in a committee room in the Palace of Westminster and once at a meeting in Manchester chaired by the former (and future) Sheffield MP Frank Hooley, and wrote occasional letters to the national press in opposition to what I saw then, as I see now, as Israeli intransigence and aggression. I also lent my name both to the Council for the Advancement of Arab-British Understanding and Unipal, which formed and maintained links between British universities and Palestinians. I would sometimes receive or see in print angry letters from Jews denouncing my 'crazy Communism' as one put it, or attacking me for 'self-hatred'.

I rejected this view, though I do think it advisable to maintain a healthy scepticism about the perfect rectitude of oneself as of one's country. I cannot believe that because one has been born into a particular sub-group the exact nature of which is in any case difficult to define, one's convictions must be fixed in a particular mould. Acceptance of such an attitude seems to me unpleasantly racist. 'Self-hatred' like 'the politics of envy', on which phrase Conservative publicity agencies were so delighted to have hit, is an all-purpose term of abuse which assumes that the views of the person attacked can be ignored since they stem from personal inadequacy. Both terms deserve nothing but rejection and contempt.

I believed that Zionism after 1945 was a regrettable necessity but that the state of Israel was deeply blameworthy for its intransigence vis-a-vis its Arab neighbours. I have never been able to understand why Israeli governments are willing to expose their citizens to sudden, terrifying attack and to resort to no other response than the use of overwhelming military force which can only exacerbate hostility between Israeli Jews and Arabs. 'Giving peace a chance', no matter whose hand has to be shaken, has always seemed to me the most elementary common sense.

By the later 1960s (and indeed long before) my loose connection with the pro-Arab cause and opposition to Israeli behaviour constituted my only connection with my ancestral Judaism. John Parker had tried to persuade me to change my name when I moved to Hull, but this seemed cowardly and a concession to an unnecessary and undesirable uniformity. Foreign immigration into Britain, after all, is much older than some British people wish to think. From time to time people still make unwelcome comments such as 'envy[ing my] rich emotional life', a comment supported in context only by my surname, or apologising to me because they do not like Michael Howard (I choose actual examples), but which life is free from pinpricks of some kind? And I hope that I have done something at least among my friends and contacts to combat the lazy resort to stereotype which can so easily lead to prejudice and then to the racism which disfigures our society (see Hampstead Friends *Newsletter*, November-December 1997).

My most significant political-cum-educational activity in my first few years at Hull was to edit, with Colin Stoneman, the Penguin book we called *Education for Democracy* and which was published in 1970 (with a second edition in 1972). The educational and political worlds had both been shaken in 1969 by the publication of the first of several so-called *Black Papers* whose authors, academics and journalists, were strongly opposed to modern trends in education. (By 1970 three had been published.) Progressive methods in the primary schools, incorporation of grammar schools into comprehensive schools and revolting students were among the targets. The *Black Papers* aroused enormous publicity and controversy, appearing as they did towards the end of the six years of Wilson-led Labour government, which had initially raised so many hopes and had led to such disillusionment. As for me I felt that my early career and nearly ten years of my life were being challenged.

Education for Democracy was a book containing two dozen short but, we hoped, pungent and radical articles covering the whole range of educational provision apart from pre-primary. The contributors, who shared a broadly common approach to educational questions, were experts in their fields. Nick Tucker, by now teaching education and psychology at the University of Sussex, wrote about deprived children in deprived areas, Brian Simon about streaming and unstreaming in the comprehensive school. There were contributions from Hull colleagues including the theologian Alistair Kee whose *The Way of Transcendence* was to receive widespread notice and acclaim when and long after it appeared in 1971. My own contribution dealt with the public schools, their exclusivity and stranglehold over the power levers of the national life.

Colin was particularly concerned with the nature of intelligence, which had been used by *Black Paper* writers such as Cyril Burt (whose own researches were later largely discredited) to advocate grammar schools for the supposedly more intelligent pupils.

Colin's view, which was that of most educational psychologists, was that it was impossible to separate native from acquired intelligence and that an examination like the 11-plus was chiefly an assessment of social class and the parental home. Intelligence, as Brian Simon and other writers had observed, could be defined in circular fashion as the entity which was measured by intelligence tests, but in no more objective form.

All of the authors were concerned to raise the standards of achievement of ordinary pupils and to democratise the context of education, notably higher education, which in 1968 and after was in a state of ferment, notably at the University of Hull. (I had, typically recklessly, played a part in the Hull sit-in of 1968 and was to do so again in 1972.) We felt that raising the highest levels of attainment, in which we all believed, could not be achieved without raising the levels of the average. As to the grammar school, which was the subject of impassioned debate (as, in a changed context, it still is), we did not feel that educating pupils termed 'clever' at the age of ten in a segregated secondary school would do much either for them or for the country as a whole. Events had moved in our direction. The Labour Party, with Anthony Crosland as Secretary of State for Education from 1965 to 1967, had declared its support for a national system of comprehensive education, and secondary education in England and Wales was being reorganised along comprehensive lines. (It is well known that greater strides were made once Margaret Thatcher became secretary of state in 1970.)

Education for Democracy was well received on the political and educational left, and resulted in a number of invitations to Colin and me to address conferences or student meetings. It secured much less publicity than the *Black Papers*, however, because our defence of steady, progressive educational advance was not as sensational as wholesale denunciation of new trends. Nearly thirty years later the situation seems less clear-cut than it did then. Educational progressives believed as I believed in my years in the classroom that the comprehensive school would lead to much greater educational attainment. And it has. In the twenty-five years after the publication of *Education for Democracy* in 1970 numbers of students enrolling in courses in higher education more than trebled. The number of female students rose particularly sharply and there are now more women in higher education than men. The percentage of girls securing five or more good GSCE passes doubled in the twenty years from 1975; the comparable figures for boys were lower but still impressive. A level passes also rose sharply (see *Social Trends 1997*, p. 55; *1998*, p. 61). Between 1970 and 1996 the percentage of state school pupils attending comprehensive schools rose from 37 per cent to 85 per cent (ibid., *1998*, p. 59). What unprejudiced observer would conclude that the advance in educational attainment is unrelated to the growth of the comprehensive school?

On the other hand the greater incidence of anti-social behaviour in and out of school over the past thirty years and the presence of large numbers of alienated young people in our cities and towns have not been a vote of confidence in the educational system. Anti-social changes in the nature of British life, often encouraged by the speeches of politicians, the arrival in many urban schools of children whose mother tongue is not English and severe restraints on local authority spending in the past twenty years have taken their toll, though we have now arrived at a situation in which the children of immigrants are often better and more ambitious pupils than their counterparts from native British families. The Labour Party now places much more importance on the individual teacher and pupil and less on educational structure and expenditure, bowing to the winds of conservative educational opinion as it has often done in the past. And selective secondary education, which has never quite disappeared, now seems to be returning gradually to the educational scene.

I have never believed that education should be a matter of teachers handing down tablets of wisdom to their pupils or students. The self-discovery and democratic methods inspired by Rousseau, John Dewey, Bertrand Russell and many other reformers remain valid in my eyes; examination results, though critically important in our society, are not the only criterion of effective education. In that context *Education for Democracy* gave support to beleaguered teachers and students and I was proud to have been associated with it.

After 1965 I had therefore had several different types of activity linked directly or indirectly with party politics, as well as the immense commitment which I had made, not entirely intentionally in the first instance, to the Ramblers' Association. I was also a

(Left to right) Paul, David, Johnny, Shirley, Peter; Land's End, August 1970.

husband and father. I took my children to the seaside and to the North York Moors National Park and on holiday to Northumberland, Scotland, Cornwall and North Wales. My sons had discovered the joys of association football, which I had played only briefly in primary school, and by the end of the 1960s I attended regularly, three boys in tow, the Boothferry Park home of Hull City (or 'ull Ci'y', as it was commonly known). There we followed keenly and vociferously the exploits of such heroes as Ken Wagstaff ('Waggy'), Chris Chilton ('Chillo') and Ian Butler. I was surprised to find, at the age of 35 or so, just what an exciting game football really is.

I was also aware that prosecuting scholarly research and publishing the results was a major part of an academic's life and the only real criterion for promotion within an extremely competitive profession. I did not have the advantage of having recently completed a doctoral thesis which could be 'milked' to produce scholarly articles or a book. I had the added problem that for my first

169

year or more my overwhelming priority was to raise my social history lectures to a level with which I felt reasonably satisfied. From my first months at Hull I was helped to 'keep up with the reading' by becoming one of the main social history reviewers for *Tribune*, the socialist weekly. (I also wrote a monthly countryside piece for the paper for some time.) I kept up this connection until my first working visit to France in 1983 made posting the books too expensive. But I knew I had to publish. What subject to choose?

In the event I began work on two separate projects. The results were mixed.

CHAPTER 7

Still at Hull: the seventies

A GOOD DEAL OF the scholarly research I have carried out has been suggested to me by other people. This was true of my first two pieces of work.

At some point shortly after I went to Hull Brian Simon asked me to write a book in a series entitled *Students* (sic) *Library of Education*. It was one of a series of short volumes divided into sections, including method, history, philosophy, psychology and sociology. I was asked to write a book on the history of the comprehensive school from its inception to the 1960s. I cannot remember exactly when I was asked, only the realisation that the book could not be written from sources available in Hull. Thus began several years of sponging off my London-based friends, including Geraldine and Mike Murray from Woodberry Down, Nick and Jackie Tucker from Tulse Hill, David and Anne Smith and Laurie and Margaret Norcross from Abbey Wood, Chris and Jennie Hall and Gerald and Peggy McGuire from the amenity movement. I was generally at home only for bed and breakfast and I tried to compensate my hosts by taking them to the theatre, but as every provincial researcher finds, it was not an ideal arrangement. (Besides, some of my friends soon moved away from London.) British universities give their staffs only tiny research grants, and unless one can find money from elsewhere staying with friends is almost inevitable.

It was a relief from this point of view when Peter Jackson's Westminster flat, which he had kept after he lost his parliamentary seat in 1970, became available to Ann and me in 1972, and it was even better when we acquired our own London flat in 1979, despite the problems involved in second-home ownership.

I sent my manuscript to Brian Simon and after an agonising wait he rejected it. As he was himself a leading expert on the comprehensive school and his mother was one of its early champions I had an exacting master to satisfy. But I am sure that he was right to impugn its scholarship, for my short apprenticeship at LSE followed by nine years of army and the classroom had taught me little of what was demanded of historians by the later 1960s. (The advent of photocopying changed everything for historical research, John Saville used to say.) Brian was an experienced and leading educational historian and I – was not. I did object, however, to his allegation that I had been too favourable to the Labour Party, for I had intended to say what in fact I felt, that much Labour history in this field, as in others, was a mixture of good aspirations, timorousness and acceptance of the assumptions and prejudices of its political enemies.

But the rejection was a salutary lesson. I could not write a satisfactory scholarly work based on my own experience as a teacher plus the manuscript which I had written and sent to Brian during my period at Abbey Wood plus additional bits and pieces of research. Whatever may be said of the slapdash methods of other historians I would have to be sure in future that I could not be faulted for work which was anything less than thorough. Better to write too little than too flimsily. None of my work was rejected in later years, whether commissioned or not. As for Brian Simon, he and I continued to be friends. I remained in touch with him to the end of my Hull days and well beyond and I stayed with Brian and his wife Joan when I was an external examiner at Leicester in the mid-eighties.

Brian rewrote the manuscript, using some of my material, and sent it to me for comment and criticism. It was published under our joint names as *The Evolution of the Comprehensive School 1926-1966* in 1969. A second, updated edition followed in 1973. The original edition was only 113 pages, and even the revised edition came to no more than 136 pages, but there were at that time few books on the subject and it was obviously useful to students and teachers. I learned from Brian's recently published memoirs (*A Life in Education*, 1998, p. 105) that it sold 15,000 copies. It is also obvious that if I had written the book alone it would not have sold nearly so many.

My other project was more successful, or would have been if its appearance had not been almost publicity-free. This was a short book for a series of monographs in economic and social history edited by John Saville for the University of Hull. Nick Tucker, then living in Hackney, had come across a fascinating and rare book (the British Museum, later British Library, then had no copy) in his local library, namely the *Recollections of a School Attendance Officer* by John Reeves, published in 1913. Reeves had been an attendance officer for the London School Board, which administered most of the elementary school education in London between 1870 and 1904, and Nick suggested that a book might lie in the subject. It did indeed. I wrote it and dedicated it to him.

I found the subject an open sesame into the social history of late nineteenth century London and British urban history in general. ('Everything is' (such an open sesame), John Saville observed.) Poverty, poor health, bad housing, the employment of children, the attitude of the upper social classes towards expenditure on the education of the lower orders, all were there. So too were demands for social reform, including free elementary education (which began in 1891), free school meals (1906) and more ambitious, wide-ranging education for older children. (Marie Lloyd's account, as related in 'The Coster Girl in Paris', was typical of many children of the period: 'At the board school I went to, they taught me to parley-voo.')

When a child did not attend school the London School Board delivered a notice (on a form labelled 'A', hence an 'A' notice) to the parental home warning that attendance at school was required by a board by-law (and by Act of Parliament from 1880 throughout England and Wales), from the ages of 5 to 10. If the child still failed to attend school its parent was summoned to a meeting on a form labelled 'B'. I had never heard of a 'B' meeting, but it was well known to the London poor of the period (and elsewhere too, for the procedure was widely copied) and to anyone interested in improving the condition of the poor in late Victorian times. G.R. Sims, now remembered (if at all) only as the author of 'Christmas Day in the Workhouse' and then a prolific and celebrated journalist, had written a good deal of *How the Poor Live* (1883) from material supplied him by the attendance officers and 'B' meetings. In turn, Andrew Mearns had pillaged *How the Poor Live* for his more famous pamphlet *The Bitter Cry of Outcast London*, published the same year. (Sims wrote that 'one or two unhappy fathers' had hanged themselves 'behind the domestic door' because they could not find money for boots for their children to attend school (pp. 18, 19) and the comment went into my manuscript. 'Where's the evidence?', asked the relentless John Saville, and the passage had to be modified.)

The Royal Commission on Housing, which sat in 1884-5, was heavily reliant on the work of the London school attendance officers. So, naturally, was the Royal Commission on Elementary Education, which reported in the later eighties. The most famous publication to rely on the work of the London 'visitors' as they were officially called was Charles Booth's massive *Life and Labour of the People in London*, published in several editions and many volumes between 1889 and 1903. Teachers, clergymen and journalists had previously reported on the 'sinks and dens' of London and other cities, but no information was as thorough and reliable as that of the attendance officers.

I did much of the work for this book in the friendly environs of the basement of County Hall. The building had formerly housed my employers, the London County Council, and was now the home of the Greater London Council. Much of the material was kept in the archives (under the prefix SBL, School Board for London) and had to be fetched. The chief fetcher, when he saw me coming, would comment jovially: 'Ah, Mr Rubinstein, more SBLs today?' I never again felt so at one with a subject as I did with the London School Board. Having taught the grandchildren and great-grandchildren of the school board pupils in the same areas (though in my case not in the same buildings, which, where they survived, were now mostly primary schools) I felt an almost mystic sense of solidarity with the school board members, teachers and attendance officers of the London School Board period. I felt that, like the attendance officers, I myself was the School Board Man.

There was then much and there has been since more criticism of the methods of discipline and the brainwashing of working-class children in huge classes, in which teaching was characterised by the unenlightened methods of the day. But I was not one of the critics. I have always been influenced by the early years I spent in the classroom and this was specially true in the late 1960s. I could not and cannot accept the view, persuasively argued by Stephen Humphries in *Hooligans or Rebels?* (1981) and others that rebellious children were fighting the good fight against middle-class oppression. For the underprivileged to rebel successfully they had to know why they were rebelling and against what. Sidney Webb in *London Education* (1904, pp. 3, 5-6) and (now a more acceptable name) Annie Besant were two of the contemporary socialists who hailed the work of the London School Board. Annie Besant wrote eloquently: 'Ignorance is a necessary condition for prolonged submission to remediable misery. The School Boards are teaching the children the beauty of order, cleanliness, and decency, and are waking up in them desire for knowledge, hopes and aspirations – plants unsuited for cultivation in the slums. They are sowing the seeds of a noble discontent with unworthy conditions...' ('The Socialist Movement', *Westminster Review*, July 1886, p. 213)

This view was unfashionable on the left in the 1970s, at least among those to whom school past and present could only be a means of social control. But I shall always think of the board schools as civilising agents and be glad that I was a lineal descendant of the overworked, underpaid teachers of that era. 'One generation stands on the previous generation's shoulders', John Saville once told me (a comment as valid and helpful as it is unoriginal), and nowhere is it more true than in education.

I was very inexperienced when I wrote that short (137 pages) book, published in 1969 as *School Attendance in London, 1870-1904: a social history*. I did not realise then that even academic books can sell, or at least sell better, if they have a catchy title. I tried to persuade Philip Larkin (who was in effect my publisher) to include illustrations (there were many to choose amongst) and reduce the price below the thirty shillings on which he insisted. In vain. He was always civil and friendly, but his verdict was: 'It will go like a bomb with everyone who's interested in school attendance in London', and that was that. The 'publicity machine' for the University of Hull, publisher, hardly existed. I did publish an article based on Annie Besant's successsful campaign in Tower Hamlets in 1888 for the London School Board ('All over the world your verdict will go') and on that of Stewart Headlam, the radical-socialist clergyman who stood for Hackney ('Vote for Headlam and Roast Beef, Free Schools and Secular Education'; *East London*

Papers, Summer 1970, pp. 11, 16), and some years later I wrote another account of the London School Board for a book edited by Phillip McCann (*Popular Education and Socialisation in the Nineteenth Century*, 1977), but I never wrote the major history of the London School Board I should have done. I had already pulled out the plums.

Most of such publicity as the book received was favourable, but Margaret Cole, herself an educationist who belonged to an older school of historians, slated it in *Tribune* (5 September 1969) as bottom-heavy with notes and sources. She praised my 'lively style', but said that in terms of the history of the London School Board (which I had not set out to write) my account was 'so scrappy as to be misleading'. I was devastated, and reflecting on my experience with Brian Simon I realised sadly the difficulties of satisfying all critics.

In the summer of 1971 my marriage to Shirley came to an end after fifteen years. Even now, over 25 years later, the memory is so green and so distressing that I do not want to dwell on the subject. I accept the major part of the blame for the break-up and I think that the broken marriage was in part the product of the demands for greater equality within marriage and elsewhere that women had rightly begun to make. Both of us later found happiness with other partners, but my divorce was much the most unhappy experience in my life and I would not wish that degree of agony on anyone. I thought that I wanted above all things to keep the marriage together and I watched myself doing everything possible to break it up. How could I behave like that, I asked Nick Tucker. He replied with a blindingly obvious statement which had not occurred to me: 'The emotions are stronger than the intellect.'

I left the marital home on August Bank Holiday Monday and spent a fortnight in a student house managed by one of my colleagues. It was empty apart from me. I then moved across the street to stay for some weeks with a young couple who belonged to the Socialist Teachers, and in the autumn to a furnished flat on Cottingham Road, all three addresses being within shouting distance of each other and of the university. Memory says that the furnished flat cost £18 a month. It belonged to an elderly woman who lived in Beverley and was in the early stages of what may have been Alzheimer's Disease. She sometimes forgot to cash my cheque, and on at least one occasion I had to contact her son to make sure that she received her money. The electricity supply operated on a coin meter; it was like being a student again.

I felt for the only time in my life the disadvantage of having no family and no other home in the United Kingdom apart from the one I had shared with Shirley. I became a burden to my friends; they must have groaned to see me coming. I found it difficult to understand what had happened to me and why it had happened. John Saville's wife Constance was an enormous help in those forlorn days and so too were Margaret Palfreman, Margaret Norcross and Jennie Hall. But one friend refused to go away on a country walking trip with me and another, who 'invited' me to his home for a weekend, made it clear that he would not have free weekends ad lib. He suggested, no doubt in desperation, that I might find it useful to spend a prolonged period in the United States. I knew that I was behaving badly in forcing other people to share the burden of my grief, but I was too distressed to be able to do much about it.

I did write to my sister Ellen to suggest that I might visit her for a period (though I don't know when it would have been, for the start of term beckoned), only to find that her own marriage was shaky and that a visit from me would not be advisable. She came to see me in Hull that autumn but her visit was not an unqualified success. I was grateful, however, that she had made the effort to cross the Atlantic to see me; whatever our failures of communication hers was an act of great generosity.

She and I had a successful weekend in Edinburgh, one of the happier events for me in that dreadful period. We stayed at a hotel, speculating on the reactions of the receptionist at being asked for single rooms by a man and woman of similar age who, as we fondly thought, did not resemble each other. I telephoned John Parker in London, I think having my first experience of the wonders of STD, which required no operator. 'Are you in London?' he asked. 'No, Edinburgh', I replied. Only those who remember waiting endlessly for an operator to connect them can appreciate the wonders of dialling all over the world (by nationalised telephone) unaided. John gallantly agreed to show Ellen round the Houses of Parliament when she returned to London.

As for my sons, of course I wanted at all costs to maintain contact with them. I realised how much the boys mattered to me, and in the face of the explosion of my world I wanted to limit the damage as much as I could. It was not easy to look after them, partly because I did not know how to cook in those days, partly because I had no real home in which to entertain them. (A student of mine made all four of us a meal on one occasion which my sons long remembered as the only decent meal that they had had at that flat.) I could not have been the only divorced father who owed an enormous amount to the local football side. Watching men chase a ball has an enormous advantage for spectators compared with such silent (for the audience) pastimes as the cinema or theatre. One can talk and shout and sing and, generally, interact. I felt and still feel that I owed Hull City, which we followed to a number of different locations in the north of England, an enormous debt.

Hull City has never been in the first division (later the Premiership). I have heard it suggested seriously that nothing would have lifted the status of the city's university so much as a first division football side and that may well be true. Certainly both town and university badly needed an element of glamour, and the later opening of the Humber Bridge (July 1981) as the then longest single-span suspension bridge in the world gave it only a temporary uplift. In later years when Peter and Johnny had gone to university and only Paul and I were left in Hull the club fell on particularly evil days; there were wide open spaces at its home at Boothferry Park. A fan told us at a match that the pitch was to be ploughed up for allotments and the produce carried away on the supporters' trains to and from Paragon Station. 'Well, ya gotta laugh, a'n ya?' he asked. You did indeed.

But in the earlier years, with the club in the second (now first) division we saw some exciting matches. We went to one with Andrew Dalby in the brief period when (it hardly seems possible now) Manchester United was in the second division. 'Waggy' scored a goal in front of our noses and another player scored a second. Manchester United beaten by Hull City 2-nil! It was the high point of our attendance at Boothferry Park.

Andrew was of great assistance during another, earlier weekend, when he came to Hull and helped me to look after the boys for a day. We went out walking on the Wolds near Hull and then returned to my flat for some sort of meal. Andrew discussed football with three boys aged 13, 10 and 8 for a solid hour or as long

178

as it took me to prepare the dinner. I have never been so grateful to him.

Andrew and my other RA connections did much for me in those months. I was away for part or the whole of a number of weekends, away from the depressing environment and the memories which I could escape more easily when I was not in Hull. I had EC meetings and other events to address or attend, and I was grateful for the good fellowship of my fellow EC members. Being on the way to a divorce, however, singled me out far more in 1971 than it would have done later, and one or two of my colleagues were shocked or disapproving.

The most valuable single act of assistance given me in those sad months was an invitation from Talal and Tanya Asad to spend Christmas 1971 with them in Cairo. Talal had leave of absence that year and was attached to the American University in Cairo. I was in doubt whether someone named Rubinstein would be granted a visa, but there was no difficulty. One of the books I took with me was, by chance, Israel Zangwill's *Children of the Ghetto* (1892). I was later to find that Zangwill was a valued ally to the women's suffrage movement before 1914, but I knew of him then only as a writer on Jewish life in East London. Hull University library's copy had a large Star of David on the cover. I wrapped it in brown paper, wrote 'Zangwill, Children' on the cover and set off. There was no difficulty about gaining admission to Egypt, for unlike the Soviet Union in those days reading matter was not examined or censored. There was also no problem about buying the whisky for which Talal and Tanya had expressed a craving, in the airport shop after I landed. (I wrote to Ellen about the Zangwill incident and she was in despair about my stupidity in taking the book. As usual I acted before thinking, and I have often suffered for behaving as if the usual rules (such as trains leaving at the scheduled hour) do not apply to me.)

This trip was my first visit to the developing world and it was of course immensely exciting. In the early morning Talal and I would converse on every subject under the sun and then Tanya would take me to visit the wonders of Cairo. To visit the Pyramids and the Sphinx, the Egyptian Museum with remains from the tomb of Tutankhamen, the magnificent mosques of the city and the main souk, the Khan El-Khalili, seemed like a dream come true. The

Asads pointed out the many small craftsmen's workplaces; it was like nineteenth-century London, as they commented. In general I found Arab and Turkish architecture less moving and impressive than Christian Gothic buildings, but the whole experience was so new and so foreign that I really had no frame of reference for comparison. (By the time I visited the Taj Mahal decades later I was less ethnocentric.) I did marvel at the intricacy of the architecture and design of the lacy mashrabiah windows. I visited the Pyramids on my own by bus, and was made much of for doing so. (I was taller than most male Egyptians, but my gender, hair and skin colour ensured that I did not stand out, nor did I feel much like Richard Burton visiting Mecca.) But the usual pattern was to visit sights with Tanya by taxi. When we arrived at least one mosque (or perhaps more) we were at once surrounded by a crowd of begging children. They were quickly dispersed by their parents, but like many Europeans I did not enjoy the experience.

We were shown remarkable hospitality by the Asads' friends, mostly Americans at the university. We would have to wait to eat until late in the evening, but then we had delicious and exciting meals. It was never more true for me than in Cairo that the best way to be a visitor in a foreign country is to keep one's ears open and mouth shut, but it is easier to bear this precept in mind than to follow it. On one occasion I managed to mistake the name of Mohammed Haikal, the famous Egyptian journalist (previously unknown to me), for that of G.W.F. Hegel, the German philosopher who had inspired Marx. I did not share the merriment which followed.

Although I had flown across the Atlantic on several occasions, I have always been frightened of flying. Returning from Cairo my plane was held up and forced to stack while awaiting a landing slot. I was terrified, certain that I was going to die, so I tried to devote my final moments to finishing the book I was reading. I did finish it and the plane landed without incident, to my great relief. Soon after my return to Hull in early 1972 there was another student sit-in, and once again I was prominent amongst the academic staff in giving it my support. (It seemed a good idea at the time.) Soon after the sit-in, in which emotions were high on all sides, I met Ann Holt.

Ann was a mature postgraduate student from the Fen country of Cambridgeshire, where the people had cold blood and webbed

180

feet, she once told me. She had studied at Hillcroft (adult) College in Surbiton and then gone to Hull to study Sociology and Psychology. She went to Hull, she said, because she had been told that the university was 'soft on mature students'. In 1971-2 she was 28 and was staying in the Asad flat looking after their cats. (I told my friend and former student David Martin later that I was living with Ann Holt. 'Does she keep cats?', he asked vaguely.)

The combination of Ann's residence at the Asad flat, my trip to Cairo and the excitement of the sit-in introduced us to each other and we began to live together on 21 March 1972, just under seven months after the break-up of my marriage. That was a Tuesday. That weekend I telephoned her from the Ramblers' Association's National Council in Liverpool to ask her to marry me. My excuse was that I was prone to act without thinking, but Ann was a mature and sensible woman who must have felt that she was in danger of being yoked to a madman. In any event, as I was still married to Shirley and under the procedure for divorce by consent of the Divorce Reform Act of 1969 would remain so until late 1973, she had not committed herself to anything irrevocable. Why, however,

Ann and David, newly-weds, Huntingdon, March 1974.

181

did she agree to come to Paris early the next month with a man she hardly knew, plus Chris and Jennie Hall? 'I could never resist an adventure', was her later reply.

In any event my good fortune was far greater than my deserts, as everyone who knows both Ann and me agrees. Not that our tastes are identical. She does not share my anachronistic fascination for the detail of party politics. Her mind is less rigid and more open to abstractions than mine, which needs the aid of proper nouns to make sense of things. It was not easy for her to begin to live with a man over ten years her elder, with three boisterous sons and friendships dating back twenty years. The course of the relationship is reminiscent in one respect of a reply which I heard a member of the Amadeus Quartet make to a questioner who wanted to know if the players had never had disagreements: 'We did have disagreements but we learned to overcome them.' And the learning process was a happy one.

On the other hand we both loved the British countryside, many parts of which we learned about together. We loved to travel, especially in western Europe and, as I shall show, in France. We both had a passion for historical architecture, which bemused some of our friends who might have been with us when we disputed whether a given window was thirteenth or fourteenth century, whether a given house had been restored out of recognition or was original Georgian. We loved music and are still ashamed to know as little about it as we do and, despite my growing deafness, we loved the theatre. I greatly admired Ann's ability to do anything, from understanding computers and repairing household gadgets to sewing, knitting, crocheting and collage. She was tolerant about my inability to do anything much other than to read books and write about what I read, though she did eventually teach me to cook and shoulder a minimum of housework. In any event living with another person is more than a question of old churches and visits to Manchester. We found that, though our temperaments were different and sometimes at odds, our views of life, politics, people and each other drew us ever closer together. And I was happily to find that, like Shakespeare's Cleopatra, 'Age [could] not wither her, nor custom stale her infinite variety'.

In fact, the only two points on which we were irreconcilable were cats and opera. Ann adored both. Cats terrified me, though

Dorothy and Horace ('George') Holt (Ann's parents) at home in St Neots, near Huntingdon, September 1998. Dorothy died on 27 December 1998.

I liked dogs. As for opera I found myself too often in the position of Mark Twain, who was said to have attended a performance of Wagner which began at 6.0, looked at his watch after two hours and found that it was 6.15. We learned to be tolerant of each other's idiosyncrasies in such matters.

Ann was the eldest of the four children of a working-class rural family in Cambridgeshire, and the only member in her generation or previous ones to stay at school past the age of 16. Her father was a plater in heavy industry, though he had been born a farmer's son, quarrelled with his family and lost his chance of the family farm. As Philip Larkin once observed graphically, family matters. Ann has not always found it easy to cross social classes or to move in self-confident bourgeois circles, in which verbal banter is a way of life. Neither of us in fact has ever found it easy to converse with strangers; I suppose that neither of us has much small talk. I did not find congenial the virtual total preoccupation of her father with cars and of her mother with her immediate family, and I have not always – or often – behaved well with them, though I have tried to compensate as far as possible by financial generosity. But the relationship between Ann and me has deepened with the years and it is gratifying to be able to write that in its 27th year it is in better shape than ever.

I will only add that despite the brief period which elapsed between the end of my marriage and the start of the relationship with Ann I remained in a distressed state about the end of my first marriage for a prolonged period. Nevertheless, from the first day of spring, 1972, I was able to concentrate on other things than myself and my woes. I must have become less than wholly intolerable to be with. John Saville went round for years afterwards telling Ann, me and anyone else who would listen how much happier I was now. And of course he was right.

Ann and I moved out of the Cottingham Road flat into a furnished house a mile or less from the university, then bought our first home on a mortgage. This was in Falmouth Street, again within a short distance of the university and handy for buses to the centre of Hull. The Falmouth Street house was cheap and small, with a yard in front and a small garden at the back. It seemed paradise to Ann and me and we spent fifteen happy years there. As I had a large room at the university for my work books, the house seemed quite large enough to me; one room was largely devoted to the work of the Ramblers' Association. Ann had never had her own house and she commented that she now had a room to cook in, another to eat in, two to live in, a bedroom, a bathroom and other rooms left over. This was not how our friends saw it. John Saville came, sat on our couch, looked round and pronounced: 'It's amazing what you can do with these rotten little houses.' (He came again and only just saved himself from repeating the same words.) Tanya Asad said that what would prevent her from living in a house like ours was the spectacle of the dustbins lined up in rows. As our dustbin was hidden away in a passage and near no other, this remark was obscure. But it should be added that this was Hull, where property was cheap; in the south of England the house would not have seemed so mean to our friends.

What made our situation worse in the eyes of the conventional was the fact that we had no car. This was at a time, 1972, when the British middle class had just completed its move to near-universal car ownership, though the two-car family was still far from common. I shared a car with a colleague for some time, a useful arrangement for us both, but one which inevitably came to an end when he felt the need for his own car. Since the summer of 1972 Ann and I have not owned a car. It was not only that we thought we were better ecologists and felt more self-righteous than other people. I was a university lecturer on a moderate salary and Ann was still the recipient of a student grant. I was paying towards the maintenance of my children and in those early years we could not have afforded a large house in a middle-class area of Hull or Cottingham or a car. In any case I had never enjoyed driving and Ann did not know how to drive.

Not having a car profoundly influenced our lives and also influenced other people's attitudes towards us. I have never been under any illusion; I have always realised that many men and a growing number of women care about their cars more than any personal relationship or any other possession. Some of our friends affected to ignore the fact that we had no car, while others felt threatened and were resentful or hostile. One of them asked: 'Haven't you got a car *at all*?' as if we might have a small one lying around half-forgotten. One of the staff at Coleg Harlech (where I was an external examiner in the 1970s), which is beautifully but remotely situated in North Wales, reflected for some time about our carless state and eventually burst out: 'You must be *rich*!'

In general we had no problem about urban life and, in a flat city like Hull, our bicycles were the answer to most transport problems. It was not so easy in the Ramblers' Association and we tended to drop out of organised rambles. We always tried to share the cost of transport whenever we were given a lift and some drivers did accept a financial contribution, to our satisfaction. We thought that in any case ramblers, having at least a nodding acquaintance with ecological issues, would see the positive side of there being at least one less car on the road. It was not that simple.

It did not take me long to appreciate the fact that everyone in society either had access to a car or – did not. I also realised that if a car owner put the case for fewer new roads and better public transport he or she was damned as a hypocrite; if a non-car owner put the case the charge was one of selfish pleading for oneself at the expense of the majority. I did not let that bother me. I was active in the later '70s both locally and nationally (representing the

Ramblers' Association) on the executive of Transport 2000, the public transport pressure group close both to the railway unions and to British Rail. We had an active local group in Hull, several of whom were ASLEF engine drivers; Ernie Prince, the branch secretary, Fred Mackrill and others were prominent among them. Tony and Kathleen Boughen, two live wires in Friends of the Earth, were also Transport 2000 stalwarts. I spent a good deal of energy in my middle years in Hull attacking road schemes, writing to the press to denounce over-generous car allowances and in general championing the cause of public transport.

Over thirty years after I took up this cause it has made some progress. It is widely admitted that Britain is unable to absorb an ever-increasing amount of traffic and that improved public transport is more efficient, more economic and better for the environment. Only public opinion is on the other side – including my father-in-law, who thinks that in wishing car usage to be restrained I want to bring back feudalism.

One of my early high points in the public transport cause was membership of the Independent Commission on Transport which had been convened and was chaired by Hugh Montefiore, then Bishop of Kingston-upon-Thames. Our executive secretary was Stephen Plowden, who was already a well-known expert on the subject. We had a number of other luminaries in the public transport field amongst our members; academics, environmentalists, members of women's groups and trade unionists. One of our members was my friend Colin Speakman, who was to become a leading figure in the field in years to come. He and a co-author wrote an excellent appendix on 'the impact on rural life of declining public transport services for communities and individuals'. They pointed out in their first sentence that between a third and half of country people in many rural areas suffered 'an isolation unprecedented since the age of the stagecoach'. (p. 323)

Hugh Montefiore was a good companion, with whom I kept in intermittent touch after his report was published in 1974. He seemed to me the very prototype of a benevolent, sometimes rather vague bishop, exemplified by his delight in the posters displayed in an urban street plagued by heavy lorries: 'Jugger off!' It was at first somewhat surprising to hear him reminisce about his Jewish childhood. Hugh (the age of surnames was now long gone) asked me

186

about a report on *Rural Transport in Crisis* (1973) which Colin, Chris Hall and I had written for the Ramblers' Association, and how the report of his committee could be prevented from sinking into oblivion as soon as published. The answer was, of course, that it could not, but I have in front of me sympathetic reviews in the *Times, Guardian, Sunday Times* and the *Observer,* and the Montefiore commission can claim to be among the early influences on a changing zeitgeist.

Despite my father-in-law's later accusation I faithfully explained to commission members how the motor car had transformed the lives of working-class people like my in-laws, and in discussion round the table this became abbreviated to 'David's parents'. The discussion survived in such a sentence as this one: 'Clearly we are witnessing a vast social transformation giving great convenience and pleasure to millions of people, but only at a huge sacrifice of some of the true riches of life and, indeed, of life itself.' (p. 260) But the Great British Public was at one with Edward Heath, who in 1966 had condemned any suggestion of restricting the motorist. 'Instead we must learn to cope with the motor car and to care for the motorist.' (quoted in *The Times,* 18 June 1974) Was this the only instance of Heath agreeing with Margaret Thatcher, who later proclaimed her allegiance to the Great Car Economy?

Meanwhile, other aspects of life went on. The boys stayed with Ann and me one or two nights a week and we took them on holiday. I was conscious of the fact that a divorced father could not rival a mother whose children thought of her large suburban home as theirs, as indeed it was. I felt, with my small house, like a character in an American film I saw during the period, who scrimped and saved to buy a second-hand car for his children, only to see their mother's new boyfriend present them with a large new one. The situation was not so crude in my case but I must be among many fathers who know that, once divorced, their position becomes more like that of favourite uncle than parent.

Ann and I took the boys to the United States for Christmas 1973 to spend Christmas with Ellen and her family. We also visited the Gaeblers in Chicago and Ann and I went to Washington and Philadelphia on our own before meeting the boys in New York. To this day I cannot recall without the sharpest anguish taking the boys to a Chicago museum and returning for them at an agreed time to find that they had been waiting in the American winter cold for half an hour or more; I had misread the closing time. Paul was only ten. I hope that he has forgotten that cold wait; I have not. I did not then realise that I would not again visit my native land for nearly a quarter of a century.

In the summer of 1974 we went with the Gaeblers and their three sons to Ireland, where we had a wonderful time, mostly in Killarney. It was the first of several visits to Ireland. A Hull friend later pointed out disparagingly that it took as long to get to the west of Ireland as to the south of France, but both have their glories which demand to be seen. The next year we took Johnny and Paul (Peter, at nearly 17, was too grown up and had taken to going to the music summer schools at Dartington Hall) to Menton, which was the first time the other members of the party had seen the Mediterranean. (I had briefly been to the area in the fifties.) My reward was for Johnny to say upon our return that he had never enjoyed a holiday so much.

From that time onwards our family holidays were mainly spent in France. Paul, being my youngest son, naturally had more holidays with Ann and me than his brothers, and I felt that I could not have been a wholly neglectful father because we I took him to France six years running – to Menton, Cannes, Les Marécottes in Switzerland but close to the French border which we often crossed, St-Lary-Soulan in the Pyrenees, Dieppe and Paris. Male Rubinsteins have had a scatological sense of humour back at least as far as my father, and the high point for Paul of the Pyrenean trip was my brief attack of diarrhoea. His derisory remarks about bicycle clips, I have to admit, reduced us all to helpless laughter.

Ann and I also enjoyed holidays on our own in this period (1972-9). Much as I missed the daily company of my sons, I did appreciate the flexibility which a life without children at home allowed us. We visited several parts of Britain, staying in expensive hotels on cheap weekend deals – Edinburgh, Carlisle, Helmsley in the North Yorkshire Moors and Stamford, Lincs, come to mind. We had repeated holidays in the north-west of Scotland, especially the islands which (with Annecy, in France) I think more movingly beautiful than anywhere else I have ever seen, and where I was to celebrate my 40th, 50th and 60th birthdays. We visited Italy several times, Prague, Leningrad and Istanbul, where the marvels of the architecture and art treasures were almost eclipsed by the glories of the food. We took Ann's parents to Paris in 1976; it was Dorothy's first foreign visit, at the age of 56, and George's first since his wartime service in India. We also stayed regularly at the Jackson flat in Westminster, which was useful both for research purposes and to attend concerts and the theatre.

Life at the university was not happy for me in the 1970s. My department, Economic and Social History, was divided into factions, partly over matters of policy, partly over personality. Academics are good at being bitchy, and I am alas better than most, but for a variety of reasons I belonged to no faction and life was increasingly lonely. If it had not been for my friends in the Sociology department and Colin Stoneman I would have felt very isolated. John Saville, for quite different reasons, shared my unpopularity and he and I in consequence drew closer to each other. It was in this context that David Martin and I edited John's festschrift, *Ideology and the Labour Movement* three years before he retired in 1982. The contributors were suitably starry, as befitted our dedicatee. They included the leading scholars Asa Briggs, Victor Kiernan, Sidney Pollard and Ralph Miliband, with whom John had been editing the *Socialist Register* for fifteen years. Margaret Cole was another contributor. By this time she and I had become correspondents and, on that level, friends. She wrote me a fascinating series of letters on the personalities and problems of Labour intellectuals in the 1930s and their relations with Ernest Bevin and other trade unionists. Other contributors were John's students or colleagues, and the book enjoyed reasonable critical success.

My own article dealt with the travails of the Labour left during the majority Attlee government of 1945-50. As with my school board work I felt that I was writing my own history or pre-history, for the people involved, some of whom like Michael Foot and Ian Mikardo were still alive, were the names with which I had grown up or knew of at LSE. It was a sad story, how the triumphant left gradually became an ineffective minority, partly through confusion over aims and inadequate leadership, partly because of their divisions over relations with the Soviet Union and other aspects of Communism, partly because of American influence – but chiefly because the British people had little passion for socialism as opposed to their desire for higher wages and more consumer goods.

The article, I think, has stood the test of time reasonably well, though the context of the period, though still only fifty years ago, is now a vanished world.

The article was one example of the fact that despite the downs and ups of my personal life in the 1970s I did not neglect research. I edited and contributed to a series of articles on British socialist, labour and radical history which had first been published in the weekly *Tribune*. It appeared in book form in 1973 as *People for the People* and consisted of short articles by experts written for a non-academic readership. I also edited a book of contemporary extracts on *Victorian Homes*, which was published in 1974. Though shorter than I had hoped it was quite comprehensive. It included sections on architecture and design, the homes of rich and poor, bathrooms and toilets, lighting and heating, the legal framework, houses and flats built for the respectable working class by employers, charitable agencies and local authorities, the efforts of Octavia Hill to house the very poor and the advent of garden cities. It was intended as a first step towards a bigger book on housing which never materialised, though several were published by other historians during the period.

I wrote an introduction and notes to the reprinted (first edition, 1913) autobiography of Frederick Rogers, trade unionist, advocate of old age pensions and founding chairman of the Labour Party (in its earlier incarnation as the Labour Representation Committee). I also wrote entries for the *Dictionary of Labour Biography* edited by John Saville and another colleague, Joyce Bellamy, on Rogers, Stewart Headlam, Annie Besant and Hubert Bland. I was grateful for the assistance with Headlam given me by Kenneth Leech, the Christian Socialist clergyman based in the East End of London; I was not to meet him for another twenty years, by which time I was working in the East End myself.

It will be seen that my publications in this period were either editing and/or articles, each time on a new subject. I have already mentioned that I wrote two more pieces on the London School Board. I spent ages writing an article on the impact of the bicycle on British society in the 1890s. The article was published in *Victorian Studies* in 1977 and working on it gave me enormous pleasure. Another article was on the Barnsley parliamentary by-election of 1897, when the Independent Labour Party put up Pete

Curran to stand against the miners' candidate in a mining stronghold. Not surprisingly Curran was badly beaten. I carried out part of the research at the Barnsley headquarters of the National Union of Mineworkers, Yorkshire branch. Arthur Scargill was then President, but I did not see him. The things I remember best about working there were the free photocopying facilities which I was given and being asked why, since I was what later came to be known as a tenured university teacher, I was still searching in the archives instead of leaving that work to young scholars (the article was published in the *International Review of Social History* in 1978, when I was 46).

I also wrote a piece about Ellen Wilkinson in *History Workshop Journal* (1979) discussing in some detail her sceptical attitude to the comprehensive school while Minister of Education in 1945-7. The article was commissioned after John Parker's sister Beryl had heard me criticise Wilkinson in a talk to a seminar at a History Workshop (the marvellous innovation masterminded by Raphael Samuel at Ruskin College Oxford) in November 1978. She reported me in somewhat misleading terms to her husband Billy, principal of Ruskin, who did not allow his absence from the lecture to prevent him from attacking me in such of the educational press as would publish his denunciation – one journal, I believe. (See *Education*, 1 December 1978, p. 535. He did not inform me of what he was doing and I knew nothing of it until told by one of my students.) It was a touching indication of the affection which Wilkinson had attracted from her juniors (Billy Hughes had been her parliamentary private secretary in 1945-7 and Beryl had been her private secretary) and also an illustration of the fact that most Labour people who were adults before 1945 thought that their principal educational aim should be a universal, free, divided system of secondary education. The grammar school was the working-class boy's path to success and nothing should be done to interfere with it. My article led to a flurry of others on the same subject in *History Workshop Journal*.

My other main publication (as editor) in the period was a new version of *Education for Democracy*, this one called *Education and Equality* and published by Penguin in 1979. The *Black Paper* writers were still active, and with the first election of the Thatcher government in 1979 some of their ideas (though not yet the reintroduction of grammar schools) came back into vogue. At the start Colin Stoneman agreed to co-edit again, but his interests had moved on, and Penguin's insistence on a shorter book with fewer articles than we had planned caused his resignation, much to my dismay. Like its predecessor, *Education for Equality* put a progressive view of educational questions at all levels in two dozen chapters. Brian Simon again contributed and there were also pieces by Howard Glennerster, Hilary and Steven Rose, A.H. Halsey, Caroline Benn and Ken Coates. This time there were articles on the education of girls and women, on black pupils and on educational practice in other countries. There was still, however, strong emphasis on the relationship between social class and education. As before the book was widely noticed, but it had little practical effect in an era of rampant Thatcherism.

Meanwhile I had been promoted to senior lecturer and, after the resignation of John Saville from the post of head of department of Economic and Social History in 1978, I took his place. It was a thankless task but the alternative seemed to be the break-up of the department, for which I could see no justification. Three of my colleagues refused to attend departmental meetings almost until the end of my three years as head of department for reasons which were not made explicit; partly, I think, because they thought the department should break up, partly because they thought John Saville had been badly treated, partly because they did not think that I should be his successor if successor there had to be. But I enjoyed the post in a perverse kind of way, got along well with the secretaries and the students and enjoyed also being on the University Senate.

By this time student representatives had found a place on Senate and it was amusing to listen to their duels with Stanley Dennison, the Vice Chancellor. Dennison liked to make the students lose their thread by constant interruptions and I have not forgotten one Students' Union president who said coolly: 'Please don't interrupt me, Vice Chancellor', and went on to make his point most effectively. In general my recollection of the Senate was that it was a body of old, male reactionaries, Hull having at that benighted time still to appoint its first woman professor. (All professors were members of Senate, plus non-professors who like myself were heads of department and a few elected representatives of other staff.) I frequently found myself in hot water for putting forward progressive views about this or that subject, and did myself no services. In general Senate was a grim affair and only J.P. Kenyon, the well-known professor of seventeenth-century history and *Observer* reviewer, and Philip Larkin could make the members laugh.

My reward for my three years as head of department was to receive a silver cup from the department's two secretaries inscribed to 'David Rubinstein, world's best boss'. It was a tribute of which I was of course hugely proud and remain so. My own epitaph for myself would have been 'He did his best', for I feel that during those tense years nobody could have carried out the head of department's task satisfactorily. I was, however, grateful for John Saville's steady support, even though he obviously felt the anomaly of being a member of a department which he did not head.

Meanwhile I was still active in the Ramblers' Association. My first major undertaking in this decade was to write a guide to the Wolds Way (1972), the route of which was still not definite, to popularise the concept and encourage walkers to use it. It was not social history, but as a member of our committee said, it was certainly the next thing to it. I took the reader across the 70 miles of the route from north to south (the reverse of the usual direction of guidebooks), telling them to turn left at the end of the field and so on, but I also provided a good deal of historical, architectural and some geological information about the Yorkshire Wolds. In that way I read up on the history and buildings of the area where I had lived since 1965 and grew to understand and love the Wolds more than I had done previously. Alan Dalton, who had been active in the East Riding Ramblers long before me, was a frequent and welcome companion on my walks along the route. The history, it must be said, was more reliable than other aspects of the book, and any account of flora and fauna of the area was largely absent. My recollection is that I identified four trees, at least two of them wrongly, in one case because I thought that any weeping tree must be a willow. Nor did I include map references, because I was not then confident in using them. One reader wrote to my publishers, Dalesman of Clapham (Yorks), impugning my 'sincerity' because of the absence of map references.

I wrote another account of *The Wolds Way* for the same publishers in 1979, correcting my earlier mistakes, adding map references, changing the route where necessary and, this time, following the route from south to north. (Why do things the easy way?) My walking companion was now Geoff Eastwood, who since my resignation as Area secretary in 1972 had become the titan of the East Riding ramblers, a member of the RA's national executive (eventually its chairman) and almost as much the local farmers' hate figure of the '70s as I had been in the '60s. Geoff was also a leading personality in Ramblers' Holidays, a separate organisation whose profits subsidised the RA and, in his spare time (as we all tended to feel about our jobs) a lecturer at Humberside College (later polytechnic, later still, university). In a real sense Geoff was for a prolonged period the Chris Hall of our Area.

The second edition of *The Wolds Way* was, as indicated, a more professional job than the first, and it was still strong on history and architecture. The greatest tribute paid it was by a local journalist who wrote that it could be 'read with much pleasure by those who have never walked the Wolds Way and who never intend to!' (*Hull Daily Mail*, 17 August 1979). (My preferred comment on the first edition had been a note from Philip Larkin, who had prettily acknowledged my gift to the university library of 'your charming, though pedestrian' guide.) Although the Countryside Commission published its own guide after the Wolds Way was officially opened my version was read for years afterwards. And the publicity given to the route by these two editions did have the intended effect of pushing the project towards a successful conclusion. By the time that my second edition was published in 1979 the Wolds Way was only three years away from opening.

Meanwhile I was still a member of the RA national executive, and in 1972 I was elected the association's vice chairman. Unusually there were two candidates for this post. National Council took place in Liverpool, where on the Friday night I left Chris Hall to canvas for me if he chose while I went with a show of insouciance to Birkenhead to visit Clive and Masha Davies. The next day the vote took place, Tom Stephenson as president in the chair. My name was called, and after identifying myself I left the room. (The other candidate did not.) I was told that Tom held his own ballot paper up to show the delegates the form on which they had to vote; he had already marked the paper with a cross for my opponent which at least the front rows of delegates could see. Despite this I was elected by 38 votes to 28, and in the normal course of events would have been elected the association's chair three years later.

That National Council was also notable for me in debating with Frank Head in public session our attitude to industry in national parks. My view was that suitable small-scale industry should be encouraged and subsidised in the parks, to ward off the threat of mining (like the potash I had tried to stop in the North York Moors), afforestation and other industries incompatible with protecting natural beauty. Frank took the more purist line that for the RA to welcome industry, even carefully selected, would 'open the door to industries of all kinds' in national parks (reported in *Rucksack*, Spring 1972, p. 17). Shortly thereafter Frank and I, good friends at the time, were the chairman (for the second time in his case) and vice chairman of the RA.

I enjoyed being RA vice chair and I liked working with Frank Head, who was a retired research chemist and a veteran of the walking movement from before the RA's birth in 1935. He was to serve for forty unbroken years on the RA executive and to die in May 1984 in his late 70s while walking in his beloved Peak District. He was a gentle, kindly, witty, dedicated man, who was not without a due measure of stubbornness when required. It fell to me be the principal speaker when a ceremony was held late in 1987 to mark the purchase by the National Trust (with funds provided by the RA) of South Head hill (1600') near Hayfield in his honour. I used to tell him that when he said he was 'Head of the National Executive' it gave him an unfair advantage in elections.

It also fell to me to ring up Frank and tell him in early 1974 that Chris Hall, our secretary, was leaving us for an appointment as director of the Council for the Protection of Rural England. A long pause and then: 'You've knocked me sideways.' My recollection is that Chris left us for a salary of £7,000 a year, considerably more than we were paying him. (My own salary as a university lecturer at the time was just over £4,200.) At the time the CPRE job also seemed a bigger challenge, though I doubt that it would do today. Chris had also had his differences of opinion with the RA's 'Old Guard', differences which seemed severe at the time but which I find difficult to recall in detail now. I have already given some idea of the RA's debt to Chris, which was to extend far beyond his period as secretary.

The person appointed to replace Chris decided not to take up the position and we appointed Alan Mattingly, a youthful member of the EC, without readvertising. Alan took up the post on or close to his 25th birthday. He already had given much valued service to countryside causes and wanted to respond to what he regarded, he wrote, as 'a rare if not unique opportunity'. If there were those who thought him rather young they could be consoled by thinking that time would mitigate that problem, but they were not to know that Alan would serve us for 24 years before retiring, still below the age of 50, in 1998. Alan had a different and less spiky personality than Chris (come to that, a less spiky personality than almost anyone) and he trained himself to become a witty and effective speaker. He was similar to Chris, however, in having a razor sharp mind, comprehensive knowledge of countryside issues and total dedication to the work of the RA. His value to the RA was inestimable and his departure a severe blow even if, as he said modestly, no one was indispensable. I have known three RA secretaries (Alan later became director); Tom Stephenson, Chris Hall and Alan Mattingly, the last two very well, and I think the RA has been almost uniquely fortunate to have had staff of their calibre. Their personalities and

Alan Mattingly at the end of his 24-year tenure at the Ramblers' Association; Aberdeen, April 1998.

196

experiences were different, but their dedication and achievements were in all three cases immense.

It would not have occurred to me in 1972 that I would have resigned from the RA's executive without becoming chairman. But I did so, and the cause was the failure of the responsible quango, the Countryside Commission, to make greater progress with developing the route of the Wolds Way, a subject which was naturally dearer to me than it was to other EC members. The matter came to a head in late 1974. I was particularly angry that the Commission had bent the knee to my old antagonist Lord Middleton by keeping the Wolds Way largely off his land and, in the beautiful Wharram Percy area, following a minor road.

I have no wish to examine the details of the row which followed. What is pertinent is that I wrote a press statement in November 1974 in the name of Geoff Eastwood, East Riding Area Secretary (with his permission of course). Drawing on a famous attack on the House of Lords by David Lloyd George I referred to the Commission as 'the landowner's poodle' and was disowned (or at least not supported) by my colleagues on the executive. I resigned angrily almost on the eve of the National Council at which I was due to be elected chairman. Thunderous silence followed; members of Council did not want a fight over what seemed an arcane issue and I had an object lesson in the truth of the adage: 'Never resign.' The incident did provide me, however, with one of my best stories. A friend on the executive (whom I am tempted to name) told me: 'Even people who don't like you admire your powerful brain.' I don't know how I refrained from replying: 'Even people who like you think you're an idiot.'

My recollection is that I behaved extremely badly over an incident which a degree of commonsense and proportion would have prevented from taking place at all. I was rude to or snubbed at least two EC members whom I met by chance, and I had to write a grovelling letter of apology to Wally Smith, our universally loved treasurer, for walking past him without speaking near my old stamping ground, the London School of Economics.

Apart from (I hope) learning something from this incident, I had the last laugh in two respects. The first was that I persuaded our Area president, by that time Kevin McNamara, to initiate a short parliamentary debate on the Wolds Way. This took place on

19 June 1975 and I wrote his speech. The landowner's poodle was paraded for all the world to see, and though Kevin would not go so far as to adopt it as his own, he quoted the relevant section of Geoff Eastwood's press statement verbatim and commented that his 'strong words...in the circumstances seem entirely appropriate'. He did say off his own bat that 'the creation of the Wolds Way has been delayed and betrayed by the Countryside Commission, the body charged with bringing it into existence.' He also called for the membership of the commission to include representatives of 'the interests of countrygoers – principally walkers, pedal cyclists and nature lovers.' In his reply Denis Howell, the Minister of Sport, rejected the poodle, defended the Commission but acknowledged that it should be more representative. 'As and when I can', he said, 'I shall broaden [its] membership.' (893 *HC Deb.*, 5s., 19 June 1975, cols 1804-20.)

The following year my friend Gerald McGuire was appointed a member of the Countryside Commission. He did not like to think, and did not think, that the poodle was responsible for his appointment – but I did. When the Thatcher government was elected in 1979 and he lost his place on the Commission he may have become a little more reconciled to the poodle. And my figure of speech was echoed in more respectable circles. I was pleased to note that Christopher Brasher, a leading figure in the outdoor world, charged that the Commission had 'never had any bite and it is known not to use its bark' (*Observer*, 9 February 1975). I wondered, but not for long, about the source of his metaphor.

My other 'last laugh' was that after three years sulking in my tent (during part of which time I represented the RA on Transport 2000's executive), though continuing my work at Area level, I attended National Council at Keele in 1978 and was re-elected to the EC. In 1981 I again became vice chairman and in 1984-7, the association's chairman. I enjoyed enormously my service in this period, especially being chairman in 1985, jubilee year, but I was sometimes reminded of the reader who reputedly told Arthur Conan Doyle that when Sherlock Holmes fell off the Reichenbach Falls he may not have died, 'but he was never the same man afterwards'. Neither was I. It had been a mistake to resign.

CHAPTER 8

Hull and Tours: the eighties

ANN AND I SPENT a gloomy election night 3-4 May 1979 at Valdo Pons's house, watching on television the ineluctable victory of the Conservatives and Mrs Thatcher's accession to Downing Street. After the election transmission ended we cycled home in the grey dawn; we have often commented subsequently that we could not have known that our lives had changed irrevocably. Among the disasters which befell us as the direct result of that election and its successors was the loss of my job in 1988 (followed by the loss of another in 1992). It was, however, time for me to feel personally the effect of the political process. It had been in a sense uncomfortable to pontificate about the wickedness of the Tories while not suffering directly from their policies. And we had little real understanding before 1979 of just how wicked the actions of the Tories would be after that date.

Many of the Labour-voting middle class now feel that there was much to be said for Mrs Thatcher, that her behaviour and rhetoric may have been extreme but that some or many of the things she did were necessary. I am not among those who hold this view. Kingsley Martin, for many years editor of the *New Statesman*, wrote a quarter of a century after Franco's victory in the Spanish Civil War that it had been a tragedy 'unalloyed with any comfort that I can find' (*New Statesman*, 20 April 1962, p. 556). In the milder British context I similarly find no comfort in thinking of the profound and apparently permanent changes of the Thatcher period.

Britain in 1979 was not a country on the way to oblivion. Its failures were not a numbing equality, an approximation to bureaucratic Soviet Communism. Rather it suffered from too great economic inequality, injustice to women and racial minorities, and too little concern for the environment. Strikes (days lost through industrial disputes) were unremarkable on an international comparison and declining in the 1970s; only 1979 itself showed a sharp rise and the ineptitude of the Callaghan government bears much of the responsibility for that (see *Social Trends 1980*, p. 127; *1988*, p. 76). In many cases, moreover, the strikes of the 1970s resulted from a period of inflation from which the whole of the industrialised world suffered. In any event the withdrawal of labour, however inconvenient for the middle classes, is a fundamental human right which any government should be very careful of abridging.

Conservative policy between 1979 and 1997 had four main aims. These were privatisation of publicly owned industries, reducing the social services, increasing economic inequality and destroying the bases of a pluralist society. They were aided by a press overwhelmingly supportive of the Conservatives and anxious to put the best gloss on whatever the government did. Privatisation has led to reduced prices or lower price increases in some cases. But often, as with telecommunications, this was the result of technological change which would have come about whether the industries were publicly (as in France) or privately owned. Privatisation has increased unemployment, led to difficulties in the servicing of appliances, and made more arduous and expensive other forms of travelling than by private car. It has enormously increased the power and wealth of the handful of (almost exclusively) men at the head of privatised industries.

The unemployment which the Conservatives set out to increase from 1979 was paralleled by deterioration in the social services. Pensions and other benefits were tied to prices, not earnings, so that pensioners in particular became poorer relative to other people. The unemployed were blamed for their unemployment; I recall no talk of a 'dependency culture' in the fifties and sixties when there were jobs for all those who wanted them. Benefits became ever more restrictive and services declined. The results included huge waiting lists and cancelled operations (as I know to my cost) in hospitals, larger class sizes in schools, the decay of council houses and increased homelessness.

As to economic inequality, this was fostered partly because the Conservatives believed that the spread of income was too narrow, partly because they thought the triumphant rich would give work to the poor. This is the oldest of 'economic doctrines' and should be the most discredited, because providing jobs to service the rich leads neither to economic nor social stability. A good summary of this gloomy creed was given by Nicholas Scott, then Social Security Minister, when he said in 1991: 'This government deliberately set out in 1979 to increase the ability of people to earn more, to retain more of what they earn, and to contribute to the general prosperity. This has happened. There have been some people who in a sense have been left behind in that movement. Their standard of living has still gone up, but not nearly as fast, and the gap has widened.' (quoted in the *Guardian*, 9 April 1991). Apart from the hotly challenged statement that the standard of living of the bottom group rose over the period, the doctrine claims that only by making the rich richer can 'the general prosperity' increase. The kindest description of this point of view is wishful thinking.

As to Conservative attacks on pluralism, one thinks of the systematic way in which they greatly reduced the powers of local government and the trade unions, and their outraged attacks on clergy brave enough to point out the reality of what their policies were doing to society, particularly the inner city. A country without a written constitution necessarily depends on the forbearance of its governors to prevent all power from being concentrated at the top. It is perhaps the gravest indictment of the Thatcher and Major governments that they should have regarded any other centres of power as illegitimate and that they should have done so much to strengthen what was already the most unchallenged central government in the western world.

One adds to the above indictment the deliberate fostering during these years of the crudest forms of xenophobia, except in relation to the United States, where the bulldog continued to be a lapdog. One thinks more generally of the manner in which the ethos of public service was replaced by self-service, and the growth of crime and anti-social behaviour in the past twenty years. One thinks of the way in which the somewhat self-satisfied notion of the 'typical British compromise' disappeared to be replaced by 'conviction politics'.

Most people experienced in the period a rising living standard which owed little or nothing to government action. Indeed, it was due in some part to the fact that trade unions had not been entirely destroyed and continued to exercise their legitimate role of working to improve working conditions. The movement for greater rights for women and ethnic minorities had a measure of success despite, not because of the government. Much of the population did not think that they were directly affected by the actions of the government but those who did, apart from the rich, usually suffered.

It must be said, however, that the Conservatives had a much clearer (even if evolving) idea of their political aims and especially how to achieve them than Labour has ever had (perhaps one should stipulate the pre-Blair Labour Party). It must also be added that they worked during their years of power with the grain of economic and social change which destroyed so much of heavy industry and with it so much of the traditional working class. The Britain of the computer and the global economy, the Britain of the middle-class majority, in which the percentage of the workforce employed in manufacturing has declined from 37 per cent in 1961 to 18 per cent in 1991 (Alissa Goodman, Paul Johnson, Steven Webb, *Inequality in the UK*, 1997, p. 90) was bound to see important changes. The charge against the Conservatives is that they pushed forward these changes as brutally and divisively as they could. As the Labour Party's 1997 election manifesto put it, 'our society is more divided than it has been for generations' (*New Labour because Britain deserves better*, p. 11).

Over the Conservative years while the social services were cut taxes rose, though the advent of North Sea oil should have enabled the government both to improve services and reduce taxes. Their publicity machine and the compliant press, however, managed to persuade many voters that income tax, the fairest tax, was the only one levied on the population (apart from the extravagant levies of 'high-spending Labour [local] authorities'), and that the percentage of income taken in all forms of taxation consequently declined. The reality was that total taxation as a percentage of income steadily rose during the period and its incidence became steadily less fair. (See Christopher Johnson, *The Economy under Mrs Thatcher 1979-90*, 1991, p. 292; *Labour Research*, March 1997, p. 27.)

But in the spring of 1979 all this lay ahead. An early taste was the introduction of cuts in grants to universities which began as early as 1981 and seemed to be based on a 'Baedeker principle', that the more beautiful the location of the university (or perhaps the more successful its football side) the safer it was from cuts in its grant. If I recall correctly, such is (or at least was) the secretive nature of British government that it was very difficult even to discover who were the members of the University Grants Committee.

Hull scored badly either on the Baedeker or the football criterion, and in 1981 the cuts hit it hard. The over 60s (one was then appointed until the age of 67) disappeared from the campus, but at the time we thought that there would be no more cuts. It was not to be so. There was a strong case for saying that British universities provided too luxurious an education for too few students, that higher education should be a right, not a privilege, that numbers of students would have to rise and conditions amongst university staff would necessarily have to worsen. There was no case, however, for dismissing hundreds if not thousands of university staff in the middle of their careers for reasons of political dogma.

One highly placed official of the University of Hull told me in 1981: 'Let us choose the staff to get rid of. We know whom to pick.' I thought to myself: 'I'll bet you do.' I was then and remain convinced that the government wanted to rid the universities of troublesome departments (e.g., sociology) and individuals (i.e., left-wingers). It failed to take into account, however, the nature of universities, in which both heads of departments and vice chancellors were academics who had risen through the ranks and who had to co-operate daily with their junior colleagues. None of these people wanted to see their universities go up in flames as outraged staff and students protested against the sacking of popular colleagues. It was not possible to select for the chop the troublemakers or even the non-publishers, who might contribute greatly to the lives of their universities in a variety of other ways. There was only one means of getting rid of staff which had any semblance of objectivity and that was on grounds of age. Senior staff, often in the nature of things highly conservative, were those who lost their jobs – and for what? Can it be argued that British higher education gained in consequence?

*   *   *

Ann and I suffered a severe personal loss at the end of 1980 by the death of our friend Margaret 'Espinasse. She was a retired reader in English Language at Hull whose husband Paul had been a professor of zoology there. She had perhaps both the virtues and limitations of a middle-class Scotswoman of her generation. She was one of the most upright and honest people I have ever met (as was my mother; they were born a few days apart in December 1903). She was an intellectual of intellectuals, passionate about reading, left-wing politics and serious music, insistent on 'hard work, plain facts and sound judgment' in the words of her *Times* obituary (12 February 1981). She was a great Hull patriot, in terms both of the town and, particularly, its university. The range of her knowledge put to shame the younger lecturers of my day. She had visited New York in the late 1920s and loved it. She kept her subscription to the *New Yorker* until almost the end of her life, but she never returned to the USA.

She had visited France and Italy repeatedly but hardly ever gone to any other country. Her attitude to Germany was that of someone who had suffered deeply from war and could not forgive the other side. Indeed, compassion was not prominent among her attributes. She was often ill in later life and after the death of her husband I tentatively suggested to her on one occasion that she might wish to live with or near one of her two daughters. 'Why should I ruin their lives?' was the characteristic reply. But we loved her and she loved us, especially Ann. We learned a great deal from her, both factually and personally, and her death was a grievous blow, as it was to my colleagues Joyce Bellamy and John Saville with whom as editors she had worked on the pioneer and massive venture the *Dictionary of Labour Biography* towards the end of her life. Ann had also worked with her during the period when both of them were involved with the dictionary.

*   *   *

I realised by the early 1980s that though editing books and writing articles was fun it achieved little or nothing (at least at that time at Hull) in terms of promotion. The only way to rise was to write books. It had taken me fifteen years to understand this, and perhaps that amount of time before I felt ready to undertake the formidable research involved in writing a book-length work of social history which, because of the immense amount of available primary and secondary sources, must be one of the more difficult disciplines for would-be authors.

Before this time I had considered myself a social historian of modern Britain whose special interest was labour history. As is often said, historians are not insensitive to the times in which they live; indeed, because of their occupation they are likely to be more sensitive than other people. I had rejoined the Labour Party but was pessimistic about its future. I knew enough labour history and understood British society well enough to be aware that the Labour Party would die very hard and that it would certainly not be superseded by the new Social Democratic Party which the media were pushing so strongly, but I thought of Labour as a basically conservative organisation. The socialist past which had so fascinated historians, including me, was ancient history. In any event its importance had often been exaggerated. The organised working class was in the process of emancipating itself, not by throwing off its chains and conquering power, but by disappearing. Labour history, in short, began to seem to me to smack of antiquarianism.

My last contribution to the field was an article on 'Trade unions, politicians and public opinion, 1906-1914', concentrating on reactions to the great strike wave of 1910-13, for *Trade Unions in British Politics*, edited by Chris Cook and Ben Pimlott and published in 1982. I was particularly glad to write the article both because I had long been interested in the subject and period and because I had failed to write a similar article for *Essays in Labour History*, edited by Asa Briggs and John Saville a decade earlier. I had then been engaged in amenity work, probably writing my Fabian pamphlet with Colin Speakman, and having agreed to John Saville's request to write an article had to tell him that I could not complete it in the allotted time. I was also far more experienced and well read in labour history by the end of the 1970s than I had been when asked to write the earlier article. My recollection is that Ben Pimlott (not yet famous as the biographer of Hugh Dalton, Harold Wilson and the Queen) asked me to contribute because he thought that, though a left-winger, I was a sensible one. Was this a compliment?!

By 1980 the women's movement had gathered strength. A new school of feminist historians had begun to change radically and permanently our understanding of social history by supplying the most important missing element, the lives, aspirations and activities of women. I found my social history teaching more and more dominated by women's history, which I had taught in one form or another

205

since I first arrived in Hull. There were not many of us in the field in the 1960s but interest and numbers increased with the rise of the women's movement. The appearance not only of works by new historians but of Virago reprints transformed understanding of the subject.

In consequence I put on a course wholly devoted to women's history. My chief research interest was the study of disadvantaged groups and the way in which they had striven to improve their conditions and change society. Although the working-class movement was the outstanding example, the outcome in modern times was, in my eyes, disappointing. (The miners' strike of 1984-5 had not then taken place, but it can be seen as the last gasp of an older tradition.) The modern women's movement was a reality, the most hopeful feature of modern British society, and it drew support from its past. This seemed to me to be the most promising field for an academic of my way of thinking. I make no claim to be the only British male historian in the field of women's history nor the most prominent of such (both such claims would obviously be false), but I am one of the few who is motivated by sympathy for the manifestations of the women's movement, including the militant suffragists of the early twentieth century.

It was not an easy field to enter. Feminist historians were generally uneasy about male colleagues. I was not asked to contribute articles to books in the field in the way I had often been asked to contribute to books on other topics within my range of interest. I did not always agree with the methods or conclusions of feminists. I wondered at an advertisement I once saw for an adult education course on women's studies in Hull, inviting prospective students to understand how and why women were disadvantaged and what they could do to change their lives. (What, I wondered, would have been the reaction to advertising a course in labour history in the same way?) But women's history is a field from which I have gained enormously and I have never regretted the ten years or so which I devoted to it from the end of the 1970s in terms of research and writing.

The jubilee of the Ramblers' Association was due to take place in 1985. Andrew Dalby and I had planned to write jointly a book on its history, when a proposal I had circulated to publishers was accepted and I dropped the plan for the RA book. I had, after all, given up enough of my career prospects and leisure to the interests of the RA. The person chosen to take my place was Ann Holt. Ann had followed a number of different occupations since we had joined forces in 1972 and she was soon to undertake a detailed study of girls' prospects and ambitions in East Riding secondary schools. She had always been interested in the rambling movement, however, and has now (1998) a long list of publications on the subject.

The book she edited was entitled *Making Tracks: a celebration of fifty years of the Ramblers' Association* (1985). I was by that time the RA national chairman and the list of contributors reads like a list of my friends in the RA. They included Andrew Dalby, Tom Stephenson, Chris Hall, Alan Howard, Alan Mattingly and Colin Speakman. (I wrote a brief final chapter.) Another contributor was Peter Melchett, whose trajectory through the RA was like a rising meteor before he finally found his niche as executive director of Greenpeace. I was initially prejudiced against him as a descendant of Alfred Mond of ICI and a hereditary peer, which demonstrates just how wrongheaded one (I at least) can be. I felt properly chastened when Peter came to meetings of the EC in 1984-5 in his shorts, having travelled by bicycle, and sporting a large COAL NOT DOLE badge in support of the striking miners.

As for me my choice of a topic in women's history was initially inspired by the early twentieth-century writer Holbrook Jackson, whose book *The Eighteen Nineties*, originally published in 1913, I had owned in a Penguin version since my undergraduate days. Jackson's book was fascinating but despite his title he had devoted himself largely to discussion of literary trends. I too saw the 1890s as a watershed, not only in literature but also in much else. Shamelessly pinching a title from Royden Harrison, whose groundbreaking study of the mid-Victorian labour movement *Before the Socialists* had been published in 1965, I called my book *Before the Suffragettes: women's emancipation in the 1890s*.

I had two terms' study leave during the course of the research for the book, and Ann and I were glad that we had bought our first London flat in 1979, about the time that I began work on it. The flat was a tiny one in St John's Wood, in a block built in the 1930s when there was a fashion in certain 'advanced' circles for minimal possessions and minimal living accommodation. I would have been far too terrified and Ann far too fond to have tried to swing a cat, but had we wished to do so the only room in our studio flat would have been too small. We had a sofa-bed which occupied a third of the living area when extended and Ann commented that our ability to survive ten weeks in such limited accommodation was a good reflection on our relationship. But we were both relieved when we moved to a larger flat (two rooms, both of cat-swinging size) in West Hampstead on Ann's fortieth birthday in 1983. We kept the latter flat for over fifteen years, sometimes using it as our main home.

I wrote mainly about new developments in the lives of women of the 1890s, or about earlier initiatives which took firmer root in that decade. These included employment of middle-class women as journalists, factory inspectors, doctors and in other occupations. They included the growth of women's trade unionism and participation in the political process as suffragists, canvassers in general elections and candidates for local office. They included notable success in higher education and leisure activities among which bicycling, the subject of my earlier article, and hockey loomed large. I wrote about literature, the phenomenon known as 'the revolt of the daughters' (who wanted their own lives, uncensored reading matter, adventures and latchkeys) and the so-called 'New Woman' of the period, on whom I hoped to have shed new light. I also wrote about love and marriage and about women's legal position. My conclusion was that the many forms which the women's movement took in the 1890s laid the ground for the revolt in the next decade of the militant suffragists, known vulgarly as the suffragette movement.

The book was favourably noticed then and later, but one reviewer commented sourly that I had written about women in the 1890s simply because that was the period which I knew about. I hope that the content of the book shows that he was wrong. In any case I learned a good deal from writing it. The book was published in 1986 by the Harvester Press. I had not anticipated that I would write the first draft in France.

In 1977, when I was external examiner at the Polytechnic of Central London, now the University of Westminster, I learned that my friend Philip Bagwell, the much-loved professor of Economic History, was retiring from that institution. I applied for his post when it was advertised and was appointed to it by a committee to whom John Saville acted as external assessor. It was then that my difficulties began. I wanted to move from Hull and to be promoted, for though the job was not advertised as a chair I would presumably have become a professor in due course. I would also have had all the research and other advantages which London had to offer.

On the other hand I had a cushy billet in Hull. I taught what I wanted to teach, had a large office, a splendid library close at hand and walked to work. Property and living costs were cheap and the glorious scenery of the north of England was within easy reach. At the poly I would have much less generous accommodation, longer teaching hours and a wider range of teaching, much of which I would have had to prepare first. My research too would have suffered, for hardly anyone teaching history in a polytechnic in those days apart from Philip Bagwell himself managed to combine the heavy teaching and administrative load with writing. Both Ann and I were uncertain but in the end, causing myself maximum embarrassment and the people at the poly maximum irritation, I declined the post. The refusal sentenced me to remain at Hull till I was asked to retire, long before I would have had to leave the poly. But it allowed me to continue my research and to live and work (as professor) in France four times.

Andrée Shepherd had been a lecturer in the French department at Hull in the 1960s where she had been a livewire in the university's socialist group and had made many long-term friends. Among them was John Saville. Andrée returned to France in the early 1970s and a decade later was teaching in the English Department of the University of Tours, in the Loire Valley. She contacted John Saville in 1982 to ask for his assistance in finding a temporary replacement for a newly-appointed professor at Tours who had accepted a post as chef de cabinet to a minister in the socialist government led by Pierre Mauroy. John suggested Stephen Kirby, a Politics lecturer who duly took up the post. A year later Andrée again contacted him. The absent professor, a M. Loing, was still 'loin', in Paris. Could John suggest another name? He racked his brains and fell back on me. His suggestion of my name to Andrée was the work of a moment but the most momentous and best thing he ever did for me after my initial appointment at Hull.

Ann and I were to have in all some four experiences of living and working in France. Before accepting each one we suffered from

*Ann and David, ramblers; Col de la Forclaz, Switzerland
(near Chamonix), July 1987.*

*Ann and David, ramblers;
below La Meije (near
Briançon), August 1995.*

the acutest indecision, but the experiences were hugely successful and irrevocably changed the course of our lives. (Among other things it determined the destination of most of our holidays in later years.) Ann had little French in the summer of 1983, though she learned a lot subsequently, and the level of my French, while not bad, has always been a disappointment to me. We had no prospects for a home, knew nobody in France except Andrée Shepherd (and her not well) and had no idea of what to expect. Stephen Kirby was helpful in telling us about Tours and the English department, but in the end it was for Ann and me to 'weird our ain drang'. Shortly before we were due to leave I met on the station platform at Doncaster Howard Elcock, a former member of the Hull Politics department who had moved to become Professor of Politics at Newcastle Polytechnic. I told him what Ann and I were going to do. 'You jammy bugger!', he said. 'You lucky sod!' He was right, but it did not seem so to us at the time.

I was then 51; Ann was just 40. By that time we were already visiting France regularly, as described in the last chapter, and in the summer of 1983 we took a long rail tour as far as Biarritz and Marseille, with many stops on the way. Among them was Tours, which we liked at once and which I had not seen since my introduction to France during my bicycling holiday in 1952. But our return there the following autumn, to begin our year's residence, was inauspicious. We had decided to break our journey in Paris but found to our consternation that there was no room at the inn, or at least at no hotel which we passed and could afford. (A huge medical conference was taking place at the time.) And so we walked through Paris overnight, watching a moon which looked as though it was suspended just above the roof of Notre Dame, spending a long period on the steps below Sacré Coeur and helping a river barge to cast off in the dawn. We thought it was a marvellous, romantic experience, but when we told friends in Tours what we had done they were aghast at our foolhardiness. In any event we took the first train from the Gare d'Austerlitz to Tours to begin our new life. Since that day we have counted ourselves as francophiles, and it must be said that love of a country must have some basis if it increases with knowledge of it.

Andrée and Bob Shepherd, who had met each other at Hull, were away from Tours for family reasons when we arrived there.

They were to be of the greatest assistance to us during that year, 1983-4, but in terms of finding a flat we were on our own. We had left it too late to find a furnished flat and had to settle for something unfurnished. What we found was, as Bob said later, 'banal enough'; a ground floor flat with a bedroom, bathroom, kitchen and sitting room. The wallpaper was hideous. So far so bad, because the flat had to be furnished and we had no furniture, but it was located close to Les Studios, a cinema with several screens which showed many classic French and foreign films. (I could understand the French sub-titles to foreign films but French films were beyond me. Ann, who studied French systematically, soon had no problem with them.) It was near to one of the most charming markets in Tours, in Place Blanqui surrounded by half-timbered houses, and also close to the cathedral and the rue Colbert, the 'Latin Quarter of Tours' as I have heard it called. There were also substantial remains of a Roman wall and the town's castle nearby.

Andrée and Bob, once returned, leapt into the breach. They lent us many items of furniture and introduced us to Danièle and Jean-Pierre Bourgoin, who lent us more. Among the things we borrowed from the Shepherds was a stove fuelled by bottled gas. I would carry the empty bottle to a nearby garage and wheel the full one back. Apart from running out of gas unexpectedly on occasion the system worked perfectly. They lent us also two desk ends; we provided the writing and typing surface by buying a suitably-sized board from a shop called Faites-le-vous-même in town. We walked home carrying the board between us, a procedure to which we were already well accustomed from furnishing our London flats. (On one occasion when we carried shelves and furniture Ann had walked in front, I in the middle and my son Paul behind.) We slept, surprisingly comfortably, on mattresses, and our visitors did too. Chris Hall when visiting us slept on several and once fell off during the night. By day the visitors' bed became a couch, misleadingly attractive until one tried to sit on it. But though the flat did have some of the elements of camping we got on well there and were sorry to leave it.

My principal memory of 1983-4 in Tours and our second visit there in 1988-90 was of the overwhelming hospitality which we had from my colleagues. The Bourgoins were firm friends from the start and the friendship has deepened over the years, with annual visits on each side. We also became friendly with an English-born couple

212

Danièle Bourgoin, David, Ann at Montreuil-Bellay (near Saumur), June 1997.

named Rodney and Lesley (born Holt) Coward, who had lived in France for many years and who smoothed our path in a variety of ways. I do not want to reel off a list of names but rather to say that I have never been the subject of such assiduous hospitality over so short a period. The head of department, André Bordeaux, did all he could to make me at home. He had built up the department in the 1960s and was adored by his colleagues. He told me many stories about his early life and other topics. Once, soon after the war, when he was teaching in England his hostess noted that his Utility trousers were too long. She called upstairs to him that if he would give her the trousers she would shorten them. He came downstairs to find the family in helpless laughter. Instead of saying: 'I'll bring them down' he had replied 'I'll take them down.' (How does one ever learn a foreign language?!)

The English department at Tours had over thirty members. They were accustomed to seeing lecteurs and lectrices (young graduates from Britain, Ireland and the United States who took 'TD', or seminars) and visiting professors like me come and go, but we were treated during our brief stay like old friends. We had difficulty in repaying all the hospitality we had received, and in September 1984, our final month in Tours, we visited one colleague or another almost every night. We left with many happy memories.

I should add that the young academic who replaced me at Hull in 1983-4 was treated with nothing like the cordiality by my small department which Ann and I experienced in the much larger one in Tours. I am tempted to reflect on differing French and British standards of treatment of visitors, but will only conclude that it was stark on this occasion.

As a French friend told us universities were part of the popular education system. The number of students was huge, staff accommodation very limited; shared rooms were universal and one did not linger in the office, as one's desk would soon be required by somebody else. The English library was far inferior to Hull's and the students were far more chatty and inattentive during lectures (many left the university at the end of each semester) than was the norm in England. (I needed all my schoolteaching skills to keep them in order.) Nor was my department wholly free from the kind of backbiting and ill feeling to which I had alas been accustomed in Hull. But I was not involved in that. I had the time of my life, liked the students, liked my colleagues and the secretaries, and grew quickly accustomed to the different conditions. In broad terms British students had a better if narrower education in the 1980s than their French counterparts, but far more of the latter were able to go to university, and those who survived to take their degree (called 'licence') received a good education.

The year was not very far advanced when I said to my colleague Jean-Paul Régis: 'I am very happy here but I don't know anybody who is not at the university. How can I get involved in politics?' He quickly arranged for us to meet Claude and Pierre Pujol, who were to become and long remained our closest friends in Tours. They were the lifeblood of the Parti Socialiste (or PS) in the constituency of Tours Centre, and under their tutelage we had a happy and stimulating political year. We attended meetings regularly and took full part in election campaigns, which we greatly enjoyed. Workers in French elections have a different role from those in Britain. There is no canvassing and there are no window bills. Instead, there is relentless 'distribution de tracts' and constant fly-posting of election material, often stuck over opposing notices. (There are also

214

Pierre Pujol (centre) at his country cottage, Les Puits Bérault (near Loches), April 1986.

David and Ann with Claude Pujol (right), at home of Bob and Andrée Shepherd near Tours, October 1988.

215

official boards for the posters of each party, which are not over-pasted by opponents.) We tried to stick our posters in places which opponents could not reach but which would be highly visible to passers-by, and I was pleased that in my early fifties I was still agile enough to do this. This type of activity could lead on occasion to altercation with site owners or 'the other side'.

Everyone in the local PS was friendly, but our friendship with Claude and Pierre was something special. They were school teachers in local secondary schools and students for higher degrees at the university, Claude in English, Pierre in history. They were also, as I said to Ann, 'a dishy couple'. We visited them often and stayed both with and without them in their country cottage about thirty-five kilometres away in the heart of the Touraine countryside, 'la France profonde'. We also visited the Pujols on several occasions after our return to England and they came to see us in Hull and in London. I dedicated my next book to them and the break-up of their marriage in 1994, shortly after our last visit to them, was deeply upsetting to us. I need not stress how profound was the effect on them and on their two beloved daughters. Pierre found renewed happiness and a new home with Marie-Joëlle Castello, whom we liked enormously as soon as we met her. His sudden and unexpected death in February 1998 at the early age of 54 was an almost unbearable blow.

We found with Claude and Pierre, with the Bourgoins and others that friendship with people who do not share one's own language is both easy and difficult. Obviously difficult because there is always at our level of proficiency a language barrier, but easy because the usual constraints of one's own culture weigh less heavily. It is of course true that many common assumptions are missing but when there is good will on both sides it is relatively easy to surmount the barriers and reach a real and gratifying intimacy. This is a somewhat hamfisted explanation, but I can only repeat that we made more friends in a shorter period in France than we had ever done before. My Abbey Wood friend David Smith told me at about this time that Italian friends had said to his wife and him that the Smiths were their closest friends, so our experience was not unique.

We did not feel happy with the changes of policy which took place under François Mitterrand and Laurent Fabius in 1983, after the heady days of the election triumph of 1981 which had produced such heartfelt jubilation not only in France but on the British left as well. But the militants in Tours Centre did not share these reservations. If they were divided by support for the different 'courants' led by Fabius, Michel Rocard and others, they were overjoyed to have a socialist government and not disposed to criticise either it or their president. We were told that in 1981 there had been dancing in the streets of Tours (and elsewhere) and we were sorry to have missed it. We joined several demonstrations in Tours, for the Alain Savary education bill (which was withdrawn after opposition protests), against Jean-Marie Le Pen and his Front National and so on. We also heard Lionel Jospin address a huge meeting at the Palais des Sports in Tours. We were impressed by him and have remained so ever since. He was an excellent speaker with wide knowledge and experience, and exuded conviction. From that point onwards Jospin was my own choice as successor to Mitterrand.

We of course took advantage of our year in Tours to widen our knowledge of France. We were somewhat bewildered to find that at every available winter holiday my colleagues headed for the Alps and Pyrenees. Things have changed in Britain, but I remembered Peter Jackson telling me that in the later 1960s he was one of only two Labour members of the House of Commons Skiing Club. It was not like that in France, for skiing in particular was widely popular. We did not take up winter sports but we visited Paris in the February holiday, enjoying cold, wonderfully sunny weather, and a feast of culture and food. We returned to Paris the following September for the Fête de l'Humanité, which we greatly enjoyed, listened to a rousing speech by Georges Marchais, the Communist party leader, and acquired the usual souvenirs. Later Pierre Pujol asked where we had acquired a fine medallion of Jean Jaurès, one of my (and Pierre's) heroes, struck for his centenary in 1959. I was much relieved by his tolerant response to the revelation that I had bought it at the Fête de l'Huma.

In the spring we visited Brittany and enjoyed it enormously despite a good deal of cold rain. I was especially pleased to visit Quimper and its famous pottery, which I had known about since earliest childhood, as my parents had owned several Quimper pieces. Ann and I were given a somewhat comic tour by one of the new American owners, who spoke halting French. We replied in our own halting French, not daring to embarrass her by admitting that we also were Anglophones, and to our great relief she remained ignorant of our guilty secret. Our greatest adventure was visiting the extensive, mystic standing stones around Carnac, and we also enjoyed walking down the Presqu'île de Quiberon, while giant waves dashed around us. It was on that trip that we visited Mont-St-Michel. We travelled by bicycle, the mount and its buildings steadily growing larger and more dramatic as we approached. We had wanted to see it for years and the reality was even more gratifying than the anticipation.

In the summer we spent a week on foot in the mountains of the Vosges area of Alsace, walking through a chain of charming half-timbered villages and ending up in the beautiful town of Colmar. We then went to Geneva, where we had a hospitable welcome from my long-standing friend Liaqat Ali and his wife Sehba. Liaqat, who was originally from India, had boarded as a student with Frida Laski and I had first met him at her house. He too had been a school teacher before finding his true vocation as an economist. By this time he was working for UNCTAD, the United Nations trade and development agency; later he returned to the World Bank in Washington where he had worked in youth. We went on to Annecy, which is built around canals, on its indescribably beautiful lake with the Alps as a background. (We were nearly benighted there too, but a resourceful taxi driver managed to find a hotel room for us. The next day we found for ourselves accommodation in a 16th-century hotel in the heart of Annecy's old town.) Annecy, with its combination of townscape, water and mountains, is my favourite place, my own candidate as the most beautiful spot in the world.

I should add that in our experience the French were sometimes almost naive in their attitude to money. Our hotel in Annecy had an exterior spiral staircase so that there was no need to pass the reception desk; one could easily have left without paying. When we left Tours in September 1984 I bought flowers for a number of people as a gesture of thanks for kindnesses during our stay. I bought the flowers in the market from a stallholder whom I had never seen before. I returned later for another bunch to be told that I had been overcharged, that the new bunch was free and I was owed a small sum. This was typical of the behaviour of the French to us. And it was certainly not the case that local shopkeepers and hoteliers mistook our nationality after the first syllable escaped our lips.

And so we returned to Hull after a wonderful year abroad. The fact that we lived in a 'rotten little house', which sin we had compounded by buying a flat in one of the more expensive parts of London, had done nothing for our popularity. We encountered derision at times and occasionally refusal to accept the fact that Ann had never contemplated changing her surname to mine. (I supported this decision wholeheartedly.) As already mentioned the fact that we did not own a car was often greeted by scarcely disguised hostility. Now we had lived for a year in France and returned with nothing but praise for that country and its people. This also aroused opposition, partly because we had had an enviable experience, partly because of the British ambivalence towards France which appears to permeate all social classes. We were prepared, however, to change neither our lifestyle nor our preferences to please other people.

One has to tread carefully in discussing this subject because it is complex, and facile judgments are usually wrong. My sister Ellen, who moved to London in the later 1970s and remarried, told me that she had heard many English people say that they liked France but disliked the French. That remark corresponded with my own experience. I returned after a happy year, enthusiastic about both France and the French people whom I had met. But the comments we heard from individuals and read in the press were often negative or, at least, competitive. If there was a demonstration by farmers or a strike by lorry drivers it was deliberately aimed at the British. French food was not what it used to be. 'I was cheated, they took advantage of me, they were rude.' Such remarks were by no means universal, but in an age of increasing xenophobia they were common. In part they arose from a feeling of sour grapes on the part of people who had not been lucky enough to live in France for a year. In part they were a response to an alleged feeling on the part of a small, supposedly sophisticated minority (to which we now perforce belonged) that everything was better in France. But they could also have been indicative of a certain national malaise. Perhaps Dean Acheson had been right to say in 1962 that Britain had lost an empire and not found a role.

This is probably a good place to add that one of the most disturbing features to me in over forty years of life in Britain has been the constant need to insist on the superiority of everything British.

('Bigger' was American, 'better' was British, I noticed.) Long ago I thought that I should keep a scrapbook and paste in articles which asserted that something British was 'the best in the world'. If I had done so it would now be a fat volume, especially with cuttings from recent years. I am sure that a week does not pass that I do not read such a comment in the 'quality' press or hear it on the radio. If British (really, English) education is behind the levels of other countries and we need to improve it, politicians do not talk about catching up but about 'creating an education system which will lead the world'. If we are not doing our best to subvert the European Union we are talking about our intention to lead it, or both simultaneously. Number 10 Downing Street has 'the most famous door in the world' (how many other famous doors are there?).

There is nothing wrong with patriotism properly conceived. Patriotism in my view should be about pride in the beauty of one's country, the compassion and generosity of its citizens, the absence of gross disparities of wealth and income, the level of social solidarity (including the social services), care for the environment, realisation that none of us is an island and that relationships between fellow citizens should be marked by co-operation. It has nothing to do with being 'better' than other countries except in the limited field of international sport, which seems to arouse more bad behaviour and mutual hostility than mutual understanding. It is a sad commmentary that British patriotism in the final quarter of the twentieth century seems so often to be based on hostility to foreigners, though we have had so many catastrophic lessons in our tragic century about where that hostility leads. And boasting that our institutions are 'the best in the world' can be embarrassing when reality replaces platitude. I think of the revelations of brutality and corruption amongst our police, our system of justice which has convicted and imprisoned so many innocent people, and our centralised form of government with its over-mighty executive.

*　　*　　*

The remainder of the eighties is quickly summarised. I had four more years at Hull (1984-8). During the first three of these I was chair of the Ramblers' Association. Between October 1988 and spring 1990 Ann and I were again in Tours.

I enjoyed the years at the head of the RA, though I often had trouble controlling the Executive Committee, with its twin hammers of Chris Hall and Peter Melchett. There was also staff trouble which ended in the departure of two employees, one of whom had long and faithful service and was popular in the Areas. (The remainder of the staff then quickly joined a trade union.) My misfortune was to be chair at the time, not to have initiated or desired their departure. I visited many Areas and some Groups and attended a variety of events, notably during our golden jubilee year, 1985. I was pleased that, shortly before my period as chair began, David Beskine, one of my outstanding students at Hull, was appointed to a post with the RA. He is still there, now Assistant Director (Access) and, as everyone agrees, an inspired appointment.

A highlight of the jubilee was the walk around England (there was another across Wales) which attracted many participants and great enthusiasm during its 181 days. I joined the walk in several parts of Yorkshire, in Derbyshire, Kent and at the end in London, enjoying it enormously. Another jubilee event was a lunch at the Festival Hall for veterans of the RA. Barbara Castle was guest speaker and I told the meeting that her appearance was unchanged from our drinking days at the Flask in 1954. I also apologised in advance to Alan Mattingly for absence from the RA centenary celebrations in 2035; I am sure that he will be there aged 86, but the centenary will have its work cut out to arouse more enthusiasm and publicity than the jubilee.

On 6 October 1985, immediately after the end of the jubilee Tom Stephenson, then aged 92, addressed the first meeting of a new access campaign from the steps of the Rambler Inn at Edale in the Peak District before we walked to the top of Lose Hill not far away. Alan Mattingly told the gathering that our membership had risen to 50,000, which seems derisory now but was a lot in those days. The weather on that walk could kindly be described as execrable and our speeches at the summit could hardly be heard; John Trevelyan, our Deputy Secretary, told me later that his feet were still wet when his train reached London. Roy Bullen of the South Yorkshire and North-East Derbyshire Ramblers, best summed up the situation after I told him, tongue in cheek, that it was a good rambling day: 'All days are good for the hills, but some are better than others.'

I served another year on the RA EC after my term as chair ended in 1987. A few months after that final year I returned to France and when I came back to England I lived not in Hull but in London, where I had few contacts at Area level. My close connection with the RA had ended: 'You *are* out of touch', my friend Alan Howard told me in the early 1990s and it was alas true. I was, however, overjoyed to be elected a national vice-president in 1988 and president of my own (renamed) East Yorkshire and Derwent Area in 1991. I retain many friends in the RA, attend its annual General Council when not in France, and keep in some kind of contact thanks to Ann's continued research and writing on amenity matters.

Before I leave the RA I should mention two events held in Hull in the 1980s. East Riding ramblers held a celebratory dinner in February 1988 to mark the golden jubilee of the founding of the area in 1938. Chris Hall and Peter Melchett were the guest speakers and their speeches went down well among the audience. The dinner, held at the University of Hull, was largely attended and enjoyed by everyone.

It had been quite a different kind of function seven years earlier almost to the day when Ann and I were invited to the annual dinner and prize-giving of the Hull and East Riding branch of the Cyclists' Touring Club. The occasion was complete with the loyal toast ('God bless her', a voice muttered), a ceremony I have never encountered among ramblers. (Nor has anyone been awarded a prize, though a few honorary national members were created in later years.) I should have been prepared because I had visited the national headquarters of the CTC in Godalming and found the secretary's wall dominated by a large photograph of the Queen. Ann and I had to sing for our suppers; I made a short speech and she was called upon to read names and award prizes. She found this difficult, since names and descriptions of the feats of the prize winners were typed in capital letters without punctuation, but she carried off her part with apparent aplomb. At the end of the evening we were ourselves awarded a prize, a shield with the CTC symbol recording the occasion. My name was mis-spelt, a common occurrence, but we were startled to see that the plaque had recorded the date as 1980 rather than 1981. We were treated with extreme kindness but we reflected that the RA and CTC inhabited different worlds.

My remaining years at Hull were dominated by my 'Milly book', which was a logical outcome of my previous book. It was a biography of Millicent Garrett Fawcett (1847-1929), the feminist who was for many years the leader of the women's suffrage movement. I had been surprised when writing *Before the Suffragettes* to note how often Mrs Fawcett's name cropped up, whether in the campaign for the parliamentary vote, employment, education of women or related topics. She had written her autobiography in 1924 and her disciple Ray Strachey had written her life in 1931, two years after her death. Both books had their moments but both were bland and necessarily lacked an historian's perspective.

I greatly enjoyed researching and writing the book, which took me to Carlisle, Manchester, Sheffield, Wiltshire, Oxford, Cambridge, Surrey, Suffolk and Jersey, apart from long periods in London. (I also acquired documents from other repositories, including some in the United States, in part thanks to the intellectual curiosity, kindness and indefatigability of my friend Gail Malmgreen.) One reviewer criticised me for disliking my subject, which was only partly true. I did find her super-patriotism both during the Boer War and the Great War hard to take, particularly when she refused to support the ending of the Allied blockade on starving Germany after the end of the war. She wrote to her former international women's suffrage colleague Marie Stritt (and copied her letter to *The Times*), explaining her refusal and offering the consolatory thought that if German women before the war had shared political power 'the criminal conspiracy of the autocratic rulers of Germany, which brought about the war, would have been an impossibility' (*A Different World for Women*, pp. 252-3).

But, though moralistic, she was not always so heartless and I found much to admire in Millicent Garrett Fawcett. She spent over sixty years of her life working for women in many different fields and she was the most persuasive and effective advocate of the women's cause over a prolonged period. Of how many people could it be said, as of Mrs Fawcett, that they were present at their last public function sixty years (and a day) after their first, and that the cause, the political advancement of women, was the same? Of how many could it be said that they began a campaign for a near-impossible cause, the parliamentary vote for women, in mid-Victorian times and saw it to a triumphant conclusion under Stanley Baldwin?

The book took me into many byways and I learned a great deal from it. The research had two high points, in neither of which I was directly involved. Ann and I had gone to Jersey to examine the papers of Elizabeth Garrett Anderson, the first woman doctor who was Mrs Fawcett's sister. (The papers belonged to Catriona Williams, Mrs Anderson's great grand-daughter. She and her husband treated us as if we were their own family.) There had long been a family tradition, which was incorporated into Jo Manton's biography of Mrs Anderson (*Elizabeth Garrett Anderson*, 1965, p. 156), that Henry Fawcett, the blind Cambridge professor of political economy and budding politician, had proposed marriage to Elizabeth (who had declined the offer) before asking Millicent, fourteen years her junior, to marry him. (In fact he had also proposed to at least two other early feminists or intellectuals.) Jo Manton's account had frequently been repeated by historians, but Ann was the researcher who discovered the letter from Elizabeth dated 8 May 1865 which told her parents: 'Mr Fawcett came up from Cambridge to ask me to be his wife.' (quoted in *A Different World for Women*, p. 15.)

Likewise I had always wondered about the story told by Mrs Fawcett herself, who described the theft of her purse at Waterloo Station and the subsequent apprehension and trial of the thief for stealing the property of Henry Fawcett. 'I felt', she wrote, 'as if I had been charged with theft myself.' (*What I Remember*, 1924, p. 62) The incident took place in 1876 when the perpetrator might conceivably have been so charged, though after 1870 property gained by a wife's own earnings (in her case by authorship) belonged to her rather than to her husband if she could demonstrate the source of the money involved. The story had been repeated in many historical works; nobody had checked it. I was again in Tours at the time, but an agent examined the records of Surrey Quarter Sessions and I later read the report in *The Times*. The charge had in fact been 'feloniously stealing one purse and the sum of 14 shillings from the person of Millicent Garrett Fawcett' (ibid., 53, 57).

The book was published in 1991 as *A Different World for Women: the life of Millicent Garrett Fawcett*. The typescript was read by my former students and present friends David Martin and Graham Johnson, both of whom had also read the draft of *Before the Suffragettes*, and also by Gail Malmgreen. All three gave me such valuable assistance that I felt inclined to write in the preface: 'They have taken such care on my behalf that they must share the blame for any remaining errors.'

David Martin and Ann Frain, newly-weds, Sheffield, December 1997.

I was asked to leave the University of Hull in 1988. I was 56 that summer, more cuts were taking place and I was the oldest member of my department. I had been in Hull for 23 years, including the year in Tours, and I was very resentful that I was asked to go. I had worked hard, often seven days a week for the University of Hull, I was well up to the average both as teacher and as scholar, and my RA work had not interfered with my university life. I felt like writing to the minister for higher education to ask just what I had done to deserve having my career cut short. On the other hand I was still unhappy in my department and by 1988 I felt that I had 'done' both Hull and its university. It was time to go.

The university subsidised my departure with a lump sum and granted me extra contributions which took me nearly to maximum pension level (half final salary). Ann and I planned to move to York and I was to return to Hull for two or three years of part-time teaching. Our plans were disrupted one June day in 1988 when I received a phone call from Nicole Vigouroux-Frey, head of the English Department at Tours, which (as there had been similar calls in earlier years and I had made clear that I was available for 1988/9 if required) I had half-expected. Andrée and Bob Shepherd, who like me had taught British civilisation, were leaving Tours. Would I return for another year? I asked for a short period to make a decision, and after anxious discussion with Ann I rang back the next day to say that I would come. This time we were to remain in Tours for eighteen months, and the draft of the Fawcett book was written there.

We left Hull on 10 July 1988, a week after my former student Peter Hibbert was ordained deacon in the Church of England. (Our impending departure from Hull meant that we could not attend the ceremony.) Leaving Hull was momentous for us but hardly a leaf stirred in Hull itself. The Vice Chancellor had written me a warm letter of thanks for my many contributions to the university, but a moment's examination showed that it was identical, apart from the top line, to the letters sent to all other departing staff. I took it between thumb and forefinger and, as my Swarthmore friend John Purnell used to say, deposited it in the circular file.

We spent the summer in London and left for Tours late in September, this time taking a furnished flat which had been found for us in a different part of the town. It was not such an interesting area, the furniture was rather old and worn and, worst of all,

Ann with Peter Hibbert, Manchester, October 1997.

226

cockroaches – till checked – roamed through the central heating ducts and across our floors. But it was a nice flat and we had pleasant walks on the banks of the Cher. Nearby too was a lovely garden with an attractive lake; it was called the Jardin des Prébendes and we never tired of it.

I was greeted warmly by my colleagues at the university and comrades in the PS and felt as though I had never been away, so easily did I pick up the reins. There were many old friends, for few people had retired or moved since my first visit to Tours, and there were at least two new ones. The first was Catherine Joncheray, a young member of staff who travelled from her home in Angers to Tours. Our two teaching days overlapped and we lunched together every week. This was fortunate for me, as she could be described impartially as young and attractive, highly intelligent, full of fun and interest, and willing to put up with my French. I was later to discover that she also had a charming husband and two lovely children. The only odd thing about her was that she seemed not to mind giving half her lunch times to me. Catherine was to be directly responsible for my next working stay in France.

The other friend was also to influence my future life. He was Bernard Escarbelt, a newly appointed professor of British civilisation from the University of Lille III. He was somewhat self-conscious about his northern origins, for the Nord-Pas-de-Calais is not the most interesting part of France in the eyes of most of the French (though it was to become so to Ann and me). Bernard was a highly likeable man and had no trouble making other friends, but he was on his own every week in Tours, and as we shared a teaching room and taught British civilisation, including sharing one course, we quickly became firm friends. His wife Nicole visited Tours on several occasions and we liked her too. Her personality and Bernard's, both appealing, presented an amusing contrast, tending to call to mind the hare and the tortoise.

In the summer of 1989 Ann and I set out to follow on foot Robert Louis Stevenson's *Travels with a Donkey in the Cévennes*, which he had undertaken in 1878. (I unkindly told friends that I had provided myself with my own âne (donkey)). Much of what Stevenson had seen we too were able to visit, and though the area had naturally changed, it was still wholly rural and the scenery was magnificent. Among the places which Stevenson had visited and described I best remember the monastery at Notre-Dame des Neiges (now a tourist centre), the charming village of Florac and Pont-de-Montvert, the scene in 1702 of the rebellion of the Camisards. The story of the Protestant martyr Pierre Séguier, movingly told by Stevenson, ended with his inquisition, torture and and death by burning. Asked why he was known as Spirit he replied 'Because the Spirit of the Lord is with me.'...'Have you no remorse for your crimes?' 'I have committed none. My soul is like a garden full of shelter and of fountains.' (*Travels with a Donkey in the Cévennes*, 1879; 1924 ed. with *An Inland Voyage*, pp. 220-3). Some of the sites of the events of 1702 were still recognisable.

After our return to Tours we were visited by Graham Johnson and his wife Pamela. As I told them the story of the events at Pont-de-Montvert ('my soul is like a garden') I began to weep, to their astonishment and embarrassment. The incident of the burning of Séguier for his convictions (and, it must be said, his bloody deeds) exemplifies for me the otiose nature of genealogy, which has so many passionate practitioners in our day. I know that, if Stevenson's

Pamela Johnson, David, Graham Johnson at the Johnson home in Mossley, near Manchester, October 1997.

*Nicole and Bernard Escarbelt (seated) at home in Sainghin-en-Weppes
(near Lille), celebrating their thirtieth wedding anniversary,
September 1996.*

account can (as I hope) be relied on, I am in the truest sense
descended from Séguier and other Protestant martyrs. We owe our
freedoms to people like him, even if they would if triumphant have
been little more tolerant of dissent than the Catholics they fought.
In comparison, the search for unknown people from whom one can
calculate a descent by blood seems to me comic if not dangerous.

That trip to a part of France relatively unknown to British
tourists was full of incident and excitement. We revelled in the glories of the cathedrals at Le Puy-en-Velay and Mende. On 14 July
1989, the bicentenary of the storming of the Bastille, we found ourselves in the attractive village of Ste-Enimie, which put on an astonishing display of outdoor sport and fireworks for so small a place.
Ste-Enimie is on the Gorge du Tarn, which allowed me a rare indul-
gement in one of my passions, canoeing. Ann and I set out with
joy in one heart, the severest (and most justified) apprehension in
the other. Within 120 seconds or so of our departure we had cap-
sized our canoe. We were neither drowned nor hurt and we spent

229

the remainder of the day in the canoe, once emptied of water, following the magnificent gorge. I am still, however, hoping that Ann will forgive me for this incident.

We have found four times in France that all good things come to an end. We had hoped, however, that this particular stay would not. I had applied for a permanent position as professor of British civilisation at Tours and was delighted to be nominated by my colleagues as their first choice for the post. The decision, however, was to be made by the Conseil National Universitaire, a national body which endorsed or rejected the nominations made locally. We left Tours in April 1990 and returned to London not knowing what would follow. What followed was that my nomination was not endorsed because, I was told, I was the recipient of a British university pension. (I could not take up a British university appointment for the same reason.) In the summer of 1990, therefore, I was approaching my 58th birthday, struggling to complete my 'Milly book' – and unemployed.

CHAPTER 9

New Career, New Religion: 1990-4

THAT SUMMER WAS a bad period for Ann and me. We had expected to return to France, possibly for good, and that option was suddenly and definitively withdrawn. My pension was not enormous and I had no job. (It should be remembered that even a sizeable amount of capital produces only a relatively low income, unless one is lucky or obsessed with money-making or both. I was neither.) We had personal difficulties. I had that summer a violent quarrel with Ellen, after which she and I did not meet for a long period, and which left me feeling exhausted and depressed. Our tiny house in York, which we had acquired at the end of 1988, was let and would be occupied till late in 1990. We could therefore not move to York and begin a new life there. After completion of my Fawcett book I had only minor research on hand; I would have to think of a bigger project. Things were at a low ebb.

One of my colleagues had asked me when I left Hull about my future plans. I told him that I intended to continue to do what I had been doing for many years: 'research some of the time, not-research some of the time'. Following that plan, after I presented the manuscript of the Fawcett biography to my publisher I applied for two part-time jobs. One of them was a post as political assistant to the Labour Group of councillors in Maidstone, in mid-Kent. To my astonishment I was appointed; in the event no more than a month or two elapsed between finishing my manuscript and starting the new job and a new career in local government in Maidstone and later at Tower Hamlets.

I should have guessed that part-time work would ineluctably become full-time and that the result would be that the kind of serious research in which I had been engaged for over twenty years would have to be abandoned. I did not. I enjoyed the work in local government and I liked the people with whom I worked, who were generally less tense and competitive than those in university life. I did have my usual problems with personal relations at times; wholly inexcusably I lost my temper with the leader of another local authority while working at Maidstone and shouted at him over the phone. There were also incidents I regretted at Tower Hamlets, even if they were less dramatic.

But in terms of day-to-day work I had no objection to being demoted from social class A to class C1. I did not mind and sometimes even enjoyed clerical work, to which there were often parallels in university life. I enjoyed working with people much younger than myself whose formal education was in some cases at a lower level. I take no credit for any of this because it was not the result of conscious effort, but I am glad of it. As I wrote to a Tower Hamlets colleague years later, I (unconsciously) made up my mind that I would apply for any post at any level which I thought I could fulfil reasonably satisfactorily. Among the jobs for which I had thought of applying was giving out railway information; I have always loved sorting though timetables. I discovered also that I would rather try to do a useful job of work and draw a salary than spend all my time on scholarly research. Research was absorbing, but if I was forced to choose I preferred a job which interested me with congenial colleagues to working on my own on a scholarly book which few people would read.

I was interviewed at Maidstone by three councillors. These were Mark Watts, the youthful leader of the eight-strong Labour Group on the 55-member Maidstone council and his two leading and much older colleagues, Geoff Ellis and Jack Hazelgrove. Mark was a bright young town planner with a London borough, Geoff had had a variety of types of employment and Jack was a part-time teacher and lecturer. I had a good interview. I was asked what I was not good at and I replied: 'selling myself'. When, later, I was asked if I wanted to say or ask anything, I showed the panel my accumulated Labour Party membership cards since 1954, neglecting to point out that there was a ten year membership gap in the 36 years since I had first joined the party. But they were impressed. 'I thought that you said you weren't good at selling yourself', one said. My own gloss on my appointment was that the movement had looked after me. (I had, after all, tried to look after it for many years.) I was somewhat apprehensive but delighted to accept the job; my 58th birthday was about six weeks behind me when I started work in September 1990.

I discovered later that the Maidstone Labour triumvirate was attracted to the idea of appointing two part-timers because they thought that they gain two assistants for the price of one. I hope that they were not disillusioned subsequently. My job-share partner was Stella Clarke, a Nottinghamshire woman in her late twenties who had a polytechnic degree in French and Spanish and who was then employed in market research. She lived in South London and, like me, took three full days to get to Maidstone to work for 2½ days a week. Accordingly, Stella gave up 60 per cent of her previous salary to gain 50 per cent of a new one, but for her, like me, the job was an initial stage in a new career. We got on well (I only fully realised how well when she announced that she was leaving) and were duly grateful to each other for making it possible to work half-time.

Maidstone in 1990 (as before and subsequently) had a council without a majority. There was a loose arrangement under which the Labour Group co-operated with the Liberal Democrats who had a little over twenty councillors, against the Conservatives who had approximately the same number. (In parliamentary terms the area was heavily Conservative; Ann Widdecombe was one of the local MPs, but the party representation in local government was much more equal.) I got on very well with Paula Yates, the (Liberal) Council leader who had been a student at Hull in my time (as had her husband Nigel, the Kent County archivist). I also got on well, despite disputes about national and local politics, with Tom Wilson, who was even younger than Stella, and who had been lucky to land the Liberal Democrat political assistant's job straight after leaving university. I do not know at this stage whether Tom was as blithely unaware as I was of the significance of the fact that the Conservatives had appointed no political assistant, and had denounced as a gross waste of money the appointments made by the other two parties.

The council was entitled to make the appointments in 1990 under section 9 of the Local Government and Housing Act, which had become law only in the autumn of 1989. Though Conservative legislation it was perfectly sensible. Councillors were busy people;

some of them, like Mark Watts, had full-time jobs and young families. They could not keep up to date with all the necessary background reading; they needed to be briefed and they needed secretarial assistance. The appointment of assistants who shared the same aims as the councillors for whom they worked was no more than common sense.

I think it was Mark who was first aware of the passage of the legislation and persuaded his Labour and Liberal colleagues of the advantages of acquiring assistance. Local government had been subject to such severe financial constraints that it was not surprising that relatively few appointments of this type were made, at least initially, although our salaries were not large. Mark, as leader of the Labour Group, had presumably the final word in the appointment of the Labour assistant, and I am still both surprised and grateful (neither word is strong enough) that he was prepared to appoint a man old enough to be his father to the post. Would I have been bold enough to do the same if I had been in his shoes?

I did not know much about contemporary local government when I was appointed, though I knew a good deal about Victorian school boards and poor law guardians. I had always been interested in the subject and sometimes thought that I should have chosen a career in local government. (My subsequent experience made me feel pleased, on the whole, that I had not done so. Too many high-ranking officers did not survive even to 56, the age at which I had left Hull.) It was not an easy job, especially for the leading officers, to work with intensely political councillors and satisfy the law's requirements about political impartiality at the same time. It does not surprise me that officers are sometimes dragged into the political arena, not due to their own convictions but to the desire to carry out satisfactorily the requirements of the politicians; doing the job properly has its own momentum.

Fortunately this kind of constraint did not affect political assistants, whose job (uniquely in local government) it was to carry out the instructions of the members of one political party only. Stella and I divided up the work between us, though we did both take part in certain activities, including a weekly newsletter which went out to all our members and which contained condensed information from our researches on relevant topics. The fact that we went to conferences in a number of different parts of the country helped to make the newsletter of interest. I remember attending an absorbing conference on public and private transport and planning held in Bath, and one on uses for redundant churches (we had a very prominent one in Maidstone) held in Huddersfield. (My former student Peter Hibbert was at that time a curate in Huddersfield and I was able to see both him and his church on that trip.) My longest-lasting memory of the Bath conference, at which all sorts of different and hopeful schemes were put forward for reviving public transport, was of a speech by a disabled woman who described graphically and amusingly how disabled people were often treated by the ablebodied. 'Here, Bill, could you look after this wheelchair?' meant looking after *her*.

Stella specialised in health issues and had initial success in preventing at least one of the local hospitals being converted into a trust. My specialisms were transport and housing. I assisted both Jack Hazelgrove, leader of the Labour Group on the Housing Committee and then his successor Wendy Marlow, one of my favourite members, in the campaign to prevent Maidstone's housing stock being alienated to a housing association. Several authorities in Kent had already got rid of their houses in this manner by the time of my appointment.

I obtained a good deal of information from other local authorities, notably ones where the transfer of the stock had been defeated in the required ballot of tenants, and helped to devise leaflets and other ammunition. I also secured outside speakers to address the Labour Group on this and other subjects. It was neither Stella nor I, however, but Wendy and other party members who had to undertake the long hard slog involved in persuading occupants of council houses and flats that it was better to stay with the devil they knew than move to the devil they didn't know – the housing association, in which the Council's housing staff would become leading figures with much inflated salaries. And it was Wendy who deserved the credit for the vote to stay with the council after I had left: 'game, set and match to Wendy', Ann said rightly.

Transfer of stock was not at that time an issue in the great cities because their housing debt and the bad state of the houses and flats meant that they were not an economic proposition for housing associations. The main attraction of transfer was that associations could borrow on the open market from private financial institutions, but local authorities also had important advantages if the government did not limit their power of borrowing or insist that their rents go through the roof. To the extent that the housing associations were attractive to council tenants it was because central government could move the goalposts at will, but the cuts which have subsequently taken place in housing association finance show that transfer was no panacea. It was not possible to repair stock without heavy expenditure, and local authorities with their vast expertise were in an excellent position if they were allowed to raise the money to do so. I was, however, somewhat shocked to find that one attraction to at least some tenants was simply that after transfer they would no longer be labelled council tenants.

One of the many attractions of the job was working with the members. Stella and I attended all the meetings of the Labour Group and both of us found the members unstuffy, politically and personally congenial. This was specially true of the four already mentioned. It was a joy to work with Mark Watts, with his quick mind, his maturity far beyond his years (I was embarrassed to have to be calmed down by him in crises) and his understanding both of local government and of people. He had an enviable knowledge of how to treat subordinates and was certainly one of the best bosses I ever had. He had his due reward when he was elected member of the European Parliament for East Kent in 1994. East Kent gained a public servant of rare quality.

Jack Hazelgrove had taught history for many years and we were attracted to each other as practitioners of the same subject; I hope that his vote for my appointment was not influenced by my plan to write a short life of Stafford Cripps for a series of socialist lives, because the plan fell through for reasons never made clear to me. Geoff Ellis was a genial, congenial type, who, like Mark Watts (and me) was a passionate supporter of urban planning, public transport and pedestrianisation, and opponent of all-power-to-the-motor-car. Members were often liberal with praise, but I never had another letter like the one Geoff sent me when I wrote a news release for him in his absence in April 1992. He wrote generously: 'I have returned from holiday and found your Labour Group News Release headed "Maidstone says no". I must say I write a better letter when I am on holiday than when I am at home. Congratulations.' I cannot recall anything nicer in my 41 years of employment.

Stella left Maidstone at the end of 1991 for a full-time post with the London Borough of Lewisham, close to her home in Brixton. She now had one job rather than two, a higher salary and payment for one hundred per cent of her working time rather than 90 per cent, but she missed the members and Maidstone, which we both liked greatly, and the relative independence which she and I had enjoyed. I have a reproduction of an eighteenth-century print of Maidstone High Street. Thanks to people like Mark Watts and Geoff Ellis it was still easily recognisable when I left Maidstone in July 1992.

I was, flatteringly, asked to take Stella's place and work full-time when she left. I declined, partly because given the journey times it would have effectively taken me six days to do a five-day job, partly because I still wanted to undertake scholarly research. (I was now working on a book on women in the labour movement between the wars.) We had well over one hundred applicants for half a job, some of whom if appointed would have had to travel from London and would not, like Stella in her Maidstone days, have another job or, like me, a pension. Their post-journey salaries would have been correspondingly low. I had a hint of why I might have been appointed originally when one young short-listed candidate told me that she didn't know which party she supported but that she thought Labour was probably the best. This was in application for a post as Labour political assistant. The quality of the candidates was on the whole good, but their political commitment was limited.

In the end the appointment was between two young women, both of whom came from the mid-Kent area, and it was very hard to decide between them. (Though I was not a member of the interviewing panel, I was generously allowed to see the candidates informally and give my advice.) We appointed Claire Britcher, who was even younger than Stella, good-humoured and easy to work with. She had formerly been a journalist in the Medway area, but was now a young mother and was looking for part-time work. She learned quickly and had no trouble in picking up the threads of Stella's job. Though I had begun to think that it might be a good idea for me to start to look elsewhere for something better paid with a shorter journey to work, I had not yet applied for any other job. I expected to continue for some time to work happily with

Claire (and more cordially with Tom Wilson than the Labour members might wish) and to enjoy the good fellowship of the Labour members. I reckoned without the general election of 1992.

Maidstone was one of the many towns which elected its borough council three years in every four. (The fourth year was the county council election.) I had started work in 1990 and the composition of the council changed little after the 1991 election. But 1992 was quite different. Stella and I had agreed with Mark, Geoff and Jack when we returned to Maidstone after our initial appointment for an informal chat that a Conservative general election victory would be a disaster. We did not realise how right we were and what a personal disaster (for me at least) a Conservative victory would prove. The Major victory in April was followed a month later by local elections, and in Maidstone the Conservatives won a majority in alliance with Conservative-inclined independents. (Labour in Maidstone had fallen out with the Liberals and denounced them publicly, but the general election had in my view a much greater impact on the borough election result than the Lib-Lab spat.) I rang Ann after the count and woke her up to tell her that there had been a Conservative victory and a Liberal defeat (Labour had kept its eight members), but I did not yet realise that in less than three months Tom, Claire and I would be on the streets.

Both Labour and Liberal Democrat members did what they could to prevent our dismissal. So did we, or at least so did I. I dug out the report of the parliamentary debate in which the Conservative government decided to authorise the appointment of research assistants, as 'helpful – and indeed desirable' (Nicholas Ridley, 14 February 1989, col. 167). The borough secretary asked Tom and me to write memos to him explaining the nature of our work. As might be expected, mine (dated 28 May 1992) was much less formal than Tom's. I pointed out that Claire and I were employed to help the Labour members carry out their statutory tasks and become more efficient councillors. All our activities were authorised or agreed by the leader of the Labour Group or his colleagues. The work was interesting and productive. I concluded pugnaciously and, as I fondly thought, dramatically: 'Any idea that we are some kind of Rasputin or Svengali pulling the strings and giving the councillors their instructions from some mysterious revolutionary headquarters would be risible were it not our jobs which are at stake.'

I authorised the memo to be passed on to the relevant council committee, so I should not have been surprised to have read my final sentence quoted in the local press (*Kent Today*, 9 July 1992). (But I was; also embarrassed and, I must admit, rather pleased.) If we had been entitled research assistants, as Ridley proposed, or administrative assistants (either of which terms would have fitted our roles more exactly than political assistants) the appointments might have been less controversial, but the new council majority wanted to assert itself and at the end of July we were ousted. I bought small presents for Tom and Claire and they thoughtfully took me out to lunch.

There was more than one leaving do for us, including one with speeches and presentations which we greatly appreciated. I went to another function at the pub run by Wendy Marlow and her husband Alan. The evening had been ominous and the air was full of insects. 'A storm is coming', Claire said. By the time I left the pub, which was not far from the station, it was raining with an intensity which I had seldom if ever experienced. Water swirled through the streets, too much for the drains to accommodate. When I arrived at the station I was as wet as if I had jumped in the Medway. Tom Wilson arrived by car from his own leaving do to catch the same train. He looked at me and said: 'You're wet.' I still treasure that perceptive observation. When I reached home ninety minutes later I was nearly as wet as I had been at Maidstone East.

The political assistants got along well with most of the council officers, though some were doubtful about fraternising with officers who worked for a minority political group. The one I liked best was Richard Snaith, who was promoted borough secretary after my arrival at Maidstone. Nobody could have wished for a more friendly and helpful chief officer, and it is hard to imagine that one existed. Richard was thoughtful enough to obtain three-year contracts for the political assistants (from 2 May 1991) and our dismissal before the expiry of the contracts meant that we were eligible for compensation. Tom, the full-timer, received £8,000 and Claire and I shared another £8,000 between us. It seemed a reasonable amount of money at the time and it seemed even more so later, when my period of unemployment proved to be only 3½ weeks. I am still in touch with Richard Snaith and grateful for his many kindnesses. His secretary Judy May and the other staff in his section were also helpful and friendly colleagues.

Meanwhile our home in York was vacated late in 1990 and we went to examine it and consider what work needed to be done, as we had never lived there. We spent much of our spare time in 1991 supervising alterations, putting up bookshelves and filling them with my books from the university which had been kept for me in Hull. By mid-1991 we had a home in which we were very happy and spent long weekends there every second week. We were to keep up this split-level existence for nearly six years. We had long loved York, which as everyone knows is one of the finest cities in the country, and when we left Hull in 1988 had already decided that we wanted to live in York (37 miles from Hull) when I retired. It was also within easy reach of three national parks and, despite all the reductions in services remained a good railway centre, not only for journeys to London on the fastest line in Britain but to many other places as well.

It was on Saturday 9 February 1991 that we passed the Friends' Meeting House in Friargate, close to the castle and the city centre. I had suggested to Ann over the years that we should attend Friends' meeting 'some time', but we had never put the vague impulse into practice. In earliest 1991 'Britain and the United States', as the BBC likes to say, had geared themselves up to attempt to bomb Iraq into the stone age. We had taken part in a great London demonstration against the proposed war and watched with dismay the Labour Party abandon its initial anti-war stand. Passing the meeting house we saw a small sticker which is still in the window as I write: 'Quakers Say NO to ALL War.' A religious organisation did not have to respond to the requirements of the tabloid press. We looked around the meeting house and wondered whether we should go to meeting the next day.

We did, and from that point onwards we attended Friargate Meeting every second Sunday. On 27 May 1991 we began to attend Hampstead Meeting, North London, as well and after that we were faithful attenders at either Friargate or Hampstead, except when we lived in France. Even then we attended meeting in Paris or the nearest point in England when we could. Both of us soon joined the Religious Society of Friends, I in 1992 and Ann the following year. We had moved, apart from our Ramblers' contacts, largely in left-wing intellectual circles, where agnosticism or atheism are virtually universal. My Methodist-Marxist friend Philip Bagwell was a notable exception. Even most of the Ramblers we knew, apart from Andrew Dalby, were non-churchgoers. My sons and most of our friends greeted our announcement that we were attending a Christian religious service each week with disbelief, derision or hostility. My son John and his partner Caroline Burgess said that we were joining the Quakers because we had given up hope of the revolution; the Friends, they said, were the Socialist Workers Party for grown-ups. There was something in that assertion.

My mother had wanted me to attend the Quaker-founded (and influenced) Swarthmore College because she knew of and admired the Friends. I had always retained an interest in both the social impact and theology of Christianity and had belonged to religious discussion groups both as an undergraduate and at Hull. Ann and I did not, as Friends are wont to say somewhat fatuously, feel that we had 'come home' when we met the Quakers, but we found both many of the members and the philosophy of Quakerism congenial. (It was in any case good for us to meet people who, while over-whelmingly middle class, were generally not intellectuals and were closer to the 'real world' than we had been in university circles.)

We had no trouble in accepting the various Quaker 'testi-monies'. We were, if not initially out-and-out pacifists, convinced that wars were seldom able to resolve relations between states and peoples; pacifism was pragmatic good sense. We did not gamble, we drank in moderation. We did not believe in swearing oaths in a court or elsewhere, believing that one should tell the truth without ceremony. We disliked the use of titles. We accepted the Quaker business method, that one should try to find the will of God or the sense of the meeting, rather than to argue a case and change a policy as one tries to do in a political party. (We found much more good will and much less mutual hostility among Friends than among socialists.) We did not think that convictions were things which could or should be shuffled on and off according to the dictates of fashion or opinion polls.

We shared the Quaker view of the seriousness of life and believed that theirs was a 'religion for adults', as they had no creed or dogma. In this stark version of Protestantism (though some Quakers like to think that they are neither Protestant nor Catholic) the individual must approach God without the aid of clergy. And we were inspired by the message of the founder of Quakerism,

George Fox (1667): '[B]e patterns, be examples in all countries, places, islands, nations, wherever you come, that your carriage and life may preach among all sorts of people, and to them; then you will come to walk cheerfully over the world, answering that of God in every one.' (*Quaker Faith and Practice*, 1995, 19.32).

This brings me to the thorny problem of God and Christianity, and it is time to use the first person singular, for no two people view the great issues of human and divine existence identically. I had never been able to accept belief in a deity independent of human agency who has a specific effect on human affairs, whether through war and plague or any other form of punishment or reward. As David Boulton, who is closely associated with both the Quakers and the Sea of Faith Network, wrote subsequently: 'God is, and always was, a metaphor for the values which, though we understand them to be generated by human culture, we have come to think of as 'ultimate' and 'eternal'... (*A Reasonable Faith*, Sea of Faith Network, 1996, p. 9). God, in short, was for me the sum of human belief in good conduct and permanent values. As for a broad interpretation of Christianity, I had little problem. As an historian properly sceptical of sources I was highly dubious about the contents of the Bible. The preachings attributed to Jesus give good though difficult guidance as to how to lead one's life. But one need not be an historian to appreciate that the majority culture in the west has been shaped or at least influenced by Christian values for many hundreds of years.

Our art, architecture and music are impregnated with Christian assumptions and beliefs. Many of our greatest writers and thinkers, whether scholastic theologians or people with much less formal education like John Bunyan and George Fox, have been inspired by the precepts of Christianity. Most of the founders of the Labour Party and many of the social reformers of the same (1880-1914) period drew their strength from Christian beliefs. It seems to me that one needs a very good reason, if one lives in a western country, and is attracted by organised religion, not to choose one or another Christian denomination. And the faith of one's forebears and the sad history of religious intolerance and persecution do not constitute, in my eyes, a very good reason.

I have said that I am uneasy about facile talk of 'coming home' to the Quakers. It is, I believe, of the essence of Protestantism that the individual worshipper must find his/her own way and this means that no two people will follow an identical spiritual journey. I do not believe that, although a Quaker, one need abandon the power of thought or that the heart must always rule the head. The absence of dogma or a creed means that some Quakers are prone to accept almost any religious or (in my view) even superstitious belief as 'not my own but legitimate'. Quakers oppose such evils as war or homelessness but many of them have little idea of how to combat them except by being nice to other people. (But the political option, one must admit, has been little more successful.) Quakers in the past attracted many hard-headed businessmen, but hard-headedness and the ability to make decisions are often absent from the political outlook of contemporary Friends.

Most Quakers, as I have known them, think of themselves as fairly orthodox Christians, though they often do not accept particular aspects of Christian dogma. But there is a thinking minority on the humanist wing, and most Friends are content to live and let live in loyalty to each other and to the society. Be that as it may, I am a committed Quaker and intend to remain so, ready to sustain the jibes of friends and family as required until my death, or unless those within the society who wish to adopt a more orthodox version of Christianity common to all Friends succeed in their aim. I hope and believe that they will not.

And so, since the start of 1991, Ann and I have attended silent meeting for worship, punctuated by the periodic ministry of those present, on most Sunday mornings. We attended a variety of business meetings and were pleased to become librarians at Hampstead for a couple of years before we left for Boulogne at the end of September 1996. We have been welcomed both by our own two 'home' meetings and by the many others which we have attended on occasional Sundays, though our pilgrimages to York have meant that we could be in neither meeting on more than a half-time basis, and this has prevented us from meeting as many people as we could wish.

In the meantime, I was jobless at the end of July 1992 and a week later I turned 60. This time I really did seem to be a permanent victim of the Tory passion for depriving people of employment. We had, however, arranged to go to the Isle of Mull for a holiday and to celebrate my birthday, and this we duly did. We delighted in Tobermory, Ben More, Iona and much else. Before going away I had made several job applications, though I had little hope of any of them succeeding. I was surprised to be interviewed by Tower Hamlets Borough Council in East London for the post of political adviser (sic) to the Labour Group, for I imagined that the Council would be swamped by applications. (Also, I had searched the *Municipal Year Book* and found a number of councillors with Muslim names whom I imagined in my ignorance would not want to employ an adviser named Rubinstein. Not for the first time in my life my preconceptions were to be embarrassingly rebuked.)

I was not surprised that I was not appointed, because I found it difficult to make much of an impression on the equal opportunities interviewing system (everyone on the panel asked the same questions of each candidate). I was therefore astonished when I was telephoned to be told that the successful candidate had failed to turn up and asked if I would take on the post on a temporary basis while it was readvertised. I began work on 24 August 1992. The joke was that because I was now working full-time in a better-paid job and was owed holiday pay by Maidstone, I actually received a higher salary in August than in July, my last month at Maidstone. I had in addition a bonus of £4,000 as described above, and my journey to work was shorter and cheaper. Ann was temporarily working regularly for the Ramblers' Association, and while the two jobs lasted, that is until the end of the year, we were unusually affluent.

Alan Mattingly, who had been a Newham councillor, had told Ann in patronising metropolitan fashion that I would find Tower Hamlets very different from 'sleepy Maidstone'. There was nothing sleepy about Maidstone, but Tower Hamlets was certainly different. The Tower Hamlets population was larger (about 165,000 as against 136,000 in Maidstone in 1991) and the density much greater. Ethnic minorities formed 35.6 per cent of the Tower Hamlets population while Maidstone was over 98 per cent white. Just under 23 per cent of the whole population of Tower Hamlets was of Bangladeshi origin, which made it proportionately the largest single ethnic minority in any borough in the country. The number of Conservatives on the Council was nil. In fact, since the formation of Tower Hamlets in 1965 from the old metropolitan boroughs of Stepney, Poplar and Bethnal Green, it had never had a Conservative councillor.

I was happy at Maidstone and was very well treated, but for sheer fascination Tower Hamlets was difficult to equal. In fact, though I had previously visited the borough on numerous occasions I was soon to wish that I had moved there when I had the opportunity to do so, instead of to a leafier part of London. (I used to feel that, whatever their skin colour, wealth or poverty, all residents of Tower Hamlets enjoyed a singular good fortune. It was as if they proudly wore an invisible badge: 'I belong to Tower Hamlets.') For Tower Hamlets had virtually everything that someone like myself could seek in an urban setting, from the Tower itself to large numbers of fine Georgian houses, three splendid Hawksmoor churches, the river front, Victoria Park and the Grand Union Canal.

Many warehouses had been turned into flats, which would have provided a welcome middle-class element in the borough had not the Council been too short of money to keep its own homes repaired. (There was thus great luxury on the one hand and increasing squalor on the other.) There was industrial archaeology in abundance, the former homes of many famous people (and the present homes of some) and endless associations with the history of the labour movement. In fact the National Museum of Labour History had been based in Limehouse Town Hall (I had lectured there on several occasions) where I was later to work, until it was ejected by the triumphant Liberals after 1986. The Bangladeshi influence provided a magnificent mosque and several smaller places of Muslim worship, shops and restaurants. The Jewish past of the borough had left traces in several places. Tower Hamlets pulsated with artistic and literary activities, and only the alien intrusion of Canary Wharf and neighbouring buildings cast a serious blight. On the other hand, it must be said that Canary Wharf had been well planned and built and in time attracted many shops and other amenities. There was endless interest in pottering around the old docks on which it had been constructed. Finally, the view from Island Gardens at the end of the Isle of Dogs, across to Greenwich is one of the very best in London. This is an inadequate summary of the highlights of one of the most exciting parts of London.

Tower Hamlets was natural Labour territory and it was at best anomalous that the Liberal Democrats controlled it for the eight years between 1986 and 1994. There were allegations that they had gained and kept control because of racist appeals to the white working class, and having read the speeches of Liberal councillors and the newsletters of their local party I find it hard to dissent from this view. On the other hand no party in Tower Hamlets was free from division on racial lines or the need to satisfy conflicting groups, and none could cope adequately with the racial tensions which too often manifested themselves in violence on the streets.

It was the boast of the Liberals that they were taking local government to the people, and to this end they had divided Tower Hamlets into seven so-called 'neighbourhoods'. When I began to work there, five were Liberal-controlled. The virtue of the neighbourhood system was that the population could identify with a particular small area (as, it should be pointed out, they could before 1965 at which date London boroughs had been amalgamated, supposedly to provide more efficient and less party-biased services). A major defect lay in the cost of providing seven town halls, seven housing and planning policies, seven social services, and the absence of unified control, except perhaps in education. (Local management of schools made that difficult too, though the schools were to make steady progress over the years.) It was difficult if not impossible, for example, to move from a rented council home in Stepney to one in Wapping. In any event the neighbourhood system was bitterly contested and a chief point of cleavage between Liberal and Labour. The poverty and variety of Tower Hamlets would have made it very difficult to govern given the best will and conditions, which it did not enjoy. It is a tribute to hard-working members and officers that conditions in the borough did not deteriorate further than they did.

The leader of the Labour Group when I began to work for the borough at its old headquarters, Bethnal Green Town Hall, was Councillor John Biggs, much the most controversial figure in my life since leaving Hull and John Saville four years earlier. I found John, then aged about 35, an engaging and attractive character, honest, bright and wholly absorbed in the political process. Like many of his colleagues he had parliamentary ambitions; like all of them, in 1997 at least, he failed to secure selection. He was to lead the Labour Party to victory in the 1994 Council elections and lead the majority group for a year before being narrowly defeated in his bid for re-election. It says something for his positive qualities that I not only liked John but went on liking him even after he went out of his way to tell me that he had not voted for me as permanent political adviser.

His drawbacks were first lack of tact, second inability to secure the support of the Bangladeshi members of the Labour Group, and thirdly his wit, which was funny and painful. People quickly grew weary of being used for target practice. (I wished him goodbye and Merry Christmas in mid-afternoon on Friday 23 December 1994, when we were again working in the same office; though the only officer present I was not John's personal assistant. My work was finished, the last post of the year had left the building and he was interviewing a senior officer. 'Thanks for dropping in', said John.) He was also, for all his bluster, thin-skinned and unsure of himself. But while many members of the Labour Group were at daggers drawn and attacked each other without reserve at meetings, John was in my experience seldom malicious or unfair to those junior council staff who were unable to defend themselves. I was perfectly able to defend myself but his malicious wit was of the gentlest even with me.

I learned a lot through working for him, though the work was (as Stella Clarke had found at Lewisham) intrinsically less interesting than at Maidstone. There were few or no conferences to attend and the duties were more strictly clerical than they had been previously. (I began to wish that the photo-copying machine had never been invented.) This was a particular drawback as I was now working full-time. There was less fraternising with the Liberal political adviser than at Maidstone, for the Liberals were now The Enemy, though the adviser (Steve Charters) and I were on good if somewhat wary terms when we met.

I think that John Biggs decided early on that he did not want me as permanent adviser. At any rate he soon introduced me to Ian Orton, the Chief Executive of Wapping, one of the two Labour neighbourhoods in the borough. Ian came to interview me and we hit it off at once. He had hesitated about entering academic life himself and had many intellectual and artistic interests. He also invited me to meet the other neighbourhood chief executives – just over five years later almost all had left the employ of the borough. (The meeting was something of an ordeal for I was still very green, but they were all kind.) It was Ian who rescued me from renewed unemployment after a permanent political adviser was appointed to the Labour Group. He and John Biggs arranged between them for me to apply for the new position of (temporary) personal assistant to the neighbourhood chair in Wapping. I did, and just before Christmas 1992 I was appointed. I thus began yet another new job, once again half-time, at the start of 1993.

I had hitherto led a sheltered life. I had always had a room or office nearly or completely to myself. At Maidstone, Stella (later Claire) and I were usually not at work on the same day, and at Bethnal Green Town Hall John Biggs was away as often as he was there. Now I went to Wapping in an office which had about a dozen occupants, our desks at close quarters. I worked at Limehouse Town Hall, a name which was a holdover from an earlier age. There had never been a borough of Limehouse, and the vestry of that name had been abolished with the other London vestries and district boards in 1899 (when Limehouse became part of the metropolitan borough of Stepney). As so often in London (and English) history, functions changed but names endured.

Limehouse Town Hall dated from 1879 but, like St George's Town Hall, Wapping's other municipal building which dated from 1860, it was described by Nikolaus Pevsner as 'exceptionally uninteresting' (*London*, 2, 1952, p. 419). Still, it was much the oldest building in which I had ever worked (Bethnal Green Town Hall had been built thirty years later), and I thought of the Victorian clerks who had travelled to the building in their frock coats, trying to survive on meagre salaries and escape the desperate poverty of their time. St George's, which I visited from time to time to work with my neighbourhood chairs, was well worth a visit because of its exterior mural painting of the 'Battle of Cable Street' in October 1936, executed in socialist realist style and damaged occasionally by local fascists or vandals.

Like the rest of the East End Limehouse had been badly bombed and some of its more interesting buildings had gone. The finest, however, still remained, though badly knocked about by several fires and later bombing. This was the church of St Anne, designed by Nicholas Hawksmoor and built between 1712 and 1730. It was next door to the town hall and was a most welcome neighbour. Even Pevsner, always sparing in his superlatives, termed the west tower 'a spectacular sight from a distance and...more so when all the surrounding buildings were still low' (ibid., p. 414).

It was a sight to lift the heart as I travelled to work on the Docklands Light Railway, and I later became and remained a Friend of St Anne's. Limehouse also had other fascinating nooks and crannies, including Narrow Street, where the homes of theatrical stars and politicians jostled each other and fashionable pubs, and Newell Street, with a row of fine Georgian houses and Dickens connections. It was an interesting and evocative area to roam around during my lunch break, though Limehouse's former renown as the centre of London's small Chinese quarter had ended with the twin cataclysms of war and the London Docklands Development Corporation.

My job as assistant to the neighbourhood chair, a kind of sub-mayor, took a variety of forms but did not occupy the whole of my time. The chair was one of the six Labour councillors and in 1993/4 the position was occupied by Abdul Asad, a good-looking young and ambitious Bangladeshi, and Albert Lilley, a former docker who told me that he had landed in France on D-Day; he had had a long career in London politics. During the whole of the time that I was at Tower Hamlets one of my chief jobs was writing letters in the name of councillors to the local and national press. I used to say that I had far more letters printed in the press under other names than I had ever had under my own. It was not difficult to get letters published, for most papers had a soft spot for Tower Hamlets. One sensitive task was to write letters from Asad (male Bangladeshis were usually known by their surnames) to Ian Orton to demand more prominent representation within the neighbourhood hierarchy for ethnic minorities, a demand which Ian was sometimes reluctant or unable to grant. The idea for the letters was Asad's and the words were often his and often very strong, but the amanuensis and part-author was his assistant, whose job was temporary (as it was to remain during the whole of my time at Tower Hamlets) and dependent on Ian Orton's good will.

Happily for me there was plenty of that. Ian was a little monarch in Wapping; one of my colleagues used to call him the seventh councillor, but that was a misnomer because he really had more power than all the other six put together. Being chief executive of a neighbourhood was a rewarding position, for it was small enough for a single person to have an effective finger in all or most pies. Ian was always kindness personified to me. I never forgot either that I wanted very much indeed to remain employed or that without Ian I would have been jobless at the end of 1992. He was not always popular with everyone, but he certainly was with me.

I was also friendly with Jenny Green, Ian's secretary, and with Tony Buckley, a leader of our economic development team. I never heard anyone speak other than kindly of Jenny; she was a former teacher but now the ideal secretary, interested in people, discreet, reliable and hard-working. I remember being in her semi-partitioned office one day in winter and commenting on the daffodils growing startlingly early in St Anne's churchyard next door. 'They're always early here', Jenny said. 'It's the bodies', said Ian suddenly and succinctly as he entered the office unobserved by me. As for Tony, he always had a good and friendly word for everybody and seemed to know local political events as soon as they happened. He was later to be (Labour) leader of the council of his home borough of Waltham Forest.

My closest friend in Wapping was Brian Oakaby, the Arts and Events officer, who had a surprisingly wide range of abilities and many different types of events to lay on. I remember particularly helping him to prepare an exhibition in Limehouse Library, I fixing photographs to Brian's instructions. When we reached the 24th and final photograph, one twenty-fourth of the available wall space was left; if I had done it alone either I would have run out of space half-way through or else half of the space would have remained blank when all the photos were in place. Brian was particularly good at organising festivals and pop concerts, and he came into his own when he took over this kind of event in the whole borough after 1994. I sometimes acted as his research assistant, particularly enjoying the spadework for an exhibition on the history of Limehouse; the more work I did on it the more fascinated I became.

It was during the course of this research that I realised that opposite Limehouse Town Hall there had been a row of shops in the early part of this century. One of them had had an owner with a German name; it was sacked in one of the riots which took place in East London (and elsewhere) during the Great War. I knew of course about these riots, but not that they had taken place so close to where I spent my working day. The people of Limehouse had had no reason to feel loyalty to a country in which they were

250

regarded by their rulers as dregs; they were the more patriotic for all that.

Brian often took me out to lunch and we visited a wide variety of local pubs. I had half expected East End pubs to be full of aggressive men who, if one brushed them would say ''ere, mite, you do that agen and you wish you 'adn't', but in fact the pubs were generally sedate and the food excellent. It was Brian who did more than anyone else to make my life at Wapping Neighbourhood as agreeable as it was.

I was also on good terms with all of the Wapping councillors, who were a singularly engaging lot. Four of the six members were Bangladeshis, including the popular S.I. Shiraz and Rajan Uddin Jalal, who was the strongest but ultimately unsuccessful Bangladeshi candidate to replace Peter Shore as the local MP. John Riley was a former leader of the council and I was later to interview him (and others) to write short biographies when they became Freemen of the Borough. (I was surprised when an administrative officer rang me up to ask what I had meant when I wrote that one recipient of this honour would as a youth 'dun' his family for money for foreign travel. '"Beg", I suppose', I said, 'but it isn't the exact meaning.' 'Can I say "beg" then?' he asked.) John was another former docker, whose proudest posssession was a photograph of himself when mayor walking down a Tower Hamlets street with the Queen. 'The Queen should be saying to people "that's me with John Riley"', I would say. 'John Riley has actually done good work for the people of Tower Hamlets. What good has the Queen done?' (Republicanism had grown on me over the decades since I was a starry-eyed young American.) I used to meet John on my way to work after I had left Wapping and he was no longer a member. He was a man of the utmost charm and good fellowship.

Of all the Wapping members, however, I was closest to Pola Manzila Uddin, who was then and remained after the local elections in 1994 the only woman Bangladeshi member of the Council. I think that it is fair to say that nobody was ever the same again after getting to know her. When I first met Pola she was still in her early thirties, with a charming husband and four lively children. Her spoken English was much superior to that of most of her male Bangladeshi colleagues, though Jalal was her (and almost everyone else's, including the English-born members') superior in written

English. She was, as I once told her, equally lovable and infuriating. (She told me quite properly that a council officer should not speak to a member in such a manner.) Her demands were considerable and sometimes last-minute. She could be imperious (but always friendly and polite) and importunate, but sometimes quite diffident. 'Do you think you could...', she would ask. 'But Pola, I'm here expressly to do that', I would reply.

She sometimes wanted things which could not be done. Like many other members she would sometimes fail to turn up to events which she had agreed to attend. But I quickly grew to love her, did what I could to help her to further her parliamentary ambitions and was delighted that she survived to the Bethnal Green and Bow parliamentary shortlist, the only local councillor who did so. (She was not then to know that she would be appointed a member of the House of Lords by the Blair government in 1998.) With a single exception she was the person of whom I was fondest in my Tower Hamlets days. And it was she who was ultimately to ensure that though I remained a temporary member of staff, my work became more and more enjoyable, exciting and close to the sources of power.

When I was not working for the neighbourhood chair I helped in the policy section; sometimes I had more work, sometimes less. I spent a good deal of time analysing the figures of the 1991 census, which were available on a borough, neighbourhood and ward basis; our wards were St Katharine's and Shadwell. I published details of poverty, education, employment and unemployment and related matters, and circulated them to key officers and outsiders. Tony Buckley would view my latest effort sardonically. 'Is there *still* something to squeeze out of the census?!' he would ask sceptically.

I spent fourteen months in Wapping. The most sensational event took place on 16 September 1993 when, after a near miss the previous year, the British National Party won a council by-election on the Isle of Dogs, which was the other Labour neighbourhood in the borough. (We were almost within shouting distance of the Isle of Dogs boundary and Tony Buckley warned me jokingly not to visit the neighbourhood after the BNP candidate, Derek Beackon, was elected.) As French Communists also found, voters could move from supporting the left to voting for fascists with no intermediate stage. It was a sensation for the racist BNP to elect a councillor anywhere, but the Isle of Dogs was in London and on the doorstep of the media, many of which were then or soon afterwards located in the western parts of Tower Hamlets or even on the Isle of Dogs itself. The publicity was immense. It included a letter which appeared in *The Times* on 25 September, drafted by me and signed by Councillors Albert Lilley and Albert Asad on behalf of Wapping Neighbourhood. The letter called for more and better housing, repairs to schools, more jobs and, in general, 'more [government] resources for the inner city'.

I had become by stages Wapping's lead officer on race relations and was the neighbourhood representative on the borough-wide Tower Hamlets Inter-Agency Panel on community relations, chaired by the Rev. David Paton, Dean of Tower Hamlets. (I had written a detailed report on race relations in other London boroughs in an effort to discover how common problems were faced

Conference at Wapping Neighbourhood on racial violence, late 1993. Standing, from left, David McFarland, David, Councillor John Biggs, John Goodwin, Kevin Constable (both Wapping colleagues), the Rev. Ian Hamilton. Seated, from left, Ian Orton, Councillor Abdul Asad, Home Office official, John Shepherd (local police chief).

elsewhere and with what degree of success.) Another stalwart was David McFarland, a former probation officer who headed a government task force on community safety in the borough. There was in reality not a great deal that we could do in the short term about the critical situation which had suddenly arisen in the borough, but we at least provided a forum whose membership suddenly soared, and a means of contact between officialdom and representatives of the rightly apprehensive ethnic minorities in the borough.

I am bound to say that I was acutely conscious of being an educated white middle-class male who went home to West Hampstead every night, deploring the violence between the poor whites and Bangladeshis of the East End. There was an unpleasant whiff of Pecksniffery about it. But I had at least not voted for a government which had set out to increase unemployment while refusing to allow councils to build new homes or repair existing ones. The consciences of the Conservative government should have been much more troubled than mine.

Racially motivated attacks in the streets and elsewhere increased at the same time, and there was one particularly shocking case of the near-murder of a Bangladeshi youth. This also aroused enormous publicity. Letters to the press multiplied, we wrote to put our case to Michael Howard the Home Secretary when he visited Tower Hamlets, we staged a conference attended by a high-ranking Home Office official, we pushed (unavailingly) for racial attacks to be made a specific crime. The BNP by-election victory, which was not repeated at the general local election in May 1994 (despite an alarmingly high BNP poll), must have been a contributory factor in persuading the local white electorate that it was better to live peacefully with Asian neighbours than to assert their 'rights' as East Enders of long standing. Social peace would benefit everyone, our letters in the local press insisted, and all local people were entitled to live in safety. Acceptance of this point of view was to mean, though I did not realise it at the time, reasserting old loyalties to the Labour Party and abandoning the Liberals with their lamentable policies towards race relations.

By mid-1993 I was working three days a week. The job was ill-defined and still temporary, involving assistance to the neighbourhood chair, working in the policy section, on race relations, with Brian Oakaby in his arts and events activities and providing services for the other neighbourhood members. In the earlier months I was sometimes short of things to do but this situation changed as I worked myself into the job. On the non-working days I was still doing research on women in the labour movement between the wars, but I had difficulty in finding enough time to devote to the project, and the research came to an end when I found early in 1994 that Pamela Graves, an American author, had published her work on the same subject, entitled *Labour Women: Women in British Working-Class Politics 1918-1939* (1994). The research which I had done on the subject remains my largest unfinished project and though the Graves book is of high quality there is still room for more work on the subject. Some of it may yet be done by me.

But even before *Labour Women* had appeared my scholarly attention had moved to my new religion. The Hampstead Friends' Meeting House is a charming building designed by the Quaker architect Fred Rowntree in 1907 in a style influenced by the leading contemporary architect C.F.A. Voysey. I set to work on what I regarded as my 'masterpiece', i.e., a finished piece executed by a medieval craftsman to gain entrance to the guild. My effort was an eighteen-page pamphlet on the raising of money for and construction of the meeting house, its history till the outbreak of war in 1914, an account of some of the early members (some of them quite prominent in their day) and the records of admission of new members. I also provided a social class analysis of the identifiable members, more varied then than now. The pamphlet was published early in 1994.

The records were full of interest. Of a new member admitted early in 1914 it was written that she had wanted to join because of the 'simple true fellowship' which she found among Friends. It was probable that she had not 'passed through any deep spiritual experience' but she had 'known something of the hard & uphill part of life'. (*Hampstead Quakers 1907-1914*, 1994, p. 12) So the admission of Friends of doubtful religious orthodoxy or affiliation had already begun. Another case was that of a woman who married in the meeting house in 1909. She and her husband had shared the same address before marriage and she was evidently a woman of independent mind: 'She has informed the Clerk that she is 30 years of age & has supported herself for the last 10 years without assistance from her parents, & that she does not consider that she is under any obligation of any sort to ask their consent & does not propose to do so.' (Ibid., p. 13) I paid for the publication of the pamphlet myself and covered my costs from sales, but I found to my disappointment that Hampstead Friends, especially the older ones, had little apparent interest in their own history. I had enjoyed the research and writing, however, and my appetite was whetted for further Quaker research (on attitudes to the Great War) which I was to begin a few years later.

This varied and rewarding existence, which included regular long weekends in York, came to an end after a telephone call in February 1994 from Catherine Joncheray, who had moved back from Tours to her native Angers. Would I be able to come to Angers to teach at the university during the second academic semester, beginning at the end of the month? It seemed that there really was truth in the French adage: 'jamais deux sans trois'.

CHAPTER 10

'Famous in France and Tower Hamlets': 1994-7

A S WITH OUR TWO invitations to Tours, Ann and I were highly doubtful about going to Angers. Our lives were happy and settled and there would be a great deal of disruption for a visit of less than three months. Would my job at Tower Hamlets be secure? The local government elections were to be held in early May 1994, a little more than two months after my departure. It seemed a dereliction of duty to leave my councillors in the lurch.

In the event I need not have worried. Ian Orton at once gave me unpaid leave, though had things turned out differently he might not have been in a position to honour his promise. Our friend Joyce Pickard, who had done much to welcome us to York and York Quakers, managed almost miraculously to find tenants for our house there during our absence. The councillors, as it turned out, did brilliantly without me. Ann and I went off to Angers, this time carrying all our clothes, books etc. on our backs; we were well used by now to travelling like beasts of burden. We had been offered university accommodation which consisted of a flat shared with three other people, two young Rumanians and an American lecturer in English who had been invited to teach in Angers for a rather longer period. The accommodation was adequate for so short a period and the journey to work, a short walk across parkland, was a joy in contrast to the arduous journey to Wapping by two tube trains and the DLR to which I had been accustomed.

There was a good deal of teaching material to prepare and time was short, but it was all very enjoyable. We were pleased to be quite close to Tours, to which we paid two visits; a sombre one to the

Marie-Hélène Besnault and Rodney Coward (Tours colleagues) with Ann,
chez Bourgoin, near Tours, May 1994.

Pujols, whose marriage was about to end, and a happier trip to the
Bourgoins, who treated us with their usual kindness and generosity, and invited others of our friends there to dinner to meet us.
(We have photographs which show graphically the combined effects
of wine and good fellowship.) We also visited the Escarbelts at their
home near Lille, Bernard having returned to his native region after
three years in Tours. We had an enjoyable weekend and caught the
train back from Gare Montparnasse by the skin of our teeth; I had
a class to take that afternoon.

Angers is the centre of a delightful region and the French talk
with reason of 'la douceur angevine'. The Maine (which gives its
name to the American state) flows through the town, and the cathedral and old town are situated high above the river; one reaches the
cathedral by a dramatic flight of steps. The castle, a real 'château
fort', houses a justly celebrated set of late fourteenth-century tapestries called 'Tenture de l'Apocalpyse' of which no fewer than 76
remain. On the other side of the river is the Musée Jean Lurçat,

258

which houses a collection of modern tapestries called 'le Chant du Monde', almost as splendid in their way as those in the chateau. Amongst the ancient half-timbered houses is the Maison d'Adam, on which poses a figure in an indecent posture. I was shocked by what can only be called 'this display', and sent postcards of it to a number of friends so that my moral outrage would be shared by them and by their postmen and women.

Angers has also a marvellous and extensive open air market on Sunday mornings. Closer to the university, which was at the extremity of the town, was a quarter whose centre was the Place de la Laiterie, which was also full of half-timbered houses. It was here that we daydreamed of living if we were lucky enough to return to Angers. Very close to our university flat was a narrow but very pretty lake, the Etang Saint-Nicolas, on the site of former quarries with a well-worn path round its edge. Here we used to walk through the trees on most days, dodging the joggers who were almost as numerous as walkers.

Though we were in Angers for so short a period we were treated with the same hospitality which we had enjoyed in Tours. Catherine and Dominique Joncheray showed us repeated kindnesses, doing everything they could to smooth our paths. We specially enjoyed a visit to the sports club to which they and their children Thomas and Alice belonged and to which we imagined that not many foreigners had access. Another colleague took us to a restaurant and two others invited us to their homes, including Dominique Dubois, the head of department. Our other hosts were John and Francine Cassini, who as luck would have it came from my home state of Ohio and had lived in Angers for many years. I taught American history (almost for the first time) in Angers, and John was a useful source of books and advice.

The period of my employ included the April holidays (which do not necessarily include the Easter period in France) and we visited Marseille, enjoying bouillabaisse in the vieux port, and Corsica, the beauty of which overwhelmed us. Not only the countryside and the sea, but also some of the towns, especially Bastia, were entrancing. Washing hung in rows between the houses of the old town and I reflected that the term 'the great unwashed' had become a misnomer. We were also lucky enough to witness the annual commemoration by the fishing community in traditional costume of the discovery of the Christ des Miracles, a small crucifix found in the sea in 1428, with a celebratory mass in the Chapelle Ste-Croix.

We returned to Angers on the day of the English local elections, Thursday 5 May. Ann and I lay in bed early the next morning listening to the results on the BBC. (Tower Hamlets was now so well known that the result in the borough was picked out on the Radio 4 news.) I had thought that the poor state of much Wapping housing and the loudly voiced hostility of some local residents to the administration of the neighbourhood meant that the Labour majority there was in danger, and with it my job. I was in no doubt that Liberal councillors would not want me as personal assistant; nor would I want to serve them. I was therefore surprised and delighted to learn that there had been a Labour landslide in Tower Hamlets. Not only was Wapping held by Labour and Derek Beackon washed away on the Isle of Dogs, but Labour had almost had a clean sweep throughout the borough. Only in Bow had the Liberals clung on. The overall result was Labour 43, Liberals 7; previously the Liberals had had 30 councillors to Labour's 20. There were going to be changes in Tower Hamlets. As for me, I reflected, never again would I lose a job because of the result of a local or national election, since there would be none before 1997, the year I would turn 65. The results in the borough were hailed by the Labour leader John Smith who a week later was dead.

We returned the day after his death to England. Catherine Joncheray with her usual charm and efficiency turned out in the early morning to take us to the station, though we pointed out to her that there was a bus which could take us almost door to door. No, she had met us on arrival, she would take us to the station. I told her of Hugh Dalton's story about Lord Halifax thanking an Indian station master for his excellent care. The reply was: 'It has always been a very great pleasure to see you off.' (*The Fateful Years*, 1957, p. 362). Shortly before we left Angers, Dominique Dubois told me that he thought it likely that there would be a post which could be offered to me in 1994-5 in the English department. He promised to let me know. It must have soon after our return that Ann's mother told her that I was 'famous in France and Tower Hamlets'. It would make a nice epitaph.

I returned in mid-May to a Tower Hamlets turned upside down by the local elections. Nobody knew what to expect because the triumphant Labour majority had promised to end the neighbourhood system. After two or three weeks back at Limehouse I moved to Cheviot House on Commercial Road, to work for Councillor Asad and other members in the area. But this arrangement in turn was temporary. Pola Manzila Uddin was now the deputy leader of the majority group and wanted me as her personal assistant. I was to move to the headquarters of the council at Mulberry Place, a spanking new building actually erected within the walls of the old East India Dock. The dock walls themselves constituted a listed building. The first occupants were installed in Mulberry Place in June 1993.

Mulberry Place was, as my nominal boss Dave Kingdon (Head of Corporate Services) said when he met me there in early July 1994, 'like a hotel', and a grand one at that. I had an arduous journey to work and the building was not an ideal workplace for the staff, but then neither were the refurbished Victorian and Edwardian buildings which had contained my former offices in Tower Hamlets. The windows did not open (which was as well, as the Blackwall Tunnel was near at hand), lights were on 24 hours a day in all seasons, and neither the central heating nor the air conditioning was satisfactory. More serious was the fact that the building, later styled 'the town hall', was remote from the community. Bethnal Green and Limehouse Town Halls and Cheviot House were in the middle of fascinating areas, but there was little to do or see around Mulberry Place. The most interesting church in the area was All Saints Poplar, built immediately after the Napoleonic Wars. A little further away was Chrisp Street Market with its prizewinning clock tower, surrounded by the Lansbury Estate, once a symbol of the new, egalitarian post-war London. The rebuilt docks area on the Isle of Dogs was also within reach in the other direction, but I found Canary Wharf too far away for a lunch-time walk.

I was now to work four days a week and from the start was so busy that the job became full-time from mid-November 1994. I had an informal agreement to write a pamphlet about York Quakers for a local history series. It was initially intended to cover the period of the two world wars but I was now unable to honour the agreement; research would have to await retirement. I wrote to Dominique Dubois and told him that, while I would be interested in a post in Angers in 1995 or 1996, I had just taken up a new position in London local government and did not feel that I could leave it within three months to return to France. He did not reply and the chance to live in the Place de la Laiterie disappeared forever. On the other hand I never had a contract exceeding three months in Tower Hamlets, and I could well have been making a gesture which would result in the loss of twelve months' well-remunerated employment in one of the most interesting regions of France. Fortunately, it was not to be so, and my departure from Tower Hamlets was to be my own decision.

The work at Mulberry Place was not very different from what I had done for John Biggs and at Wapping, but now I was on the fringes of the very centre of power. I worked in the leadership office and heard much of the political gossip, of which there was a good deal. As so often in Labour Party history, much of the energy of the victorious Labour group was dissipated on internecine warfare. (I was glad, as I was given reports of Group meetings lasting till midnight, that I had not after all been appointed to the permanent post of Labour Group adviser. The adviser had to be present to take the minutes of Group meetings.) Manoeuvring for position between left and right (the terms meant relatively little at local level), whites and Bangladeshis, shifting alliances and antagonistic personalities was incessant. John Biggs as the new leader of the Council felt forced to spend time calculating his chances of re-election as leader. His relations with Pola Uddin soon deteriorated and partly in consequence he narrowly lost power in the election of spring 1995. In the four years between 1994 and 1998 there were to be three Council leaders, three deputy leaders, three chairs of education and three chairs of social services.

More important than the determination of councillors to push each other off the nearest cliff was the fact that the Council was too short of money to carry out all its duties properly. The financial noose was ever tighter and it was little short of tragic that the people of the East End, plagued by poor housing, unemployment and a generally low level of educational attainment were hampered even further by the fact that the Council could not keep the streets clean and homes repaired. Shortage of money could be fairly laid at the door of the government, and the fact that the BNP challenge declined at each by-election owed little to John Major and his friends.

It was also a huge job to abolish neighbourhoods, recentralise services, appoint a new chief executive, find work for the former neighbourhood staffs and end the employment of those for whom there was no place in the new structure. I found it hard to believe, as the months passed and the tumbrils rolled, that my head was still attached to my body and I was still at work. Re-organisation followed re-organisation and there was much bitterness as established staff were forced to leave. On the other hand, there were important initiatives across the board, in terms of improving race relations, combating poverty, raising standards in schools and attempting to reunite the different communities in the borough after the divisive Liberal years. I was not in a position to judge globally how successful were the first four years of Labour administration, but I do know that both members and officers worked hard to improve community relations and services for local people.

When I left Tower Hamlets to return to university teaching a colleague and friend in the borough wrote to congratulate me on what he thought would be a greater intellectual challenge than I had enjoyed in local government. His intent was kindly, but I had no feeling at Mulberry Place of working below my capacities. Writing speeches or letters to the press for members, taking minutes of committees, attending the leader's weekly meetings with trade union representatives, answering letters from the public, undertaking odd pieces of research on race relations, public transport or other issues, added up to a varied and fascinating working life. One of my friends said rightly that I had one of the most interesting jobs of anyone who worked for the Council. I was very lucky.

There were plenty of phone calls to make and letters to write to say that 'Councillor Mrs Uddin regrets' and the like, but local government is an inherently fascinating subject, particularly in Tower Hamlets, and I only regret that my time in it was so short. I was able to meet Kenneth Leech, the famous clergyman (and old friend of my former student Peter Hibbert) previously mentioned, who had been based for decades in the East End. Ken lectured on the history of the Cable Street area to a packed St George's Town Hall one evening in autumn 1994, and later I began to participate in a discussion group which met regularly at his flat in Aldgate. That connection was rudely ended by my departure from Tower Hamlets in September 1996.

My enjoyment of the two-plus years at Mulberry Place was greatly enhanced by personal contact. Local government is certainly not free from the bickering and backstabbing which so disfigured university life for me, but I threatened nobody and my only concern was to hang on to my job. This did not mean that I never crossed swords with anyone, but such incidents were infrequent and temporary. On the other hand I made a surprising number of friends given the short period of my service and the fact that almost everyone I met was much younger than I was. When I left Tower Hamlets I was aged 64; there were very few staff on the eight floors of Mulberry Place aged over 50. Another problem was that I had enjoyed many more years of formal education than my workmates and, more important, I spent much more of my leisure in reading. I used to say that whenever someone was needed who could read and write I was called for, but I did my best to overcome the barriers of age and education without (I hope) usually displaying this degree of arrogance.

I do not want to turn this account of my working life at Mulberry Place into a list of names, and it is difficult to pick and choose between the people whom I knew and liked at Mulberry Place, but a few must be mentioned. In May 1996 my old friend Rajan Uddin Jalal succeeded Pola Manzila Uddin as deputy leader of the Labour Group. He was one of the most intelligent and well-informed of all the Labour members and I greatly enjoyed working with him. He, like Pola, made a variety of demands and I enjoyed writing speeches and letters at his behest. He was a controversial character but, as with other members, he was always thoughtful and kind in his dealings with junior (in rank!) staff. Bethnal Green and Bow acquired, by all accounts, an excellent MP in Oona King to succeed Peter Shore in 1997, but I regretted that neither Jalal nor Pola was the Labour candidate. The other member to whom I was close was Nooruddin Ahmed, chair of Equalities and Personnel, to whom I was personal assistant as I was to the deputy leader. Noor, as he was called, was fertile of ideas and an exceptionally nice and kindly man. He was one of only two people whom I met in my years in local government in whom I had total confidence that his judgment and actions towards other people were always right and fair. I felt pleased and proud that three of the members whom I knew best and to whom I felt closest were Bangladeshis.

The other person in whom I had total confidence was Clive Jacotine, who had been Chief Executive of Bow Neighbourhood and who, when I met him, was in charge of the transition from the neighbourhood system to a recentralised local government. We quickly became friendly and met often at the Sunday evening chamber music concerts at Conway Hall. I was pleased that he was able to stay occasionally at our home in York. Another friend was Cliff Stephens, who worked in Personnel policy. I was delighted when Cliff, nearly thirty years younger than I was, first invited me out to lunch. After that we became good friends and saw much of each other. Ann and I were later to be visited in Boulogne by Cliff and his charming Chinese-born, Cambridge-educated wife Ling.

However, my enjoyment of my too-brief period at Mulberry Place was largely due to my colleague Joanne Todd. She was the personal assistant to both the leader of the council and the mayor, and our desks were adjacent; we filled in for each other in holiday periods or on other occasions when one of us was absent. Joanne was an East End girl nearly 25 years my junior; her grasp of the English language was sometimes more colloquial than formal. She would make me cross at times, specially as she was as insistent on thinking in stereotypes as I was on the uniqueness of the individual. (Although she did not know it at the time, she was the inspiration for the statement which I drafted for the Equalities section and which was later widely circulated as a leaflet and poster, proclaiming: 'We are all individuals! Never make assumptions about colleagues based on their race, gender, disability, sexuality, name, religion or nationality!')

Joanne was one of the colleagues to whom I was closest in all my years of employment. It is difficult to explain 'the reason why', but it was one of those cases in which the personalities fitted. There were more objective reasons. Joanne was, as Ann (not always inclined to make this kind of judgment about people) said, the kindest person she had ever met. Nothing was too much trouble for her to do on behalf of friends. When I left Tower Hamlets she gave me a present with a note saying: 'I thought we made a good team! I've learnt such a lot from you.' More realistically but still generously, she wrote to me in France at the end of June 1997: 'I still miss you & your little moods in the office'. (Why did Ann laugh so hard when she read this?) Only Joanne would be so generous as to dismiss my displays of petulance as 'little moods'. After I left Tower Hamlets and Joanne I felt that I knew how Leigh Hunt had felt when Jenny kissed him.

Joanne had the witty and decisive last word after complaining about my illegible postcards as, alas, everyone did – and does. I told her that she ought to be grateful that I sent her cards and that if the postman could read the address she should be able to read the text. She wrote: 'Thanks for the postcard. I'm not complaining but it took me three days to decipher it – but I'm not complaining – I kept going back to it & tried again. I kept thinking about it & I felt triumphant when I finally understood, but please don't think I'm complaining; please keep sending your postcards.' For once in my life I could think of no reply.

It was not long after I first met Joanne that our families met each other. Ann and I spent a number of enjoyable evenings with her and her husband Dave, a printer with the London Borough of Southwark. Dave is not a man easily outshone by his wife; he keeps up his end with ease. They have three active and energetic children; luckily Joanne and Dave are also energetic and family-centred. To add to all her other activities Joanne is a pillar of her church, All Saints Poplar, and a school governor. We enjoyed comparing notes about our respective denominations. She was unaware until she read these lines in draft that I was to use her and her family as

David with Joanne and Dave Todd at our home in West Hampstead, London, December 1996.

an example of social mobility in my teaching of modern British society in Boulogne. A large house in Bow, two cars, family holidays in Florida and the Dominican Republic, her fortieth birthday celebrated in New York; hers is not the traditional East End working-class family. She wrote to say that she could not decide whether or not to employ a cleaner. 'Can I brush aside my working class mentality & get someone to sort me out?' (I replied that the working class would not hold it against her if she did.) And this was a couple both of whom had left school at sixteen.

I had written to all my French university contacts late in 1994 saying that I was available in 1995 if they had a temporary vacancy. I did this partly because I wanted a last year in France and partly because I wanted more security than the one, two and three month contracts I was being given at Tower Hamlets. I heard nothing and had almost given up hope of returning to France when on the evening of 20 November 1995, as Ann and I were determinedly ignoring the fact that Princess Diana was telling all to Martin Bashir on 'Panorama', I had a telephone call from Imelda Bonel-Elliott, head of the English department at the University of the Littoral in Boulogne-sur-Mer. Was I available in 1996-7 if there was a vacancy?

My friend Bernard Escarbelt, after his return to Lille, had taken charge of the English department at Boulogne, then a 'filière' of the University of Lille III. I had given lectures for him both at Boulogne and at Lille, so I was known to the colleagues in Boulogne. The centre there had since become part of the separate University of the Littoral and it seemed likely that the English department would be looking for a temporary professor of British civilisation in October 1996. Before the end of our conversation I asked Imelda if she was a republican, since she had rung during the royal interview. Being Irish by origin she had a very different understanding of that word from mine, and for a moment we were talking at hilarious cross-purposes. Ethnocentricism sets its snares for us all.

Telephone calls followed at fairly regularly intervals and by the summer of 1996 it was clear that there would be a job for me. I had never told Imelda that I would accept, only that I was interested. By the time the existence of the job was actually confirmed, however, I was too far committed to decline. It was a wrench to leave Tower Hamlets, but I told myself that I was essentially a university teacher rather than a clerk. Also, it was to be a permanent job, to last till my 65th birthday – one year away. Ann and I had our usual attack of pre-France collywobbles and as before, it was wholly unnecessary. We had the time of our lives.

Much was made of me when I left Tower Hamlets and the festivities owed a great deal to Joanne Todd's organisation. Ian Orton made a typically graceful farewell speech. As I type I can look round and see four of my presents. Another was a framed verse, a biography in parvo. My favourite line was the following: 'Not only belying his good looks, he is the author of history books'. I was also the subject of a very nice write-up in the staff newspaper. And so to France!

We left London on 30 September 1996. Our start was inauspicious. I misread the departures board at Victoria Station (I was not the only one to do so and wrote an angry letter of complaint; the train was subsequently shifted to Charing Cross) and missed the boat train. I rushed to Charing Cross and took the next train. After a hair-raising taxi ride from Ashford I caught the catamaran by the skin of my teeth and thus managed to arrive in Boulogne before the removals man. Had I missed that catamaran he would have been there before me.

The Boulogne experience was in a number of respects different from our previous sojourns in France. We had the most comfortable flat of our four French homes. It was almost in the centre of the town; Boulogne was the smallest place I had ever lived and my home was in the town centre for the first time. We were almost on top of the central police station, which had its inconveniences in summer when, with all windows wide open, we could (or at least Ann could) hear the policemen chatting and listen to their inadequately oiled barrier-gate rising and falling as vehicles arrived and left. I had never previously lived by the sea, and though it was a good twenty minute walk away it was exciting to be so close. Ann in particular revelled at being able to walk to the sea whenever she wished.

The university too was a different experience from Tours and Angers. Imelda Bonel-Elliott and I were the principal 'civilisationistes'. Not only was I not, as previously, an extra wheel, but Imelda's administrative responsibilities as head of department meant that I had an even more important role to play. I had seven courses to prepare and teach: British history from, as I liked to say, 'the primeval slime' to the nineteenth century; political, economic and cultural aspects of the reign of George III; the Victorian period; the home front during the Second World War; the British political system; the British economy; and (a course shared with colleagues) contemporary British society.

This variety was very helpful to me. The later eighteenth century was a period which I had hitherto neglected. The Second World War was a particular interest and I was fascinated by the revisionist debate about it amongst historians, in which I could see both the echoes of Thatcherism and (as it seemed to me) the unspoken resentment of younger, working-class historians towards the complacent assumptions of their servant-keeping predecessors. I could hardly have taught this course, which was part of the CAPES qualification for secondary school teachers (the contents changed annually), without the assistance of my friend David Martin of the University of Sheffield. David uncomplainingly sent me books and photocopies by return of post; with no British university library at hand I would have been crippled without him. (Graham Johnson also came to my rescue, sending several books which helped me with Victorian history.) The three courses on contemporary Britain made me undertake essential reading and order my thoughts on the nature of the modern British world.

My colleagues, while friendly, did not overwhelm Ann and me with hospitality as they had done at Tours and Angers; I am tempted to write that this was partly due to the fact that fewer of them were French, but the truth is that at the earlier universities the Anglophones were just as hospitable as my French colleagues. It was spring or early summer before we were invited to two of my colleagues' homes. Everyone was very friendly at work, however, and I had some enjoyable departmental lunches. I also enjoyed my contacts with Maggie Gillespie, our lectrice, who took the classes for one of my lecture courses. She lived in Paris, however, and was hence only in Boulogne two days each week.

There were, however, special factors which made hospitality more difficult in Boulogne than elsewhere, notably a much smaller department. Any feeling which I might have had that we were less than enthusiastically welcomed was emphatically swept aside when the end-of-year drink turned out to be a 'good-bye and thank you

David' function. For the second time in less than a year I was feted, nice things were said, presentations were made; I was overwhelmed.

Whatever we may have lost in social contacts through the university was made up elsewhere. We learned early on that the Anglican church (*not*, on the continent, the Church of England) had weekly services in a chapel belonging to a Catholic convent (relations were friendly between the two denominations). We made a number of contacts in the English and Anglo-French community which attended services. Ann served faithfully every Wednesday afternoon in the English library attached to the church and thus became friendly with Pauline Cecchin, the church warden. Pauline had married a Frenchman and lived in France for many years. She now lived in a house in the old town of Boulogne, where we visited her and Pierre on several occasions.

Our closest church contacts were the clergyman (called 'chaplain'), Don Ruddle, and his wife Pippa. Don, slightly older than I, was the former vicar of East Malling, near Maidstone, who now lived not far from St Omer in a delightful house which he and Pippa had restored and improved. The Ruddles had thought they had moved to France to retire, but they soon found that Don was in charge of several churches, to say nothing of ministering to the English-speaking prisoners in the local jail. These duties involved driving considerable distances each week. Their backgrounds and lives, which included long residence in Africa and (in Pippa's case) what is now Pakistan were very different from ours, and their interests were of course much less overwhelmingly political than mine. As with local government in Tower Hamlets, as with the Friends, this difference of background and interest was a salutary experience for me.

We knew guiltily that clergy and their spouses had a surfeit of human contact and entertaining. We knew in addition that the Ruddles were a convenient (for the visitors!) port of call for their old parishioners when on holiday, but this did not prevent us from offering and accepting hospitality from them. We felt at once at home, happy and relaxed with them, as happens all too seldom with contacts in later life.

I realised to my surprise that by the end of our time in Boulogne I had taken part in the service there more frequently than any other act of worship in my life except for the Friends' meetings in

Hampstead and York, though I had attended many Church of England services in a variety of places previously. I did not dare tell the Ruddles this, nor did I dare to say (what I implied to Peter Hibbert) that it was difficult for me to feel that the words used in the Anglican service had other than traditional, historical significance. I 'thought of it as a metaphor', however, as Ann counselled, and remembered that the Sea of Faith Network, mainly an Anglican group, took a similar line to my own. I was also much happier with Don's High Church views (as I was with Peter Hibbert's) than I could possibly have been with an evangelical clergyman.

I was glad and grateful to attend the Anglican service about once each month and listen to Don's thought-provoking sermons. I remember in particular a reference he made to St Teresa of Ávila and her lack of money. 'What could Teresa do with sixpence?' Don asked. 'Nothing. But with Teresa and her sixpence God could change the world.' I was much moved and told Ann so afterwards. She replied that Quakers and Anglicans could often speak each other's language.

We tried to attend monthly the small Friends' meeting in Folkestone, the hour's time difference between France and Britain allowing us to arrive soon after the meeting began. We also took advantage of our proximity to east Kent to attend other meetings; Dover, Canterbury and Ramsgate. We had several very enjoyable walks in east Kent, in which we visited Sandwich, Deal and St Margaret's Bay. It was a richly rewarding area, too far from London to visit easily on a day trip, too near home to spend a holiday there, but accessible without difficulty from Boulogne.

We normally spent another Sunday morning each month walking around Boulogne and district (and twice in Kent) with our rambling club, the Association Sakodo (or 'backpack'). We were made immediately welcome as the 'ami(e)s anglais(es)' and this contact greatly enhanced our enjoyment of our year in the Boulonnais and its attractive, rolling, wooded countryside, dotted with chateaux of various ages and pretty villages. The president of the association, Christian Poilly, knew everything and could do everything. The range of his interests, topographic, historical, political, was immense and he was the best of companions – and story-tellers. Christian could 'walk on water', as Ann said, and his wife Christine was 'ridiculously pretty'; the word mignonne could have been invented for her. Our closest friends in Sakodo were Guy and Thérèse Morhan, who lived opposite the theatre in the centre of Boulogne. Guy was a retired librarian and Thérèse had kept a clothing shop. They had wide interests, which in Thérèse's case included a passion for music. She was a leading member of the chorale 'Chante Joie' which we heard sing French, German, Italian and English songs on one occasion. The Morhans greatly increased the enjoyment of our year in Boulogne and offered us hospitality when I returned there to take classes in November 1997 in my role as professor emeritus.

The best thing to say about our year in the Nord-Pas-de-Calais is that the reality exceeded our wildest expectations. We felt at once at home in this unglamorous part of France, which had so suffered from war, poverty and deindustrialisation over a prolonged period. We soon found that there was far more to do and see than we had imagined. Boulogne itself had one of the most attractive markets we had ever visited and the walled old town on its hill was a constant pleasure. We visited with Sakodo the Audomarois area of canals and rivers near St-Omer, which made us think of the Norfolk Broads; long cut off from the outside, it seemed almost a secret world. It was a fertile area, however, and produced a large part of the French cauliflower crop. We also visited, with Sakodo and separately, the delightful resort of St-Valéry-sur-Somme where, as Philip Larkin might have said had he visited the area, sky and Picardy and water met, and which had luckily escaped the ravages of war. We also enjoyed the enthusiasts' railway line which went round the bay of the Somme to Le Crotoy.

We also liked all the towns which we visited in the region, specially St-Omer and Arras, admirably rebuilt after being almost wholly destroyed in the Great War. Nicole and Bernard Escarbelt, though struggling with the problems of ill and ageing parents, took us to a remarkable exhibition of art and archaeological treasures of the Nord at Valenciennes, including some from the Merovingian period which I told them that I had hitherto believed to be mythical. (I had certainly seen very few relics from that period, let alone the richness of the ones on display in Valenciennes.) On another occasion they took us to the 'braderie de Lille', a weekend-long non-stop street market in the centre of the city, one of the many old traditions, events and carnivals in which the Nord-Pas-de-Calais is so rich. Lille is a fine city and we were lucky enough to visit on another occasion the magnificent, newly-reopened Musée des Beaux Arts. On Easter Monday 1997, when my son Peter was visiting us, we were spectators at Cassel of the parade of the giants of the towns of the area. They serve as mascots and symbols of the romantic and turbulent history of the towns of the Nord and are regularly carried in procession through the streets by teams of men. This is no mean feat as they can reach a height of over eight metres and weigh more than 300 kilogrammes. They were originally made of wickerwork and pasteboard but newer versions use more modern materials.

In August 1997 we spent a fortnight in Nord-Pas-de-Calais and Picardy, entering Belgium briefly to visit Ypres and Poperinge, and Champagne to see Reims. Our purpose was to visit 'battlefields and belfries' as Maggie Gillespie amusingly commented, otherwise the Great War sites and many cathedrals of the area. We (or I, in my American army days) had visited some of them before, others not. It was a humbling fortnight. The experience of the battlefields, museums, cemeteries and monuments of 1914-18 was over-whelming. We were full of admiration for the care which had been and still is lavished on these sites, horrified by what had happened there and by the fact that bodies and artefacts are still regularly dug up from the former battlefields. We heard the Last Post at Ypres with a large crowd and were told that in November 1918 the town had been so ruined that it was said that from horseback one could see it all at a glance. The inscriptions by British tourists in the books of remembrance, however, sometimes uncomprehending, some-times militaristic, made us realise that one found in such places what one went to see. For us the visit reinforced our pacifist con-victions and our sense of outrage that millions of men could go cheerfully to slaughter at the behest of their rulers and the highly effective spin doctors of the day.

Visiting the battlefields made the statistics of the Great War come to life for us. We understood better than we had done before why the French were so insistent on German reparations after 1918 when we saw the rebuilt towns and read on placards in the war zones that, for example, the agricultural areas of the department of the Aisne had been virtually obliterated in 1914-18. We were moved when we visited the Chemin des Dames, the scene of some of the bloodiest battles, and saw at Cerny-en-Laonnois French and German cemeteries in juxtaposition; as our guidebook said, 'leurs tombes aujourd'hui fraternellement unies' (various authors, *Première Guerre Mondiale des Flandres à l'Alsace*, 1996, p. 322). And we rejoiced, at Reims, to see the memorial stone outside the cathedral commemorating the joint visit of President de Gaulle and Chancellor Adenauer in July 1962 which symbolised the end of the catastrophic enmity between France and Germany.

One can visit the cathedrals at Reims (heavily rebuilt after war damage as it is) and Amiens time after time and gain more from each visit. Visiting Amiens in particular is an almost unbearable emotional and aesthetic experience. I had not previously, however, visited the magnificent cathedral of Beauvais, which I found one of the high points of our moving and varied fortnight. We were also delighted to follow once again Robert Louis Stevenson's footsteps, to visit the cathedral at Noyon and the town hall at Compiègne, which he had lovingly described in *An Inland Voyage* in 1878. We were plunged back into the war zone by visiting the Clairière de l'Armistice near Compiègne where the Germans had surrendered in 1918 and the French in 1940, seeing the little museum with its railway carriage of the 1918 era and many horrifying slides showing the devastation of the battle sites in France and Belgium. We visited also the spot closer to Compiègne where the Germans had rounded up 1250 men as late as 17 August 1944 and transported them to Buchenwald. The anniversary had just taken place and the monument was covered in flowers.

The general election of 1997 was a high point of our year. We made sure that we arrived in London on the afternoon of 1 May and knocked up for our MP, Glenda Jackson; this was the twelfth successive general election in which I had worked for Labour. We were 'still up for Portillo' and the fall of the grisly gang which had misgoverned the country for so long, and while we had no unrealistic hopes of a Blair government we were as thrilled as millions of other people by the result. In view of the exceptional and celebratory circumstances we spent a night in a four-poster bed at the Falstaff Hotel in Canterbury en route back to Boulogne.

Imelda Bonel-Elliot, who did her best to look after us during our stay, did me an unexpected favour when she invited me to address the local Mouvement Européen in Le Touquet, where she lived. The subject was the Labour Party and the British general election. Imelda's invitation petrified me, since although we were now living and working in France for the fourth time, the only occasion on which I had spoken French before an audience was when I gave a short talk to the militants of the PS Tours Centre on British political developments in 1984. But when I recovered from my fear (and thought to myself that if I had not wanted to receive such invitations I should have remained in Ohio) and prepared the lecture, I found not only that it had been good practice but that it had forced me to concentrate my thinking on the Labour Party and its development more than I had done heretofore. I had for several months been debating vigorously with Nick Tucker by correspondence our widely differing points of view on the Blairite Labour Party, and this was of considerable assistance when I had to prepare the talk. My university lecture preparation was also helpful.

Came the night and I lectured in the crowded Maison des Associations to an audience which included some of my students. I tried to repress the periodic thought that an audience was listening to me lecture in French without giggling, and there was a lively discussion afterwards followed by a buffet reception in one of the nicest hotels in Le Touquet, at which Ann and I then spent the night. As I was paid for the talk and worked it into an article for the *Political Quarterly* I felt any thanks were owed by rather than to me.

Like many others I was unimpressed by so-called 'New Labour', because I loathed the over-emphasis on media management and was sceptical of the claimed break with Labour's past. It was easy to hoodwink journalists who, while not ignorant, had short memories and were always seeking sensation and novelty. The reality, I argued, was otherwise. Labour had always been a moderate, social-reforming party, except at certain periods of crisis (as after 1931 and 1979) and after the Second World War when the effects of the war itself, an overwhelming majority in the House of Commons, overdue social welfare measures and public ownership of ailing industries were made to seem like socialism.

It was not, I told my audience in Le Touquet, the Labour Party which had changed but British society. The working class was smaller and more affluent; the population no longer consisted, in the main, of poor manual workers and their families. An historical turning point long anticipated had finally arrived in which money was the great divide rather than, primarily, birth or education or inherited wealth. City currency dealers earning six figure salaries could come from unprivileged backgrounds. The great mass of the population shared similar preoccupations and tastes. Deindustrialisation, Americanisation, television and the cheapening of consumer durables had created a new society. Economic inequality had increased, but social inequality, which was in the end more significant, had declined. (Deference to aristocracy and monarchy was by no means dead, though I could not then have realised how soon or how spectacularly it would be manifested.) The Labour Party had had to react to this situation and, given the virtual (and unprecedented) disappearance of its left wing, pursuing the traditional Labour policies of appealing to the great bulk of the population was allowed to appear, quite inaccurately, as 'new'.

This is what I said and what I wrote for the *Political Quarterly*. Time has perhaps chipped away the edges of my thesis, but in general I stand by it. A party which had done little or nothing with its postwar majorities to take power away from the possessing classes, which introduced cuts in social services as required by the International Monetary Fund, which failed to raise the school leaving age to 16 on financial grounds, which supported every twist of American imperial policy throughout the Cold War including support for the war in Vietnam could hardly be regarded as other than the legitimate parent of the new, Blairite party. By 1997 the party was partly feminised, had greater regard for the needs and demands of the ethnic minorities and a more youthful facade, but these changes were more superficial than fundamental and were in any case the result of socio-economic, not political change. However the eighteen months following the election confirmed that even the rhetoric has changed and that the historic commitment to social justice has been replaced by promises of higher expenditure on health and education – from which the middle class have often in any case been the beneficiaries.

Butskellism reigned as it had done in the 1950s, though it was significant that whereas the Conservatives in the earlier period accepted the main outlines of the postwar Labour settlement, Labour at the end of the 1990s accepted the main outlines of Thatcherism. In both cases, however, Labour was part of the broad political orthodoxy and happy to occupy the centre ground. It was that centre ground which had moved.

★   ★   ★

By September 1997 our thoughts turned perforce to moving back to London. We gave a talk about Quakerism to our friends in the Anglican community (another present) and joined our final ramble with our friends of Sakodo (still more presents). We visited Folkestone Friends' meeting for the last time to worship and say goodbye. Our last 'outing' was a visit to Abbeville, whose church, though still impressive, had been badly damaged in 1940 and was not yet fully restored, and St-Riquier, whose gemlike church reminded me of Wells cathedral. We had lunch in the sunny town square with the church forming an exquisite background. We also admired the amusing Maison Petit, built by a Napoleonic veteran with its gabled roof shaped like the emperor's hat.

On 7 October we left Boulogne with full hearts and happy memories.

CHAPTER 11

Around the World in 154 Days: the United States: 1998

SIX MONTHS FLEW past and Ann and I prepared to start on our travels again, this time much further afield than France where, it must be said, our hearts remained. We had by April 1998 a long-standing arrangement to exchange homes with George and Elsa Struble, friends of Swarthmore days, so that we would spend a substantial period in the United States in the spring and summer of 1998.

All was ready. On Easter Monday (13 April) we walked in the Chiltern beech woods near Great Missenden. It was a cold, sunny day and the countryside and season were superb. The next day we set out for Heathrow, calling up in my mind the long, lonely journey I had made from Hampton Court and Heathrow to Cleveland over forty years before to be called up into the American army (see ch. 4 above).

This time the circumstances were very different and so too was the trip. I was now, after nearly 34 years as a British subject, using my fourth British passport. All the others had stated my place of birth simply as 'Cleveland', a place which might easily be thought to be British. (In fact, though Cleveland is the name of hills and a local government unit in north-east England, there is no British settlement of that name.) I had had no trouble entering the United States with my British passport in 1967 and 1973, but some malignant fate (or, more probably, change of policy) had led the Passport Agency to list my place of birth on my latest passport as 'Cleveland USA'.

The Strubles, our Oregon exchange partners, 1998 (photo taken at Seattle, June 1981); left to right, Elsa, George, Laura, Andrew, Jennifer.

As Ann and I went through the final pre-boarding formalities I was informed by airline security that as I had been born in the United States I needed not only a valid British passport but also either an out-of-date American passport or written permission from the American embassy to enter the USA. I had two old American passports dating from the 1950s – at home, and there we repaired, to try again the following day. This time I was allowed to fly, though only after a long telephone conversation at the boarding gate between security and the American embassy and between the embassy and me. I doggedly maintained that I had not been an American citizen for well over thirty years and the embassy was finally satisfied. The sequel was as expected. After all the anxiety and expense (which included supplementary payment on our subsequent flight from New York to Portland, Oregon), nobody at immigration in New York had the slightest interest in either my place of birth or previous nationality.

I should not, I thought to myself with as much resignation as I could muster, have been surprised. An immigration service which thought it profitable to ask even short-term visitors entering the

United States to state whether they had ever been drug traffickers, involved in terrorism or genocide, or were seeking entry to the United States to engage in criminal or terrorist activities was certainly capable of discriminating between a bona fide foreign national and a second-class former American like me. Once again I reflected that I had done the right thing in emigrating – and in changing my nationality.

The stimulus to my always latent anti-Americanism was, however, mitigated when I received a courteous letter from the American consul in London (dated 20 May 1998) explaining that American concern was not about foreigners born in the United States but about dual nationals, who were legally required to enter that country on their American passports. (Perhaps this was to prevent entry to the United States being given or sold to those who were not entitled to it.) I was still annoyed that as a British citizen and the holder of a single passport I had been prevented from travelling to a supposedly friendly country. I was not, after all, responsible for the fact that governments had delegated the interpretation of their immigration policies to airlines which faced heavy fines if they made mistakes and consequently added their own restrictions. (Had I understood what was required I could have satisfied airline security at once that I was no longer an American.) But I was lucky enough not to have suffered major inconvenience or hardship on this occasion. And I was surprised by the consul's suggestion that I might wish to apply for restitution of my lost American citizenship, the implication being that it would be granted.

George and Elsa lived in Salem, Oregon. No witches had been put to death there (that was Salem, Massachusetts) and we had heard of the American north-west as exceptionally beautiful. I was also, of course, curious to see what had happened in my former country in the 24-odd years since I had been there, and how I would react to it. It was scarcely credible that it had been longer since my last visit to the United States than the entire length of my previous residence and visits there. Our first experiences were stereotypical enough. Two strangers in New York asked whether we could sustain a walking fortnight with our fully-loaded rucksacks (our preferred luggage for ease and convenience), to which we replied that we could. It would have been more accurate to have said that we were still able to do so the last time we tried, nearly three years previously. A New York hotel clerk forty years my junior called me

David, to which greeting I later became accustomed. But I never enjoyed being addressed as half of 'you guys'.

My reaction to the United States and its people was varied but generally positive. After more than forty years living abroad and however American I might still seem to some of my British friends, I felt very much a foreigner. It was possible to communicate with Americans without speaking a foreign language, but twenty years of raging Americanisation in Britain had by no means ironed out all differences of vocabulary and idiom. Theirs was the language of the lowest common denominator. Many of the people we met or heard said: 'I have a couple things to tell you'. They did not get, they 'git'; they did not take or help themselves, they 'grabbed'. Their speech, employing words like 'thataway' without irony, recalled the Old West. Official Americanese as exemplified by television, newspapers and government notices also seemed to be characterised by a kind of conscious folksiness. And the transformation of nouns into verbs, though far from unknown in Britain, had gone much further in the United States. It was an effective but unappealing language. On the other hand we found that some colloquialisms which we knew or took to be British ('do' as in function, 'dicey' as in hazardous, 'cushy' as in cushy, and, to our surprise and amusement, 'Victorian' for architecture, artefacts and customs dating from the later nineteenth century) had crept into American English.

We found a specifically American set of thought and speech processes, a literalmindedness, portentousness and naiveté which contrasted sharply with British irreverence and satire. Educated Americans admired the British preference for the rapier rather than the bludgeon but seemed incapable of emulating it, which perhaps explained why they watched so much second-rate British television on their public service networks. A newspaper headline which I saw in the Spokane *Spokesman-Review* (4 June 1998) summed up American literalmindedness (as well as their extraordinary, wild countryside) with considerable panache: 'Grizzlies that partially ate hiker to be killed.' (A Glacier National Park spokesman was quoted: 'There's nothing to indicate the guy died any way but by bear.') We were later told that 'partially' was in any case superfluous.

The differences were not only linguistic and temperamental but practical. Middle-class, middle-aged Americans seemed to be

281

obsessed with sending their children to a 'good' university and how to find the twenty-five thousand dollars (£15 thousand) or so required annually to finance them. They found it difficult to believe that until recently young British people (for whom higher education long remained, unlike the United States, the experience of an elite) had been paid to study, but it was clear to us that the divisiveness which has so long afflicted English secondary education was reproduced in American higher education. (The Republican congressional majority was advocating during our American visit support for private education at the expense of the American public school.)

Another major concern of Americans from which we are still largely free was how to finance their health care by individual provision. (A small but significant and apparently increasing minority of the British population is covered by private insurance; *Social Trends 1997*, pp. 28, 145; *1998*, p. 148; information from Office for National Statistics, October 1998.) The *New York Times* referred to the 'heart-wrenching stories' related to President Clinton by patients whose health insurance cover was scandalously decreed inadequate for comprehensive care by private health management organisations (16 July 1998; also *West Hawaii Today*, 21 August 1998). Old people were a particularly vulnerable group and in partial consequence many stayed at work until well past the age of 65.

Inadequate health coverage was made worse by inequality between races which endured despite obvious and gratifying progress by black people in all spheres. Twelve per cent of white families were classified as poor, with annual incomes under $15,000 a year in 1995, but 30 per cent of black families fell into this category. Fourteen per cent of white adults and 26 per cent of blacks had no health insurance; the infant mortality rate for whites was 6.3 per thousand; for blacks, 14.6 (*Oregonian*, 4, 5 August 1998) or 132 per cent higher. In 1990-5 the ethnic minority infant mortality rate in Britain is likely to have exceeded the white rate by no more than 50 per cent (*Health Inequalities*, 1997, p. 90). In any case racial inequality in Britain, far-reaching and shameful though it is, is not exacerbated by treating health care mainly as a private matter to be left to individual initiative and the profit motive.

A third issue for liberal Americans was how to reform their politics and specifically the financing of political parties. Their favoured approach lay through such extra-party organisations as the League of Women Voters or Common Cause. Such people and organisations often thought of themselves as non-party political, an illustration of the current profound disillusionment with the pettiness and paralysis of the American political system. People in Britain who wish to influence the overall political process find it more natural to join parties than to try to 'take politics out of politics'.

Higher education, health care and the financing of political parties are all controversial subjects in Britain but none of them arises here in the same form as in the United States. Given the differences in thought processes, in the use of the English language and in practical concerns it is grossly inaccurate to regard Americans and British as essentially the same people, as the British press, politicians, pressure groups and even some scholars are wont to do. (Few Americans are inclined to make this mistake.) Nor were middle-class Americans devoid of resentment or reservations about foreigners, even English-speaking ones, and perhaps especially former Americans. When I apologised for initially rejecting a dinner invitation and subsequently accepting it I was told: 'You're back in the United States now, you can speak your mind freely without causing offence.' No other remark so astonished me during this visit.

And yet, I felt as we settled into our Oregon home, Anglo-American differences were perhaps more superficial than fundamental. The majority of British people, after all, had not attended public schools and did not have the ability to think quickly and react wittily so dear to the BBC – and the House of Commons. I had every reason to know that many Americans and many more of the British had crossed the ocean and settled happily enough in new surroundings.

We found more willingness in the United States to interfere with private enterprise in the name of the public good than in Britain. We saw not only cigarette advertisements carrying government health warnings but large billboards devoted to attacking smoking. In one 'he' asks: 'Mind if I smoke?' To which 'she' replies: 'Care if I die?' Other advertisements were devoted to preventing the sale of cigarettes to the young. As inveterate pedestrians we were impressed by the almost invariable courtesy shown us by motorists. It was wholly different from Britain where motorists seldom affect to notice pedestrians, especially when turning left. We were surprised that American visitors survived their first few days' exposure to British driving habits.

In the past Americans admired the sense of community which they found in Britain. It would be going too far to say that roles have been reversed at the end of the twentieth century, but it seems to be the case that the alleged British passion for private enterprise of recent years has been modified in the United States by the experience of how, unbridled, it actually works. Nobody in the United States talked about privatising the buses or, so far we knew, the Post Office. In our passion for emulating the United States we have continued to follow a path towards a goal which the Americans themselves are not pursuing.

Another reaction to the United States was to note how kind almost all strangers were to us, including shop assistants, post office clerks and bus drivers. (This was less true in the big eastern cities than in the west.) There were always smiles and courtesy and if it was sometimes cloying to be enjoined to 'have a nice day' it was, after all, identical to the 'bonne journée' to which we had been accustomed in France as a matter of course. Shop or cafe assistants treated us as equals, as if on another occasion we might be behind the counter and they in front of it. On the other hand we disliked having to whisper in public in order to prevent strangers from joining in our conversations. A country so insistent on private enterprise seemed to have little concern for personal privacy. Such a situation was seen at its worst in the obsessive media concern with the sex life of the American president; it was, as Roy Hattersley observed recently, a 'nation...desperately short of reticence' (*Guardian*, 17 September 1998).

We did not have the illusion that there were no social classes in the United States, though we knew that they were more complex than in Britain. I sometimes felt that the alleged American classless society amounted to no more than a common accent in speaking English, admittedly a matter of very considerable importance. But I was surprised and pleased to find that when George Struble took us to lunch at Willamette University, from which he had recently retired from his post as professor of computer studies, he was addressed unceremoniously as 'George' by one of the waitresses.

Would we have met in Britain a cafe assistant like Rebecca, who lived for her participation in the Portland Opera (next performance, Prokoviev's *Love of Three Oranges*) and her acting in the Oregon Shakespeare Festival held in Ashland, southern Oregon? No, she did not enjoy driving the 47 miles from Salem to Portland for rehearsals. But it was worth it for the music. We found also that the coach drivers and guides on our various trips, who had obviously had limited formal education, were not only competent and knowledgeable about the geology, natural and human history of what they were showing us, but full of contagious enthusiasm. Again we doubted that British coach drivers would have displayed the same mixture of impressive knowledge, unflagging interest and desire to learn more about their subjects.

There is more to be said about social class in the American context. We met as we had met previously middle-class resentment that skilled working-class people enjoyed high standards of living and also resentment of trade unions, though official figures (from the *Statistical Abstract of the United States 1997*) showed that the better paid jobs went to professional and managerial groups and the well educated, and that the continuing decline in trade union membership had left only one in seven employed Americans in a union in 1996 (pp. 431, 440, 473). We also read with interest a journalistic comment on a carpenter's union official named Robert Brady who had just won a by-election to the American Congress in a Philadelphia constituency. 'People find Brady's embrace of the old...tradition of machine politics...embarrassing. The fact that he's a *Youse* [as in 'youse guys'] kind of guy makes it worse. Class matters so much in America, even though we've officially banned discussion of it.' (*Philadelphia Inquirer*, 22 May 1998). We were to discover that the term was quite widely used in the American media, even if not always exactly as in Britain.

The incidence of violent crime is a feature of American life as disturbing to citizens as to visitors. In fact the number of violent crimes is, proportionately to population, quite similar to that in England and Wales if the definition and the recording of crime are also similar. In 1995 nearly 1.8 million violent crimes were known to the police in a nation of 263 million people, against 316,000 in England and Wales, whose population is about a fifth as great. But the ultimate violent crime, murder, was another matter. There were over 21,000 victims of homicide in the United States in 1995 and 699 in England and Wales. There were nearly 1.1 million prisoners in American and 57,000 in British jails in 1995 (rising to 65,000 in England and Wales in 1998; *Guardian*, 27 October 1998). There is some comfort in the fact that violent crimes and homicides have dropped in the United States; but its prison population rose by more than five times between 1970 to 1995. (*Statistical Abstract of the United States 1997*, pp. 14, 201, 204, 220; *Social Trends 1997*, pp. 28, 153; *Fact File 1998*, pp. 31-2).

During our four month stay in the 'contiguous' United States an African-American was killed in Texas in a horrifying manner, allegedly by a group of white racists. Two policemen in the national Capitol were shot dead by a gunman. Even a favoured state like Oregon was not immune. Two young men were charged with the random murder of a couple on a beach. Two schoolboys were charged with killing their parents in unrelated incidents; one of them was also accused of shooting a number of his schoolfellows. The American passion for firearms and for responding to violent crime by the use of capital punishment is repugnant to European notions of civilised society.

And yet this was not the whole story. We found that the gun culture had strong opponents who expressed their views vocally if, thus far, unsucessfully. If extreme violence was common, loutish behaviour by youths looking for trouble seemed to be less so, especially at sporting fixtures. We attended a baseball game in which the Salem-Keizer (Keizer was the adjacent town) Volcanoes played the Everett Aquasox from Washington state. This was a professional match in a purpose-built stadium and the crowd exceeded 4,000 people, a figure larger than the normal attendance of most of the clubs in the third division of the English football league. There was no hint of trouble on or off the pitch and no drunkenness, though beer was freely available. The atmosphere was that of a family occasion, since there were many women and children among the crowd. Later we attended another game, a derby match against the Portland Rockies. The atmosphere was as friendly and relaxed as it had been on the earlier occasion, and though the Volcanoes made some serious blunders and were badly beaten there was no barracking by the crowd. The fact that sport is relatively seldom an occasion for displaying male aggression in the United

States was one of the factors contributing to the success of the 1994 World Cup held there.

★   ★   ★

We were impressed by the detached wood-framed houses, wide streets, ample space around the houses, abundant bird life, lawns, bright flowers and bushes (much more garish than in Britain) and absence of fences, gates and hedges which we saw in Salem and elsewhere in the United States. These features made us homesick for the smaller, terraced homes and hedges to which we were accustomed in Britain, but they were interesting and sometimes architectually attractive. We noticed that, though the homes we visited were comfortable and well appointed, the American middle classes did not appear to live very much more luxuriously than their British counterparts, though they did have more bathrooms! In the age of central heating, computers, video recorders and two (or more) car families, western Europe had largely caught up. A friend of our Hull friend Margaret Palfreman who had emigrated to British Columbia had once irritated me by describing the principal middle-class area of Hull as 'pinched'. I could see in Oregon what he meant, but there was certainly no reason for the British to feel, as they did when I went to live amongst them in the 1950s, that they were materially in a different league from their North American counterparts.

We liked Salem at once. It was the state capital which meant that there was an array of public buildings in the town. These included the state capitol building or legislature-cum-executive offices, completed in the inter-war American ceremonial style. It was a style too often, as in this case, 'vaguely reminiscent of government buildings...in foreign dictatorships' (that is, of Mussolini's Italy) as a local guide (*Let's Go...the Pacific Northwest...1992*, p. 116) pointed out. It was, however, a building that became more attractive both inside and out the more one saw it and facilities for the legislators were admirable, as we found in the course of an enjoyable free tour. The public buildings also included schools for the blind and the deaf and other social services, as well as the Oregon State Penitentiary and Oregon Women's Correction Center. Like many other American cities (Salem's population of about 125,000 and a regional population of about 200,000 was greater than but comparable to York's) the city centre had been allowed to decay,

287

to be replaced by shopping 'malls' at the edge of town catering primarily for car-borne shoppers. But Salem had made a real and successful effort to restore its centre and there were a number of attractive shops including three department stores and several bookshops; we noted also a 'Drive-up Divorce' lawyer's office.

There were also parks and museums and we enjoyed particularly the Mission Mill, a museum based on the former Thomas Kay Woolen (sic) Mill which retained most of its machinery and provided an excellent taped guide for tourists. Ducks swam in the former mill race, it had a hospitable and well stocked cafe, a visitors' centre and shops which sold goods reminiscent of the National Trust.

Near the Mission Mill was the railway station, still within easy walking distance of the Strubles' home. The line to Seattle (north) and Los Angeles (south) passed through the centre of town with as little segregation from the public as a tram line. Barriers protected only level crossings. There were few but enormous passenger trains; the freight trains which passed at all hours of night and day were also huge and lengthy. We 'heard that lonesome whistle blow' far and wide as the trains passed through the town. Also near the Mission Mill and the town centre was George's university, Willamette. The name was of Indian, not French origin, and the emphasis was on the second syllable ('Willamette, dammit'), which was at first not easy to remember. The university was leafy and the Mission Mill stream also flowed through its grounds.

As so often at home we found that public transport in the United States was better than the local middle class (which in general did not use it) or for that matter most foreigners were willing to believe. In using the bus we discovered that Salem was not so white or middle class as we had thought. We gradually realised that in the town centre many notices were displayed in both English and Spanish (this was true of much of the country) and that while there were relatively few African-Americans there was obviously an Hispanic population. In this respect Salem resembled Oregon as a whole, for school surveys for 1997/8 showed that one pupil in twelve in the state was Hispanic, over three times the percentage of African-Americans (*Oregonian*, 8 June 1998). Nor was Salem as Protestant as we had expected, for a dozen of the many churches listed in the telephone directory were Roman Catholic, in addition to the Hispanic Iglesia de Cristo.

We attended a Unitarian service on the first Sunday we were in Salem, before George and Elsa left for London. The service took place in a fine new church in whose construction the Strubles had been moving spirits in planning and finance as well as serving as willing labourers and craftspersons. Everyone was very kind to us, but we were pleased the following Sunday to be amongst our 'ain folk' at the Quaker Meeting House located almost within shouting distance of the Strubles' home. Announcements after meeting and a leaflet urged support for a code of conduct on the sale of arms 'to help curb the global proliferation of conventional weapons', more paved roads on Indian reservations and restoration of food stamps to needy, legal immigrants. At subsequent Quaker meetings other leaflets which we welcomed as more political than we would have found in Britain opposed Nato expansion, landmines and budget proposals which harmed the poor, and encouraged the purchase of fruit harvested by unionised labour. We were aware that such causes, the province of the pre-Blair Labour Party, were often championed by church and citizens' groups in the United States.

We had been warned that American newspapers, particularly those distant from the East Coast, contained little European news and we felt somewhat isolated as we realised how cut off we were from Britain. The splendid Salem Public Library would have made any York librarian weep with envy, but there were no British or other foreign newspapers. The American press we read thought that, in terms of English-speaking Europe, only Northern Ireland was of interest. (Nor was there interest in the rest of Europe, apart from occasional reports from Russia and the football World Cup in France which was reported more fully as the competition reached its climax. But even that event was often reported in terms of the indifference of Americans to association football and their consequent inability to play it.) So we acclimatised ourselves to American news and newspapers and to half an hour of BBC World Service news (which was interested in the entire world bar Britain) in the evening, relayed on the local public service station. We told ourselves that we had left our own country voluntarily and that we should make the most of being abroad. And we tried to find British papers, sometimes successfully, when we visited the large cities. The nadir was in Seattle when we gratefully paid $3.00 (about

£1.80), at least six times the price of local papers, for a five day-old copy of the truncated international *Guardian*.

⋆　　　⋆　　　⋆

After we had been in Salem for about a fortnight and a week after the Strubles left for London we began to explore the western United States. Oregon itself was a huge state of nearly 100,000 square miles, greater than the area of the United Kingdom. Its population of about 3.2 million, however, was only half that of the 32 London boroughs, though it was concentrated mainly in the Willamette Valley which contained Portland (much the largest city), Salem, Eugene and other centres. It had a long coastline, part of the Cascade range and other mountains, Crater Lake National Park and Oregon Caves National Monument and over two hundred state parks with scenery ranging from mountains, lakes, rivers and woodland to beaches and sand dunes. The highest point in the state, Mount Hood, was an elegant snow-covered peak 11,239 feet high and near the border with Washington state. Oregon had also, suitably for a state dominated by woodland, a number of national forests and wilderness areas. (We were told, however, that the timber industry was declining in favour of computers and electronics.) It was an ideal state for holiday makers of whom there were several million in Oregon every year and a good centre for country lovers like Ann and me.

Portland, which was close to fine countryside, was well worth a visit. Its lively Saturday market was strong on crafts and it had superb Japanese and rose gardens, justifying its sobriquet as the 'City of Roses'. Pioneer Courthouse Square, the city's central meeting and idling place, had been redeveloped in the 1980s and was now used to hold public events including musical performances known as 'Peanut Butter and Jam Sessions'. In a corner of the square signposts indicated the distance in hundreds and thousands of miles to various points in the United States and around the world, with a single exception; the distance to Tipperary was stated wittily as 'a long way'. We attended a small but moving exhibition on *Palestine: fifty years of dispossession* at the central library and wondered whether any British library would be sufficiently courageous to host such a controversial event. We also visited Powell's famous bookshop in the town centre. It was said to be one of the largest bookshops in the United States and had an excellent second-hand section on British history among many other subjects, though a disproportionate amount of space was given to royalty.

Portland was also interesting and encouraging for the environmentalist. The city (or, perhaps more accurately, the state and federal governments) had constructed an extensive system of urban motorways but it was now making a serious attempt to prevent further urban sprawl and promote public transport. Travel by bus and tram (announcements in English and Spanish) in an extensive part of the city centre was free to the passenger as, we were to find later, was part of Seattle, and a smaller section was forbidden to all motor traffic except buses. (Portlanders and visitors aged 65 and over were given reduced fares as 'honored citizens', a designation I felt could reasonably be copied elsewhere.) The mayor, Vera Katz, was a non-car owner and a strong advocate of replacing travel by public transport. 'The growing number of automobiles in our region', she wrote, 'congests our roads, pollutes our air...crowds our neighbourhoods...and diminishes our overall quality of life' (*Oregonian*, 25 July 1998). Her goal was to work towards free public transport all over the Portland region. This enlightened policy, which certainly had its articulate opponents, had been framed not only in the car-mad United States but in the relatively uncrowded northwest of the country. And Portland, while particularly progressive in this respect, was not alone in understanding that the reign of the motor car could no longer continue unchallenged.

We did not see much of Oregon, however, until later in the summer. Our first trip was to California by overnight train, the Coast Starlight. We admired the magnificent scenery of the Cascades as the train climbed to a height of 5,063 feet. We were duly impressed in San Francisco by the bay, the Golden Gate bridge which we crossed on foot in both directions, and the cable cars rumbling up and down the streets of the hilly city. We were less impressed by the signs of destitution which we saw, including soup kitchens and common lodging houses in one of the richest cities of the most powerful nation in the world. I wondered what the men and women in the food queues thought of the wickedness of Saddam Hussein and whether they appreciated their government's efforts to make him bow the knee to the forces of freedom and democracy.

We greatly enjoyed our visit to Yosemite, our first experience of an American national park. We saw no bears and having no car

(Yosemite is easy to reach by nationalised Amtrak train and bus) suffered no loss from their frequent depredations. But we admired the sheer cliff faces and the waterfalls, walking to Vernal and Nevada Falls nearly 2000 feet above the valley floor in scenery reminiscent on a vaster scale of the walk up Grindsbrook from Edale in the Peak District. We appreciated the efforts of the national park authority to encourage access without destroying the park's natural beauty and the free shuttle bus service within the park. We later discovered that the national park service itself has tried to exclude most cars from the Yosemite valley, so far without success (*Oregonian*, 5 August 1998).

We were also impressed on this trip and subsequently by the remarkable comfort of the Amtrak trains, their lavish staffing, good meals served at reasonable prices and the care taken by conductors to point out natural features of interest en route. We were less impressed by the fact that in many areas, at least in the west, there was only a single service a day in each direction. If one left the train at a 'smoking stop' and wandered away, conductors pointed out gleefully, it would be necessary to to wait for 24 hours to continue one's journey. Another disadvantage of rail travel was the leisurely pace which made even British trains (to say nothing of French or Japanese ones) look fast. The consequence for the environment was severe, in terms not only of roads and cars but also aircraft noise. Forty-seven aeroplanes a day left Portland for Seattle in the summer of 1998 against a background of vociferous complaints about noise by local residents in both cities (*Oregonian*, 6 July 1998). Four trains a day made the same journey and took three-and-a-half or four hours to travel 186 miles. There is a train every half hour from London to York, 194 miles away, and the journey time is two hours or less.

* * *

A litle later we girded ourselves to cross the continental United States, both as tourists and to visit some of my old friends from school and university days. We were gone for three weeks and in that time we visited Boston, New York, Philadelphia, Washington and Chicago; we moved on, that is, from *Boston Globe* to *New York Times, Philadelphia Inquirer, Washington Post* to *Chicago Tribune*. This was odd to English (though it would not have been to French) eyes, accustomed to reading the same morning paper from Penzance to Berwick-on-Tweed.

We envied the cheapness of the local transport systems, everywhere costing less than London Transport, though it seemed to us that the London Underground must be easier for foreigners to understand than American subways. (We were always given cheerful assistance, however, whenever we needed it, often before we asked.) We appreciated the large railway stations in the eastern cities which had many passengers and frequent trains, reminding us of home. Smoking was forbidden almost everywhere on all our journeys by plane, train, subway and bus.

I enjoyed the eighteenth-century buildings in Boston and Philadelphia, often built in the style of Christopher Wren. The Old North Church (1723) in Boston, associated with Paul Revere's celebrated ride in 1775, and Christ Church (1754) in Philadelphia stand out in the mind. We also saw secular buildings dating from the eighteenth century in these cities. Boston had made the most of its colonial and rebellious tradition by establishing as long ago as 1951 a 'Freedom Trail' of old buildings, cemeteries, the Bunker Hill battle site (1775) and the old warship the USS *Constitution* (1778). Philadelphia boasted not only Independence Hall (1756), where the American Declaration of Independence had been signed in 1776, but also whole streets of eighteenth- and early nineteenth-century terraced housing. (So did Boston in the Beacon Hill district.) We were particularly impressed by the lively South Street area of Philadelphia, where we paused to pay homage on 10th Street to the birthplace of Henry George (1839-97), the inventor of the single tax who had so profound an effect on the political history of the British Isles between 1880 and 1914. We also admired the celebrated Quincy Market in Boston and the lesser known but equally exciting indoor Reading Terminal Market in Philadelphia, built on the site of a former railway station. Both pulsated with life and bore evidence to the vitality of at least part of their respective city centres.

At Cambridge, near Boston, we walked through the grounds of Harvard University, and I wondered what would have happened to my life if I had after all decided to attend Harvard in 1950. We also visited a moving monument to the Irish famine of 1845-50 unveiled by Mary Robinson when Irish president in July 1997. An inscription expressed the determination that never again should a people be allowed to starve in a world of plenty.

The visit to Philadelphia was a sentimental journey for me, though we did not visit Swarthmore, and I was glad to attend an excellent performance of the Pennsylvania Ballet in the Academy of Music where I had so often heard the Philadelphia Orchestra in the 1950s from an 80 cent seat in the amphitheatre. It was pleasing to find that one could still obtain an amphitheatre ticket for the orchestra for $5.00, an increase much lower than the rate of inflation.

In New York we felt more than anywhere else the striking contrast between great wealth and great poverty which we saw in all the American cities we visited, a curious juxtaposition of first and third worlds. We marvelled at New York harbour and the Statue of Liberty, the experience heightened by the fact that we arrived during the 11th annual Fleet Week, with many naval vessels (staffed by men and women sailors) and precision flying. We were greatly impressed by the new and moving museum of immigration on Ellis Island, with its souvenirs of the huddled masses yearning to breathe free of late nineteenth-century Europe. I imagined (rightly or wrongly) that my grandparents had passed through the halls which now carried fascinating displays of some of the prized possessions brought by the immigrants and also of the hostility which their arrival aroused in some of their future compatriots. I was dismayed, however, to find that the Barbizon-Plaza hotel on Central Park South where my parents had often stayed in New York, occasionally with me in tow, was no more; we had intended to visit it and drink a glass to the memory.

We had a ringside seat in New York for a spectacular thunder and hail storm which flooded 14 of the city's 25 subway lines within minutes, causing havoc and delaying 'tens of thousands of subway riders...in their commute [sic] home', the *New York Times* reported (21 May 1998). Not only the subways but also the streets themselves were flooded and sometimes impassable, and there was no electricity in part of Brooklyn for a short period. I would suggest that this was further evidence of 'third world New York', but in fact it is hard to imagine any city not being brought to a standstill by such a downpour.

Washington seems to the tourist more a set of monuments than a city. We visited as I had always done when in Washington the deeply moving Jefferson Memorial. High on the wall was carved an inscription drawn from a letter which Jefferson wrote in 1800, the year he was first elected president, to Benjamin Rush: 'I have sworn upon the altar of God eternal hostility against every form of tyranny over the mind of man.' In which other nation would a leading statesman have so expressed himself, publicly or privately, at that date? And which nation has done so much to attempt to enforce uniformity of thought and action at home and throughout the world since 1945?

We also visited newer monuments in Washington, including the impressive memorial to Franklin Delano Roosevelt. Its carved quotations from speeches made gratifying reading to the somewhat surprised socialist, such as this one from 1937: 'The test of our progress is not whether we add more to the abundance of those who have much; it is whether we provide enough for those who have too little.' We also visited the memorials to the dead of the Korean and Vietnamese wars. I found at the Korean memorial computer details of my old schoolmate Teddy Bonchek (complete with photograph), who had gone into the army and died in Korea aged 21 in April 1951 while I disported myself in my first year at Swarthmore. (My career as a blood donor, which lasted until I developed high blood pressure in my fifties, took an early stimulus from this tragedy.) On a less sombre note we visited George Washington's home at Mount Vernon near Washington, with splendid views across the Potomac, and noted its similarities and differences to an English country house of the eighteenth century.

We also admired Chicago, Ann more than I, for I missed the eighteenth-century buildings which we had seen in Boston, Philadelphia and even New York. But Chicago is a mighty and ever-growing city, which manages to link triumphantly its tall buildings and Lake Michigan, so that one can swim almost in the shadow of the skyscrapers. It was not thus in the Cleveland of my youth. We attended a spirited and highly enjoyable production of *The Man Who Came to Dinner* (Kaufman and Hart) which I had often heard about but never seen. If it seemed like many American films, pulsating with wisecracking energy, it would have seemed much more original when first produced in 1939. The acting was outstanding and I enjoyed it enormously. We also visited the splendid Chicago Art Institute, one of the world's great art galleries.

(Left to right) Tom Greene, Ann, David, Margaret Greene at the Franklin Delano Roosevelt Memorial, Washington, May 1998.

David and Liaqat Ali at the Vietnam Memorial, Washington, May 1998.

The sightseeing was fascinating but for me personal contact was even more gratifying. I was surprised to find that I still had so many friends in the United States and we were overwhelmed by kindness and hospitality, sometimes from people whom I had not seen for quarter of a century or longer. We saw on this eastern visit Meg Bodecker, Ellen's sister-in-law, whom I had always loved and seen too seldom, our French friend Claude Pujol who was carrying out research in Philadelphia, Joan Goodman to whom I had been close at Swarthmore when she was Joan Friendly, Tom and Margaret Greene with whom we spent more time than we had done since Tom and I were undergraduates, Liaqat Ali who had moved from Geneva to the World Bank in Washington and was now retired, Milt Cummings my close friend from Swarthmore days but unseen for over forty years, and Bob and Carol Gaebler, with whom I had had more frequent contacts than with my other American friends over the decades.

In Philadelphia we met Bob's sister Peggy Morscheck who was now the director of information at the Quaker centre there. We did not recognise each other and Bob had not told her that we would be visiting Philadelphia, but when I told her who I was she threw her arms around my neck, lunched with Ann and me, showed us around the many Quaker and non-Quaker bodies situated in the centre and invited us to her home for a meal, all without previous notice and all in one weekend. At Liaqat's home we were privileged to attend a dinner party at which two Washington-based Indian-born environmental scientists advised a subcontinental government minister on how to deal with problems of agricultural production, pesticides and relations with multi-national companies. It was a unique opportunity for us to listen to a discussion by authorities on a subject of enormous import to a large part of the world's population, and we reflected long on our own sheltered and privileged lives.

It was a shock to see how much older my friends had become but satisfying to visit them before, as we fondly thought, old age finally encircled us all in its unrelenting embrace. Certainly watching Tom Greene race up the escalator on the off chance that the bus might be late (it wasn't) left me in stunned envy of his fitness. When we returned to Salem after our three-week excursion I felt that our trip would have been justified by personal contact alone.

I was initially reluctant to return to Portland, Oregon from Chicago by train, for the 2,261-mile journey took two days and we had already been away for a considerable period. I was, however, reconciled to the journey because of Ann's desire to travel by rail, Bob Gaebler's eloquent description of the glories of the route, and also because of the high cost of air travel on a single, last-minute fare. I have never been so glad to be proved wrong. The journey of the Empire Builder was lengthy but splendid. As on the Coast Starlight to San Francisco the accommodation was comfortable, food and service of high quality and the staffing much more generous than on European trains. We encountered the only smoking carriage of our entire trip, but as the train (like the Coast Starlight) was a double-decker there was no need to walk through the (lower-deck) smoker on the way from our (upper deck) carriage to the observation and restaurant cars.

We travelled through the lakelands of Wisconsin and woke up, having missed Minnesota in the night, to the endless but fascinating prairies of North Dakota whose roads seemed mostly to be unsurfaced. The train stopped from time to time for servicing and the passengers tumbled off to admire artefacts of various kinds, including statues to pioneers and others, and at Havre, Montana, a massive S-2 locomotive which had been used on the line from 1930 until it was replaced by diesel power after 1945. We bought a copy of the *Minot Daily News* at Minot, North Dakota, a town of 35,000 people hundreds of miles away from the nearest cities. The front page had four stories, three of them local (an unseasonal frost, the mayoral election, educational expenditure), while the fourth dealt with the repercussions of India's testing of nuclear weapons. We were impressed by this indication of interest in the outside world in what seemed to us such a remote spot and wished that Europe too had been thought worthy of notice.

As the journey continued the scenery became more impressive. Eastern Montana had fine earth and rock formations and wide rivers. And then came the Rocky Mountains. The Empire Builder skirted Glacier National Park in scenery which could hardly have been more spectacular. The mountains, forests and green, green water of the Flathead River as day became twilight and then dusk were as fine a sight as we had ever seen from a train. The line reached 5,216 feet at the Marias Pass, considerably higher than anywhere in the British Isles but the lowest pass across the Rockies between New Mexico and Canada. The train made three stops at the edge of the national park and we felt almost like Ulysses tied to the mast, so strong was the impulse to stop and explore the park. We resolved to return.

Nothing could equal the journey through Glacier, but we had still to travel down the Columbia River Gorge on our way to Portland past high cliffs, dams, waterfalls and splendid views of Mount Hood. Arriving at Portland we took the Amtrak bus to Salem, arriving at the railway station after a journey of 48 hours. There are many marvels in the United States but we concluded that one of the most satisfying must be the rail journey from Chicago to Portland.

Our next trip was northwards to Seattle, Vancouver (British Columbia) and Banff National Park in the Canadian province of Alberta. For much of our rail journey to Vancouver we passed close to Puget Sound, with its wooded islands and distant mountains. We were lucky enough to see a pair of bald eagles close at hand near the sound and we also had fine views of Mount St Helens (which had erupted spectacularly and disastrously in 1980) and Mount Rainier, at 14,410 feet one of the highest and most impressive mountains in the contiguous United States. Seattle and Vancouver are located on inlets connecting them to the Pacific Ocean, but they are protected by sounds, straits and islands, and in the case of Seattle a substantial section of mainland. Both have mountain backdrops, fine waterfronts with ferries, cruise and cargo ships, fascinating markets, an active multi-cultural life and imposing modern buildings. We were greatly impressed but less so by the fact that both, especially Seattle, had their quota of down-and-outs and beggars.

My school friend Eileen Manning (previously Gelfand) met us near Vancouver, accommodated us generously for three days and gave us an excellent introduction to the area, where she had been resident since the 1960s. Eileen took us on a beautiful sea journey, irresistibly reminiscent of the Inner Hebrides, to Victoria on Vancouver Island. It was a new experience for us to visit so large a city (and provincial capital of British Columbia) as Victoria (about 100,000 people) so far from the mainland but the local population, of course, saw nothing untoward in this geographical oddity. We saw in Vancouver and elsewhere in Canada evidence of visits by royalty, the Queen's head on coins and banknotes, towns named after eminent Victorians, and in Vancouver a cricket match in progress. We also heard words and pronunciations which indicated British influence on Canadian speech. We knew that many or most Canadians (whether anglophone or francophone) were keen to preserve their national identity, but for all that the similarities between Canada and the United States were more obvious to the foreigner than the differences.

We travelled by grossly over-priced and indifferently comfortable tourist train to Banff, passing mountains, forests, rushing rivers (ideal for white-water rafting) and lakes. We were told in detail of the hardships and engineering feats, some the work of British designers, which made possible the construction of the Canadian railways through the mountains. As we reached the Rocky Mountains and drew close to Banff the scenery became even more spectacular, culminating at the Continental Divide where the train reaches 5,332 feet). I had heard about this area from my childhood without dreaming that I would ever visit it, but all anticipation was put in the shade by reality.

The greeny-turquoise Lake Louise 35 miles from Banff was one of the principal objectives of our entire trip to North America (as it is of so many other visitors) and it too lived up to its advance billing. Surrounded my mountains and glaciers it was an unforgettable sight. We walked along the lake's edge and up towards the glaciers, in places through snow. We also walked in the forest above Banff, bathed in sulphur springs and wished that we had longer to explore the area. We were, however, disappointed to find that the Canadian national highway ran from east to west through part of the national park as a motorway and that a main road crossed the park from north to south. In consequence some of the wild country had lost its character. Who could gain from this wanton damage? It was not the image of the public-spirited Canada of which I had heard in my youth, though it must be added that the federal government had vetoed a plan for a large new commercial development in Banff shortly before our visit (*Calgary Herald*, 25 June 1998). Upon our return to Salem we were met by the wholly unexpected and joyful news that Pola Manzila Uddin (see ch. 9 above) had been made a peer.

300

Our next visit was to Crater Lake, the only national park in Oregon. We again took the Coast Starlight train, this time to Klamath Falls in southernmost Oregon. 'Dinner in the diner' while gazing at mountains and lakes was a wonderfully satisfying experience. We hired a car in Klamath Falls and drove the sixty miles to Crater Lake. We had been warned that snow lay on the ground in the park into the summer, but we had not expected to find so much in early July, even at 6-7,000 feet above sea level. Footpaths (or 'hiking trails') and roads alike were still closed. Crater Lake is the deepest lake in the United States, reaching a depth of 1,932 feet. It was formed by a volcanic eruption nearly 8,000 years ago and is surrounded by a volcanic rim called a caldera. Mountains rising to nearly 9,000 feet form the backdrop. The lake's main claim to fame is its almost incredible blueness, varying from turquoise to cobalt. It is a fascinating, almost hypnotic sight.

We joined a party of 21 which walked in the woods and meadows on snowshoes; I supposed that I was the oldest member. It was a remarkable experience to tread on the deep snow while feeling the warm sunshine on one's face and arms. This excursion, free to participants, was led by an expert, congenial national park ranger who told us that the average visitor (the vast majority of whom are Americans) stayed in the park for only an hour or two. 'They spend more time in the gift shop than around the lake', he commented. 'They go to the toilet, take a couple of photographs and then leave.' At once I stopped feeling sorry for my compatriots who typically visited eight or so American national parks in a fortnight and Ann and I felt smug about the thirty hours which we spent at Crater Lake.

We spent the rest of our time based on Klamath Falls. Its population is under 20,000, but it is the largest settlement for miles around and has some attractive features. Unhappily a giant hand seems to have upended the town, leaving some of its vitals – small businesses, banks, restaurants, hotels – strung out on a main road for miles to the south. The natural result is that much of Main Street is empty or forlorn. Americans began to desert their town centres soon after 1945 and, as in Salem, there have been valiant attempts to restore them in later years. It is incomprehensible that Britain, where limited land and historic towns are so much more precious than in the United States, should so eagerly have followed the same path to urban sprawl and still be doing so.

301

The day after our return to Klamath Falls from Crater Lake was the Fourth of July, Independence Day, the first time I had been in the United States on that date since 1954. We watched the amusing, good-natured parade down Main Street in the morning and a fine fireworks display after dark. In between we took a boat trip on Upper Klamath Lake, claimed to be the largest American lake west of the Rockies, and saw both bald and golden eagles. We also walked in the Rogue River National Forest, whose lakes and footpaths are much used by visitors. Here, uniquely in the course of our American journey, we were driven away (from the surrounds of the Lake of the Woods) by swarms of mosquitoes.

The next day we visited the remarkable Lava Beds National Monument in the far north of California. We first visited Petroglyph Point, where we saw several thousand pictograms or symbols carved on the lava rock face by the ancestors of modern Indians, perhaps as long ago as 2500 BC. We then walked round the rocky, naturally fortified site where 'Captain Jack' (the Modoc Indian leader Kientpoos) and a handful of warriors held off the might of the American army before being starved into submission after nearly five months in 1872-3, 'so settlers could graze a few cows', as Lee Juillerat's official pamphlet on *Captain Jack's Stronghold* (1992 ed., n.p.) puts it. It was certainly one of the typically squalid episodes of 'how the west was won'; a contemporary account appeared in the *Illustrated London News* in April 1873. We marvelled at the wild landscape of lava flows and sagebrush against a mountainous background, especially the magnificent snow-covered Mount Shasta (14,380 feet). We also visited a few of the caves of the region which to the inexpert eye resembled those near Castleton in the Peak District.

Our appetites had been whetted to visit Mount Rainier National Park and the Columbia River Gorge by seeing them as we passed on the train. We stayed close to Mount Rainier itself at Paradise Inn, visiting a tiny, German-founded church and a lively enthusiasts' steam railway at Elbe en route. Paradise belied its name, for us at least. Though the inn was pleasant enough its surroundings were mainly a giant car park, a tribute perhaps to the common late-twentieth-century conception of paradise. The many footpaths to Mount Rainier were overcrowded because they began immediately above the car park, but led to a landscape of astonishing beauty, including alpine (as they are called) meadows, some covered with snow in late July, others with a profusion of colourful wild flowers. Mount Rainier stands isolated, head and shoulders above neighbouring mountains, and the views of the snow and immense glaciers on its slopes were, we hoped, unforgettable. We walked to a point about 1,700 feet above the inn; we had only reached the halfway point, for Mount Rainier still towered 7,000 feet above our heads.

We visited the Columbia River Gorge by coach tour, first seeing Bonneville Dam, completed in 1937 and opened by President Roosevelt as a triumph of the New Deal. (It has been greatly expanded in more recent years.) The dam does everything possible to attract visitors and explain itself to them, and also tries to counteract its own adverse effect on the fish supply by a programme of breeding and the provision of ladders. We viewed salmon and other fish from special windows as they swam up the fast-flowing river and then spent a couple of hours in the publicly-owned paddle wheeler *Columbia Gorge*. The Columbia is an important working river. It has a good deal of barge traffic, carrying timber, grain and other goods, and we saw also a large raft carrying logs downstream. Eighty goods trains a day use the railway lines which follow both sides of the river. It is sad that there should be only one passenger train in each direction. We admired the several water falls which the coach stopped for us to visit, especially Multnomah Falls, the second highest in the United States (we had seen the highest, Yosemite Falls, in full spate in the spring). On the way back we visited Crown Point, from which there is a majestic view of cliffs and the Columbia far below.

One more visit remained before we left the continental United States to continue our journey westwards. This was to Glacier National Park, to which we travelled by the same splendid rail route which we had taken in the other direction in June and where we found comfortable accommodation in the youth hostel. Rivers, lakes, waterfalls, wild flowers and mountains made a magnificent ensemble. We took a tour on a sunny day in one of the quaint red charabancs which are a feature of the park. These open-roofed vehicles dating from the 1930s were operated by knowledgeable driver-guides known as 'jammers'. The tour bus, following Going-to-the-Sun Road, reached nearly 7,000 feet at Logan Pass; it was a truly spectacular trip. We also did a fair amount of walking and particularly admired Upper Two Medicine and Josephine Lakes, which could only be reached by foot and which were surrounded by mountains of 8,500 to 9,500 feet. Taken as an ensemble we found Glacier the most satisfying of the five North American national parks we had thus far visited.

Glacier Park is a 'bear park' par excellence, and for many visitors seeing a bear is one of the aims of their trip. Rather to our surprise we were amongst this group. For long we thought that bears outside zoos were mythical beasts. We had seen none in Yosemite or Banff. Nor, we thought, were we going to see any in Glacier, despite a formidable barrage of books in the shops with such titles as *Bear Aware* and *Bear Attacks*, anti-bear spray (we wondered if we would have had the presence of mind to use it at close range) and bells. We did see massive mountain goats and various kinds of deer. We also watched people watching bears with field glasses and tried to persuade ourselves that the brown blobs in the middle or far distance were actually moving. We walked round Two Medicine Lake where the rambler had been (partially) eaten by bears in June and duly noted our guidebook's warning: 'Be alert for grizzly bears in this area' (Erik Molvar, *Best Easy* (a relative term) *Day Hikes: Glacier and Waterton Lakes*, 1998, p. 59). But never a grizzly did we see. We took a boat tour past an area known to the cognoscenti as 'the bears' picnic ground', but the boatman told us that the bears must be unionised, for they did not appear at weekends.

And then it happened. At the very last minute, as we were leaving the park to begin our return journey to Salem, we saw a little knot of cars. Ann looked past the cars and said: 'It's a bear!' There it was, a large, handsome black bear just opposite us at the edge of a wood, busy rootling around for food in a manner rather resembling a pig. It was quite unconcerned by the cars and their occupants' cameras. We watched spellbound for some considerable time until it lumbered away. So bears were not, after all, mythical beasts. Our holiday had been crowned by success.

Glacier would have been perfection had it not been for its traffic. Vehicles were supposed to be limited by length – apart from our little buses – but those permitted to enter included bulky caravans and it was hard to see just what was forbidden apart from commercial lorries. The fact that there were not many roads in the park made the crush of vehicles even worse; the roads had become rivers of traffic, car parks and 'bear jams'. Even walkers could not always get away from them, as the footpaths on occasion paralleled the roads. To us it was obvious that the constant traffic was antagonistic to the very idea of a national park and that at some stage tourists, at least day trippers and those staying in fixed accommodation would have to learn to travel by national park mini-bus charging a nominal fare. Most of the accommodation was close to but outside the park boundary, so that a ban would have been easier in Glacier than in some other parks. We thought that as many tourists would be attracted as antagonised by traffic-free roads and that well-planned mini-buses could cater satisfactorily for disabled people. The administration of American national parks is admirable in other respects, but the conflict between natural beauty and the motor vehicle is one which cannot be ignored forever.

★ ★ ★

Ten days after our return from Glacier Park the Strubles returned home from London, and three days later we left Salem for the last time with both regret and anticipation. We flew from Portland at the start of our expedition to 'the rest of the world', our first stop, still in the United States, being Hawaii.

305

CHAPTER 12

Around the World in 154 Days
(continued): the journey home: 1998

W E STAYED IN HAWAII for a week, initially with my
Swarthmore friend Carol Beaumont (now Whitesell) and
her husband Craig, a retired member of the United States Forestry
Service. Like other people whom we had met on our trip Craig had
remained employed until he was over 70. He told us that it was
illegal in the United States to force employees to retire on grounds
of age, a curious situation in the eyes of Europeans who, with better
medical care for the elderly, are so often anxious to retire before
they are compelled to do so. Carol and Craig were heartwarmingly
friendly, greeting us at Honolulu Airport with *lei* wreaths. Carol
also took a day off work, observing: 'If I have to wait 44 years to
see you it is worth a day off to do so.'

We visited the Pearl Harbor memorial to over 2,000 people who
died in the Japanese attack of 7 December 1941. The USS *Arizona*
sustained about half the loss of life and a moving memorial has
been constructed over the barely submerged and clearly visible
remains of the ship. The tour of the site was free of charge and it
was besieged by visitors of many nationalities.

We then flew to the island of Hawaii, universally known as 'the
big island', which was refreshingly free of the motorways which
blight Oahu, the island which contains Honolulu and most of the
population of the state. There we stayed at Hawaii Volcanoes, our
sixth North American national park. The park is dominated by the
massive volcano Mauna Loa (13,677 feet), which erupts every
decade or so, and the smaller Kilauea, which has no summit but
which is the most active volcano in the world. (Mark Twain had

passed that way in 1866 and described the erupting volcano in strikingly vivid detail; *Roughing It*, 1872; 1981 ed., chs. 74-5.) It has now been erupting continuously since January 1983, though the fire and brimstone were to be found closer to the sea than to the volcano crater. We drove round Crater Park Drive and also walked several miles among the astonishing caldera and craters, steam vents, sulphur banks and old lava flows. Unlike the lava beds in California this was live volcano territory, though cheek by jowl with lush tropical rain forests which were home to exotic red and yellow birds. We joined a short explanatory tour led by a national park ranger (again there was no charge) whose home was in suburban London; he was the second British ranger we had met in an American national park.

Later we visited Pu'uhonua '0 Honaunau, a national historical park commemorating the society and religion of pre-European Hawaii. In pre-European days it was a place of sanctuary for criminals and rebels; it boasted a great wall whose massive dimensions recalled the effort involved in building Stonehenge or, as Mark Twain commented (ibid., p. 524) the Pyramids. We went on to St Benedict's church, painted throughout with biblical scenes by a Belgian clergyman at the end of the nineteenth century to assist the understanding of his illiterate congregation, and a coffee mill where we saw Kona (or Cona) coffee beans roasting and heard about the conditions in which the beans were harvested, mostly by Mexican immigrants. This was close to the spot where Captain Cook was killed in 1779, quite justifiably in Mark Twain's view (ibid., pp. 512-13).

Hawaii is one of the most racially mixed of the fifty American states and all ethnic groups are minorities. Estimates of ethnic composition vary, partly because intermarriage has steadily grown. About half the population appears to be of Oriental origin, of whom Japanese are the predominant group, though Hawaiians of Filipino and Chinese descent are also numerous. About a third are of European origin and no more than an eighth Polynesian Hawaiian (*The Hutchinson Encyclopedia*, 1992 ed., p. 482; *Encyclopedia Americana*, 1992 ed., vol. 13). We read and were told that there was a measure of racial discord. Politics are to some extent racially based, with most people of Japanese origin supporting the Democrats and many whites being Republicans, but the different groups are more willing to accept each other as equals than in many other parts of the United States. The fact that white people are in a minority is no doubt part of the explanation.

We flew on to Osaka, Japan, not without some apprehension as our flimsy phrase book seemed little support in coping with a language so remote from our own. We need not have worried. Smiles, rudimentary (or better) English and a desire to help foreigners met us throughout our stay. In return, smiles, pointing and a handful of Japanese words from the phrase book smoothed our passage. We were materially aided by the fact that the west and Japan use the same characters for numbers and even more by the transliteration into our alphabet or translation into English of Japanese street and shop signs and tourist information; the use of English in outdoor advertising was common. In addition the multitude of cheap restaurants usually had pictorial representations of their fare in an outside window or on the menu, which was a godsend to us.

Our impressions of Japan as of other countries we visited on our journey home were necessarily superficial. But we found that the cities we saw, though largely the product of postwar reconstruction, had an unmistakably Japanese character. It was pleasant after months of exposure to American slovenliness to observe people who generally took a good deal of care over their appearance. The large majority of both sexes dressed in western style, though some carried parasols or fans to ward off the heat. Bicycles were numerous and ridden by all sorts and conditions of people, including smart business men and women. It was frightening at times to be borne down upon by cyclists, all riding on the pavement. We enjoyed walking down the busy Shinsaibashi-suji, a long street of shops, some old others new, covered by a continuous glass roof. It and other covered markets in Osaka seemed immensely full of character after the bland American shopping 'malls' we had seen, or was it only exciting because unfamiliar?

We visited Osaka Castle, reputedly the most popular tourist attraction in Japan. The site was magnificent, the walls were massive, but the eight-storey main keep, we discovered, had been destroyed by lightning in 1665 and rebuilt of ferro-concrete in 1931. We were undisturbed. The castle looked as a Japanese castle should look; romantic and impregnable. We also visited Shitennoji Temple, a restored, working Buddhist temple with impressive relics and a pond with, I thought, more turtles than I had seen in the whole of my previous life. There we took part in a prayer ritual, or would have done had I not been too stiff to assume the correct prayer position, sitting back on one's heels. We were less impressed by the tent cities of the homeless which we saw laid out in orderly fashion all over Osaka in green spaces and their approaches.

While in Osaka we visited Kyoto, less than an hour away. Kyoto is the former capital of Japan and it is full of temples, shrines and royal palaces, far more than we could hope to visit in a day. We settled for taking a service bus from which we visited the admirably contrasting garden temples of Kinkaku-ji, Ryoan-ji and Ninna-ji, a collection of buildings and gardens of great beauty and repose within a couple of miles of each other. Kinkaju-ji boasts the splendid Golden Pavilion, rebuilt in 1955 after a disastrous fire. The most notable feature of Ryoan-ji is its mystical rock and gravel garden first laid out, it is claimed, in the early sixteenth century. It was impressive to everyone and full of meaning to devotees of Zen. It was moving to watch young Japanese and westerners sitting in rapt silence above the garden. At Ninna-ji I was particularly impressed by the massive pagoda of seventeenth-century inspiration which made the one at Kew Gardens look like a toy, as indeed to some extent it is. The day was stifling and we were duly pleased with ourselves for ignoring the heat while searching for cultural and aesthetic experience; only tourists would suffer so much so willingly.

We took the celebrated 'shinkansen', the bullet train, from Osaka to Tokyo. The journey was comfortable and smooth, stopping twice and taking about three hours to cover 553 kilometres. It was thus significantly faster than Britain's best line, from London to Edinburgh, and some shinkansen were faster still.

Tokyo was much like Osaka to the tourist, but it was larger and there were fewer bicycles. It seemed even more modern and to boast even more neon signs than Osaka or indeed anywhere else in the world. Signs of an economy in distress were not visible with the important exception of the tent cities; indeed, it was easy to believe that 70 per cent of Asian GDP was Japanese (*Japan Times*, 29 August 1998). As in Osaka we visited gardens (Imperial Palace East Gardens), places of religious observance (Meiji and Kanda-Myojin shrines, Asakusa temple), a covered market (Nakamise) and the super-lively Shibuya district. We attended an excellent Mozart concert in Shibuya only because two separate strangers stopped to help us, one of them insisting on accompanying us until she could point out the concert hall. We saw the somewhat grotesque but impressive Diet building, the home of the Japanese parliament. Finally we visited the Tokyo National Museum, where we admired its fine collections of Japanese sculpture, paintings, textiles and pottery from many periods as well as an exhibition of Chinese lacquer art excavated from tombs in Hubei province and dating from the fifth to the third centuries BC.

Hong Kong was our next port of call. If I had harboured any illusions about its romance and mystery they would have been speedily dispelled. The juxtaposition of tall buildings, mountains and water was striking and the views from Victoria Peak at nearly 400 metres were splendid. But there were (visible) no small cafes run by expatriates who had fled from England after committing nameless crimes and not returned for forty years, nor curious shops run by Polish or German adventurers. Joseph Conrad and his creations were not in evidence. Nor were there narrow alleys sheltering opium dens or inscrutable Chinese wearing embroidered gowns and long pigtails. The reality was much more prosaic and, for the tourist, more comfortable. There was finance capitalism en masse on the Hong Kong side of Victoria Harbour and tourist traps en masse on the Kowloon side.

However, the view at night from Kowloon of the harbour with its ceaseless activity, including a huge cruise ship, the lights of the tall buildings of Hong Kong and their reflections in the water, and the lights dotting the hills beyond was romantic enough for anyone. Moreover, we enjoyed greatly visiting the jade, flower and other specialist markets in the Yau Ma Tei and Mong Kok districts of Kowloon, walking the thronged pavements and visiting the Taoist temple of Tin Hau. We felt, rightly or wrongly, that we had at last penetrated into real Chinese urban life.

We had not planned to visit Macau before we arrived in Hong Kong, sixty kilometres away, but we were glad that we did. It was the first colony we had seen, one of a fortunately fast disappearing group. It had been Portuguese since 1557, nearly three centuries before Hong Kong became British, and is destined to be returned to China at the end of 1999. We had not realised that the population numbered nearly half a million nor that there would be so many skyscrapers, but relics of the past were easy to find. The colourful A-Ma Buddhist temple had been founded in the 15th or 16th century and the Portuguese had left many signs of their long presence, though little sign that they were still nominally in charge. We admired the Largo do Senado or Senate Square, the nearby church of São Domingo, the facade of São Paolo with its Chinese influences and the forts of Monte and Guia. The São Paolo facade completed before 1640 was, we thought, the oldest building we had seen since we left London. We also walked along the waterfront and past many blocks of flats, homes of the Chinese residents. Though they smacked of gross poverty we felt that Macau was a real place and not an artificial construct like Hong Kong.

We flew on to New Delhi. We found, as so often in life, that reading was not an adequate preparation for reality. Moreover, sympathy with Indians could not modify the huge difference between our standard of living and theirs. In any event we were unprepared after the prosperity of Japan and the self-sufficiency of the Hong Kong and Macau Chinese for the poverty, the underemployment, the begging, the crumbling infrastructure and the constant importuning by taxi drivers, would-be guides and others to purchase their goods and services. It was in a sense as if we had found ourselves in Victorian London. The chaotic and noisy traffic, however, quickly reminded us that we were in the Third World at the end of the twentieth century.

New Delhi, built as a grandiose capital of the British *raj* in the early twentieth century, resembled Washington in at least one respect; there were many impressive buildings but the city was enormous and it was initially difficult to find any centre. We visited the Rashtrapati Bhavan, designed by Edwin Lutyens as the Viceregal Palace and the adjacent secretariat, the work of Herbert Baker; the two buildings were constructed between 1912 and 1931. Monkeys ran round the internal balconies of the secretariat. We also visited the massive India Gate, a war memorial to the fallen Indian soldiers of 1914-18 and the British and Indian dead of the Third Afghan War of 1919. These grandiose monuments, impressive in their way, revealed a disturbing but not unexpected proto-fascist caste of mind in their designers and builders.

We turned to the more indigenously Indian parts of the city. Historically speaking the most impressive art and architecture of this capital of a predominantly Hindu nation was the work of its Muslim rulers of the early modern period and before. We visited the Qutb Minar, the collection of splendidly worked minarets, tombs and mosques dating mostly from the thirteenth and fourteenth centuries. We visited also the Lodi Gardens, which looked very green after the monsoon and housed more fine mausoleums and mosques, this time of the Sayyid and Lodi dynasties of the fifteenth and sixteenth centuries. No visitor to Delhi misses the Lal Quila or Red Fort, erected by the Mughal Emperor Shah Jahan in the third quarter of the seventeenth century. Two hundred years later the fort was largely destroyed by the British after the rising of 1857, but the extensive remnants included fine arches, carving and inlay work, as well as the domed Moti Masjid or Pearl Mosque of the Emperor Aurangzeb (reigned 1659-1707). We were pleased to see both at Qutb Minar and the Red Fort that the large majority of the many visitors was from the Indian sub-continent. Our final stop in Delhi was at the tomb of Humayan, constructed in 1555-69 in honour of an earlier Moghul emperor. A building of red sandstone with black and white marble trimmings, it was a fitting precursor of the Taj Mahal.

We had planned to visit Delhi in fact mainly as a staging post to the Taj Mahal, 126 miles away at Agra. I had wanted to see the Taj ever since as a child in wartime America I had read the travel literature of Richard Halliburton (1900-39), the American adventurer. Built between 1638 and 1659 by Shah Jahan as the mausoleum of his wife Mumtaz, the Taj Mahal must be one of the most frequently visited and most lyrically described buildings in the non-European world. I shall not try to provide a detailed description of my own to add to all those which have come before. Suffice it to say that the Taj did not disappoint, that it was amply worth the years of anticipation and the long day trip from Delhi, and that as a poem in white marble it was fully equal to any English or French cathedral I had seen. And as we had seen so much less Muslim than western Christian architecture its impact was all the greater. The freshness of the marble and the superb state of preservation added to its dreamlike quality. Here too most of the visitors were sub-continental.

David and Ann before the Taj Mahal, Agra, September 1998.

We shall not forget the day of our visit. It began at 5.30 a.m. when we left our hotel and did not end until nearly 10.30 p.m. The road from Delhi to Agra was a dual carriageway, but the surface was rough and often under repair, necessitating single-line traffic for a good deal of the journey. The traffic was disorganised and sometimes frightening. Emaciated-looking cows wandered along or across the road. Our coach was adequate but uncomfortable and for our party of seven Australian, British, French and Indian tourists we were provided with a driver, his mate, an escort and, at Agra, a guide. Both the latter two spoke excellent English (the guide also spoke French and often accompanied French parties) and were helpful and well-informed.

The communities which we passed between Delhi and Agra were populous and poor, with inadequate housing which was frequently no more than shacks or tents. Sanitation was inadequate or non-existent. When we stopped briefly outside Delhi beggars appeared by the coach and remained beside us until we left. Sonia Gandhi, president of the Congress Party, had been quoted in that morning's *Times of India* (5 September 1998) as saying: 'The abolition of poverty within the next 10-15 years must remain our fundamental objective.' From what we saw the objective smacked heavily of wishful thinking.

The first stop of the day was at Sikandra, the mausoleum of the emperor Akhbar the Great (1542-1605). It was an impressive and elaborate monument, a foretaste of what was to come. Large numbers of monkeys, not all of them good-tempered, and several antelopes roamed through the grounds. We also visited the Red Fort of Agra, built by Akhbar and his descendants in the century after 1566. It was finer and less damaged than the complex of the same name in Delhi, an impressive mixture of a castle's strength with a palace's delicacy of interior design.

We had to fight our way into both the Taj Mahal and the Red Fort through a forest of touts selling peacock-feather fans, postcards, chess sets and other goods at prices which steadily diminished as we neared our destination. Such experiences did not add to our enjoyment and I reflected that westerners who experienced the heat, the poverty, the insistent demands of beggars and touts of all kinds, and the necessity of sighteeing by taxi, who then voluntarily returned to India for more were a special breed to which I did not belong.

Greece was our last port of call. I was ashamed of having lived so long and never having visited Greece, but not ashamed of the reason; my passion for France. We arrived in Athens and I felt like weeping when I first saw people taking leisurely, long drinks on cafe terraces and meals outside. (Outdoor eating did not seem to be popular in the United States and the summer heat was too intense in Japan, Hong Kong and India. In Greece we had most of our meals outside.) Despite the opacity of the language and obvious signs of poverty and underdevelopment we felt that we had at last returned to the common European home. Meals in restaurants were a revelation after the United States. They did not begin at or even before 6.0 p.m. and there was no coffee ad lib throughout the meal. There was no (or little!) attempt to rush the meal through as though patrons had a train to catch, the main course arriving before the first course was finished; no unrequested bill before one finished the main course despite the existence of a dessert menu. These had all been common features of American restaurants as we experienced them. As throughout most of Europe the Greeks thought of a meal as a civilised, unhurried occasion.

Our purpose in visiting Athens was to see the Acropolis. Our hearts began to pound as we caught glimpses of it from the airport bus. The next day we climbed the hill and visited the Propylaea, Parthenon, Erechtheum and Acropolis Museum. There were large numbers of tourists, the marble footing was sometimes hazardous and scaffolding enclosed much of the Parthenon, as it had apparently done since the 1980s. The weather remained very hot. Nevertheless it was an enormous thrill to visit the Acropolis, particularly the Parthenon which I had wished to see as long and as ardently as the Taj Mahal. Here was the perfection of classical Greece, a romantic classical ruin, the epitome of the civilisation which, through its language and literature had inspired the European upper classes for centuries and, through its architecture, continued to inspire wider circles to our own day. British homes, after all, are still being built to the popular taste with columns and pediments. I felt, paraphrasing Napoleon, that twenty-five centuries of history looked down on me.

By now we had been travelling for nearly four weeks and sightseeing in cities for nearly three, and we were ready for a less frenetic programme. We took the ferry from the Athenian port of Piraeus to the island of Aegina, one of the closest islands to Athens and about 30 kilometres from Piraeus. Given our arduous air journeys (we had left Delhi at 2.30 a.m.) and our constant sightseeing in intense heat we had no wish to travel further. The buildings in the little town of Aegina were mostly quite modern but they were charming and generally no more than three or four storeys. There were no tall blocks of time-share flats or international hotels. This was very enjoyable. One day we visited the inland temple of Aphaia. It dated from soon after 500 BC and enjoyed a fine hilltop site. Its Doric architecture was not quite so pure in style as the slightly later Parthenon but the difference was interesting and it was in excellent state of preservation. Local publicity claimed that it was one of the finest classical temples in Greece.

On another day we visited the archaelogical site and museum at Colonna, just north of Aegina town. Here a single broken, fluted column remained standing from the Doric temple of Apollo of the late sixth century BC as well as foundations going back to the Bronze Age. The site also contained the remains of a mosaic

315

pavement which looked Roman, but the inscription was in Greek and it belonged to a synagogue of the 7th century AD.

Having explored pagan and Jewish remains we set out by bus (Aegina buses are old but efficient; they are frequent and widely used by locals and visitors alike) in search of Christians. In the middle ages the capital of the island was removed to Paleohora in the interior, which was judged to be safer from piracy than the coast. The population moved back to the seaside in the early nineteenth century but 32 frescoed churches, dating from the 13th to the 17th centuries, remained in situ. We climbed up to visit about half of them, almost all open to visitors. The frescoes were in various states of deterioration, repair and rehabilitation; the terraced hillsides and a large modern monastery spread out dramatically below us.

On our final day in Aegina we took a ferry down the Saronic Gulf to Ydra (or Hydra), two hours distant. It was hard to imagine a better location or a more perfect spot. It had a church with a seventeenth century belltower, whitewashed houses around the harbour and climbing the several hills, no cars, a perfect swimming spot with deep water to the shore and a clean blue sea. On the return journey we stopped at Poros, another picturesque island in the Saronic Gulf. Here the main attraction was the view from the belltower about a hundred metres above the town, the green interior of the island, the harbour and the Argolid Peninsula on the mainland. Both Poros and in particular Ydra, we felt, deserved closer acquaintance.

★   ★   ★

The next day was our 154th away from home. I had lived out of a rucksack for a month, looked like a tramp and felt like one. (How was it that Ann, also living out of a rucksack, always looked fresh and lovely?) It was time to return, to sell our flat in London and pour ourselves into a life of Labour (perhaps), Quakers, Ramblers and research in York. I felt like Noel Coward, asked by Gertrude Lawrence how he had enjoyed his world tour: 'The world? very enjoyable.' (*Private Lives*, 1930, Act 1). But I was happier to arrive at Heathrow on 15 September 1998 than I had been to leave it five months earlier. 'The world' *had* been 'very enjoyable' but henceforth I would approach it on a more piecemeal basis. The trip of a lifetime had ended.

Epilogue

IN THE COURSE OF my American journey in 1998, when I met a number of old friends from my school and undergraduate years, I reflected on the 44 years since graduation and wondered whether life since Swarthmore had justified my early hopes and ambitions. My conclusion, unoriginally, was that it had been something of a curate's egg.

Certainly I have had disappointments and defeats. My first marriage was a mistake which ended in agony. In consequence I saw much less of my sons in their adolescence than I wished. The internecine warfare in my department at Hull and my failure to make lasting friendships in my years there caused me periods of unhappiness. I failed to commit myself fully without outside distractions to the life of the academic but I was not one of those for whom the countryside and its concerns were all-sufficient. I was never, in short, fully at home in either world. History has played a joke on me as economic and social change have destroyed the political structure and assumptions of my youth, leaving me as a lifelong socialist in a position uncomfortably resembling a dodo.

But life has been full and rich. I was born into a family of intellectual and aesthetic stature without financial worries, so I had no need to find my own way into the world of books, music and the arts or to seek success by amassing money. I found my three careers as schoolteacher, university teacher and local government worker rich in intellectual content and personal contact. My years in the Ramblers' Association have given me enormous gratification and cherished friendships. Although I was often unhappy at Hull I shall always be grateful for the expansion of my intellectual horizons which the life of the academic made possible. I was a successful teacher and my published research was generally received with favour by those who came across it. In any case it was the best I

Caroline Burgess and John Rubinstein with their niece Dora Rubinstein, Newcastle, summer 1993.

Four of my five grandchildren. Jo *and Caroline are the parents* *Georgia and Mariel (and of Ab* *not shown); Paul and Jane are* *parents of Dora and W*

David with Dora, York, Christmas 1994.

Paul Rubinstein and Jane Park with their son Wilf, Boulogne, December 1996.

Mariel and Georgia Rubinstein, London, about February 1998.

could produce and I found it of absorbing interest. It was thanks to Hull and in particular to John Saville, to whom I owe so much, that I was given my first chance to live and work in France. My four periods of residence there were an unforgettable experience which permanently altered my life.

I have been blessed in a second marriage which, while sometimes turbulent, has brought me enormous happiness and fulfilment, intellectual and personal companionship to an unusual degree. I am on excellent terms with all my sons, with John's partner Caroline Burgess, Paul's wife Jane Park, and, increasingly, with my five small grandchildren and two step-granddaughters. New friendships and interests have followed old ones and becoming a Quaker, while resulting in occasional frustrations has brought many rewards, increased my serenity (I believe) and tolerance (I hope). My quixotic decision aged 22 to leave the United States for England has given me a much richer life, I am convinced, than would have been possible had I remained in my native land. And like many of our friends Ann and I have travelled widely. 'You two lead a lovely life', my mother-in-law once commented. We have been very fortunate.

Looking back, therefore, on more than 66 years I think that I have had as fulfilled and happy a life as possible for one of my angular personality. The disappointment for which I have had no compensation has been neither personal nor professional but political. Nick Tucker reminds me that in Britain the majority of the population enjoys a high standard of living undreamt of by previous generations. This is of course true and a matter for satisfaction. So too is the fact that distinctions of social class have declined in the past thirty years or so. Nobody should want a society with a strong political left wing which draws its support from mass poverty, ignorance, ill health and backbreaking toil.

But the fact must be faced that most of the improvement in living standards has come about because it has been a source of profit for capitalists. Capitalism has become the greatest force in history for bringing prosperity in favoured countries to large numbers of people, though the second half of 1998 has proved once again that it has been at best a mixed blessing. Few attempts to create a fairer society by political action have succeeded, here or elsewhere. We live still in a world of gross disparities, of increasing economic inequality, but now the political will to bring about meaningful social change has largely disappeared. Britain has suffered more than other countries from the blind belief in 'market forces' which have characterised the past twenty years. A recent and authoritative United Nations report ranked the United Kingdom fifteenth of seventeen industrialised countries in a 'human poverty index', ahead only of the United States and (barely) Ireland (*Human Development Report 1998*, p. 28). A host of domestic reports come to a parallel conclusion; poverty in Britain has grown markedly since 1979. Even the welcome gains of the movements for racial and gender equality and protection of the environment have been at best incomplete; indeed, environmentalists too often find themselves engaged in damage limitation rather than fighting for new ground.

Our world is one of mass ignorance and consequent exploitation in which the social solidarity of the past, which for all its faults was real enough, has degenerated into unbalanced and selfish individualism. Our vision of reality is the product of the mass media, and much of the population has lost interest in anything other than sensation and tinsel images. For someone who has spent most of his working life primarily engaged in trying to persuade children and young adults to read and think for themselves this has been particularly disappointing.

Fortunately the disappointment of one's unrealistic hopes rarely lead to despair. One does not reject all action because it will not lead to revolution, but continues to work as circumstances permit, day by day for specific, limited objectives in a changed world. It is a world of profound potential. And though the opportunity after the Cold War ended to create juster societies in east and west was decisively lost, life carries on. Even in countries dominated by the motor car, the television and the personal computer people are not islands. Many of us believe as fervently as ever that race, religion, gender and social class cannot be allowed to divide humanity forever and that the aims of life should not be restricted to increasing one's possessions. There is still a world to win. Battered by years and disappointments I am proud to remain amongst this vigorous and unbowed comradeship.

Index of Personal Names

Index of Places, Subjects, Titles

339

WALES, 51, 116, 169
  Coleg Harlech, 185
  Hawarden Castle, 52
  Llanelly, 70
Waltham Forest Borough Council,
  250
Wars
  Algerian, 107
  Boer, 223
  Cold (*see* separate entry)
  Franco-Prussian, 12
  Great (First World War), 5, 78,
    105-6, 107, 134-5, 223, 256,
    272, 273-4
  Korean, 52, 295
  Napoleonic, 261, 277
  Second World War, 10, 17-19,
    106, 107, 249, 269, 274, 275
  Vietnamese, 60, 95, 147, 148-9,
    163, 276, 295
Washington Post, 292
Way of Transcendence, The (Kee), 166
West Hawaii Today, 282
Westminster Review, 175
What I Remember (Fawcett), 223,
  224

Where, 123
Who's Who, 52
'Wilkes and Liberty', 42
Wolds Way (*see also* Yorkshire Wolds
  under 'England, places'), 154-6,
  193, 194, 197
Wolds Way, The (Rubinstein), 193-4
Women's history, 205-6, 208
Women's suffrage, 208, 223
World Bank, 218, 297
World Cup (football)
  1994, 287
  1998, 289

XENOPHOBIA, 201, 219-20 (*see also*
  patriotism)

YHA (Youth Hostels Association,
  England and Wales), 151-2, 156,
  160
YMCA (Young Men's Christian
  Association), 51, 61

ZIONISM, 8, 23, 165